ISRAEL IN REVOLUTION: 6-74 C.E.

ISRAEL IN REVOLUTION: 6-74 C.E.

A Political History Based on the Writings of Josephus

DAVID M. RHOADS

Fortress Press   Philadelphia

Library of Congress Catalog Card Number 75–36452
ISBN 0-8006-0442-3

5406E76   Printed in U.S.A.   1-442

Josephus, Flavius
jews - history - 168 BC - 135 AD
  "   "   rebellion, 66-73 AD

CONTENTS

To
W. D. DAVIES

ACKNOWLEDGMENTS

I am grateful to the following persons who read the manuscript at various stages and made valuable suggestions about the content: Marc Borg, John Collins, Dennis Devlin, Eric Meyers, Horst Moering, Morton Smith, James Strange, and William Telford. William Gunderson, Don Michie, Sandy Rhoads, and Charles Solberg recommended numerous changes for clarification. My student assistants, Dave Echelbarger, Tom Gavoc, Mark Kruger, and Bruce Powell, were helpful in checking references and preparing footnotes. Russ Margolin, Mary Alyce Michie, Angela Zophy, and Jonathan Zophy gave ready aid in proofreading. Gwen Goldbeck prepared the indexes. The typists, Erna Williams and Mary Alyce Schmitt, were invaluable to the whole process. Don Michael Farris of Duke Divinity School Library gave ready assistance by providing research materials.

I am especially indebted to W. D. Davies for his personal support and faithful supervision of my doctoral work at Duke University.

DAVID M. RHOADS

Kenosha, Wisconsin
April, 1976

viii

INTRODUCTION

The first century was a fascinating and formative period in the history of the Jewish people. It was for the nation of Israel an era of vitality, rich with diversity, and filled with great hopes. Yet it culminated in the Roman conquest of Israel (66–74 c.e.), a conquest which resulted in the destruction of Jerusalem and the temple and which foreshadowed the dissolution of the nation some sixty years later. Judaism endured, but the great diversity of religious expression in Israel did not survive the war. Nor has there since been a temple where Jews could carry out the ritual sacrifices demanded by the law. And it was not until 1948 that Israel was reconstituted as a nation.

What were the causes of this war? What led the tiny nation of Israel to risk war with the mighty Roman Empire? Were there minor conflicts which escalated into a war unwanted by both sides, or were the Jews merely seeking the right moment for rebellion? Was the war an inevitable consequence of a clash of ideologies? And when the war did come, was the nation united in the war effort? Also, on what grounds did the Jews hope to win this war against such great odds?

There are many sources which are employed to reconstruct this important era in Israel's history. However, Josephus is the major source for our knowledge of the political events of this period. He was a Jewish participant in the early part of the war and an eyewitness to the siege of Jerusalem. As a historian, he was pro-Roman. The purpose of this book is to evaluate critically the writings of Josephus in order to explore some of the possible answers to our questions about the Jewish resistance against Rome during the period 6–74 c.e.

1

Chapter I deals with the important events of Josephus' life and the way in which his point of view has shaped his historical writing. Chapter II sketches the history of Israel from the time of the Maccabean Revolt (167–142 B.C.E.) to the beginning of the first century and explores the nature of the provincial relationship with Rome begun in 6 C.E. This chapter also includes an introduction to the major Jewish sects—Pharisees, Sadducees, and Essenes—to show more clearly their complex role in the subsequent course of events.

Chapter III deals with the prewar period from the revolt of Judas the Galilean in 6 C.E. to the initial defeat of Roman troops at the opening of the war in 66 C.E., focusing on the various forms of resistance, the overall movement of the nation, and the key events leading to the war. Chapter IV delineates the character and the social, political, and religious motivations of each of the five revolutionary factions active during the war (66–74 C.E.). In Chapter V, the purposes of the revolution are examined on the basis of Josephus' polemic against the participants. The final chapter presents the major conclusions of the study.

Before one begins such a study, it is important to clarify the vocabulary which will be used to discuss the Jewish resistance against Rome. In this book, the term "resistance" encompasses many forms of anti-Roman activity, including nonviolent as well as violent actions, official as well as popular protests. The term "revolutionaries" refers to those who engaged in armed resistance and were committed to war against the Romans. Traditionally, the title "Zealots" has been used synonymously with revolutionaries. However, there is no clear evidence that any formal group or sect by that title existed in the prewar period, and Josephus applies "Zealots" to only one of the five groups active in the war period. Thus, in this study, the title "Zealots" refers, as in Josephus' writings, to one revolutionary faction. The common noun "zealots" includes a broader classification of persons who carried out various acts of zeal which may or may not have been revolutionary.

The term "revolutionaries" further distinguishes those who were committed to a war for independence from "moderates." "Moderates" supported the war effort but would have settled for peaceful terms and accepted the return to a subordinate relationship to Rome. The moderates may also have been different from revolutionaries in their pursuit of a defensive, rather than an aggressive, war policy. "Revolutionaries" and "moderates" are distinguished from "quietists" who did not partici-

2

pate in the revolutionary movement of the war. There is always the danger of oversimplification in these distinctions, because there were a variety of views and motivations within each classification. Nevertheless, this categorization seems most helpful in clarifying to some degree the confusing narrative of events.

I

JOSEPHUS

This study is based on the works of Flavius Josephus, the major source for our knowledge of the political history of Israel during the period from 6 to 74 C.E. Josephus is an interesting historian because he participated in and witnessed many of the events he describes. Born in 37 C.E. and raised in Jerusalem, he was twenty-nine when the war broke out with the Romans. As a Jewish general and later as translator for the Roman commander during the war, he experienced the conflict from both sides. Within ten years after the destruction of Jerusalem, Josephus wrote a history of the Jewish struggle for independence entitled *The Jewish War* (75–79 C.E.).[1] Comprised of seven books, this work contains a lengthy description of the Roman-Jewish War (66–74 C.E.), preceded by a political history of the Jews from the time of the Maccabean Revolt (167–142 B.C.E.).

Josephus also wrote an extensive history of the Jews entitled *The Jewish Antiquities* completed later in his life (93–94 C.E.); this work, comprised of twenty books, contains a continuous Jewish history from its origins up to the beginning of the Jewish War in 66 C.E. As such, it contains no record of the war itself. But its history of the prewar period from the time Judea became a province in 6 C.E. parallels that of *The Jewish War* and is more detailed. Thus, the *Antiquities* is an important source for the period under study.

Attached to the published copies of the *Antiquities* is a brief work

---

1. All references to the text and translation of Josephus are from H. S. T. Thackeray, R. Marcus, A. Wikgren, and L. H. Feldman, eds. and trans., *Josephus*, 9 vols. (Cambridge: Harvard University Press, 1926–1965). On the question of the dates of these works see Emil Schürer, *History of the Jewish People in the Time of Jesus Christ*, ed. Geza Vermes and Fergus Millar (Edinburgh: T. & T. Clark, 1973), 1:46–55.

called the *Life*. Probably completed several years after the *Antiquities*, this autobiographical work is mainly a first-person account of the period when Josephus was general in Galilee, from the time of his appointment at the opening of the war to the return to the Romans under Vespasian. This narrative parallels, in a more detailed form, the third-person narrative of the same events in *The Jewish War*. At the beginning and end of the *Life*, Josephus has included some general autobiographical reflections.

A less-known work, *Against Apion*, was written shortly after the *Life*. It is a small tract containing an explanation of many Jewish traditions and is not directly relevant to our subject.

Since Josephus was a participant in and eyewitness to much which he records, a knowledge of his life and activities as revealed through his works is indispensable to an understanding of his writings and the history he relates. The present chapter summarizes the highlights of his life and includes some observations on his historical method and sources.

THE LIFE OF JOSEPHUS

Josephus was born in 37 C.E. into the Jewish priestly aristocracy. His father, Matthais, was a member of the first of the twenty-four priestly clans (*Life* 2). Through his mother, Josephus claimed to be of the royal blood of the Maccabees (*Life* 4).[2] Josephus' heritage thus identifies him with the priestly ruling class of Israel, the class which cooperated most directly with the Romans and which had the most to lose by a war with Rome. This ruling class was opposed during the war by Jewish revolutionaries who rebelled not only against Rome, but also against the traditional high priests (*War* 4:148, 152), the wealthy (*War* 2:427), and those of noble birth (*War* 4:139).

Josephus' record of his own educational background illustrates that he was an ambitious, indeed a pretentious, man. He alleges that at fourteen he was already well known among Jerusalem's chief priests and leading men for his superior knowledge of Jewish law (*Life* 8). At sixteen he presumably began a study of the Jewish sects—Pharisees, Sadducees, Essenes—and spent time in the wilderness as a disciple of Bannus, a hermit (*Life* 10). Choosing to live according to the sect of

2. For other references to Josephus' family, see *War* 5:333, 344, 419, 544; *Life* 204, 414, 416, 426–27.

5

the Pharisees, he then settled as a priest in Jerusalem in his nineteenth year (*Life* 12).

Certainly an influential part of his educational experience was a trip which he made to Rome when he was twenty-six years old to defend certain fellow priests who were sent in bonds on a "trifling charge" (*Life* 13). As a result of a shipwreck on the voyage, he met an actor who later introduced him to Poppaea, the Emperor Nero's consort. Her aid won the release of the priests, and Josephus returned home with large gifts from her (*Life* 16). Josephus had now encountered the wealth and culture of Rome. This experience, along with the fact of his growing influence in Roman circles, must have increased his own political ambition within Judaism, an ambition which was perhaps evident in his educational endeavors.

Josephus was especially impressed by the might of Rome. When he returned in 66 C.E. to a Jerusalem on the brink of revolt, he tried to dissuade those bent on revolution by reminding them of the power of Rome (*Life* 17). When it became obvious that the revolutionaries could not be stopped, Josephus met with the moderate chief priests and Pharisees (*Life* 12). This group decided to feign concurrence with the revolutionaries in order to influence them to pursue a strictly nonaggressive policy toward the Romans, hoping that "ere long Cestius would come up with a large army and quell the revolution" (*Life* 22). Cestius Gallus was the Roman governor of Syria who was sent as the military and political representative of Rome to put down the Jewish uprising at the beginning of the war. When he came before Jerusalem a group of leading Jews under Ananus, son of Jonathan, attempted to open the city gates to him (*War* 2:533). These efforts were unsuccessful because of revolutionaries who successfully defended the city against Cestius and drove him and his troops out of the country. This Jewish victory over the Romans won the nation and the city to the side of war, the chief priests themselves leading the newly organized Jewish government (*War* 2:562). However, many of these priests, including Josephus, apparently still hoped for a peaceful solution without further war (*Life* 28–29; cf. *War* 3:135ff.).

Under these circumstances Josephus was appointed to organize the defense of Upper and Lower Galilee (*War* 2:568). A part of his responsibility was to gain control over "the brigands and revolutionaries" by inducing them to lay down their weapons, which were then

6

to be reserved for the select men of the nation (*Life* 28–29). The accounts of Josephus' command in Galilee as recorded in the *Life* (95–100 C.E.) and the *War* (75–79 C.E.) differ at many significant points. What is clear, however, is that Josephus' ambiguous efforts to play the role of army general in Galilee while at the same time surreptitiously pursuing a policy of moderation resulted in great dissension among the Galilean factions. Some actions of his seemed to inspire strong anti-Roman sentiment, as, for example, when his Galilean troops confronted the loyalist forces of Agrippa II (*Life* 114–19). At other times his behavior appeared pro-Roman, as when he refused to distribute the booty seized from the caravan of the wife of Agrippa's overseer (*Life* 126–54; cf. *War* 2:595–613). Josephus was opposed by John of Gischala, who later became head of a revolutionary group in Jerusalem. Josephus was accused of being a tyrant (*Life* 260, 302); *War* 2:626), and a traitor (*War* 2:598, 599; 3:355; *Life* 129, 135), and he was charged with maladministration and deception (*Life* 314; *War* 2:602). Through John of Gischala's connections with some leading men in Jerusalem, an embassy was sent from there, without the proper sanction of the popular assembly in Jerusalem, to relieve Josephus of his Galilean post (*War* 2:629ff., *Life* 195ff.). Josephus was, however, able to outwit this plot against him by his own stratagems, along with the help of Galilean popular support which he had succeeded in winning. Even so, during this period Josephus clashed with Jewish revolutionaries who opposed Rome throughout the war.

Josephus did, however, fight the Romans when they came into Galilee under Vespasian, and he finally took refuge at Jotapata, where he commanded the defense of that city for forty-seven days (*War* 3:406). When Jotapata fell, in the summer of 67 C.E., Josephus hid with forty municipal notables in a cave under the city. He was unable to persuade the notables to surrender rather than commit suicide, so they all drew lots to kill one another in turn. Josephus was one of the last two people to draw lots, and he persuaded the other surivivor that they should capitulate to Vespasian (*War* 3:354ff.).

However one assesses Josephus' actions up to this point, he subsequently owed his life, his well-being, and his later fame to the Romans. Both his writings and his actions betray that dependence. When Josephus surrendered to Vespasian at Jotapata, he prophesied, on the basis of a dream, that Vespasian would one day be emperor (*War* 3:351–52,

399f.). In 69 C.E. that prophecy was fulfilled and Josephus, who had been a prisoner of Vespasian since his surrender, was released from his bonds (*War* 4:626). After accompanying Vespasian to Egypt, he joined Titus, Vespasian's son and military successor, in his march on Jerusalem. There he actively joined the Roman cause by serving as Titus' spokesman and interpreter, repeatedly advising his fellow-Jews from outside the wall to surrender (*War* 5:261, 362–419, 541; 6:118). After the fall of Jerusalem in 70 C.E., Josephus went with Titus for the triumphal march in Rome. He then took up residence in Titus' former house, was granted citizenship, and given a pension (*Life* 423). He took for himself the name "Flavius" from the Flavian house of the emperors Vespasian and Titus, and spent the rest of his years writing under the patronage of one Epaphroditus (*Antiquities* 1:8; *Life* 430; *Apion* 1:1; 2:1, 296). He also became friends with Agrippa II, the Jewish king who had participated in the war on the Roman side (*Life* 362). The favor of Vespasian while emperor toward Josephus was continued by Titus, Domitian, and the Empress Domitia (*Life* 428ff.). Josephus died around the turn of the century. A statue, erected in his memory at Rome, attested to his position and fame.

JOSEPHUS AS SEER

Some authors have portrayed Josephus as a traitor and an opportunist who cooperated with the Romans in order to save himself and to fulfill his own ambitions. Certainly that is how his actions were viewed by many of his compatriots during the war years (*War* 3:360, 439; 5:541). Although little is known of their reactions to his publications, his works are often viewed today as pure propaganda of self-justification in the face of accusations that he betrayed his country.[3]

Despite the hostile criticism of Josephus and his works, we need not see him as a mere opportunist. His writings reveal to us a man struggling between personal survival and a commitment to Judaism;[4] he did

3. Norman Bentwich, *Josephus* (Philadelphia: Jewish Publication Society of America, 1914); Clemens Thoma, "Die Weltanschauung des Josephus Flavius," *Kairos* 11 (1969): 39–52; Wilhelm Weber, *Josephus und Vespasian* (Berlin, 1921). Others identify him as a traitor without questioning the sincerity of his motives or the greatness of his literary achievement: Martin Braun, "The Prophet Who Became a Historian," *Listener* 56 (1956): 53–57; and Helgo Lindner, *Die Geschichtsauffassung des Flavius Josephus im Bellum Judaicum* (Leiden: E. J. Brill, 1972), pp. 13–14.

4. Lindner, *Geschichtsauffassung*, pp. 49–59.

not wish to relinquish either. This is most apparent at Jotapata where he wrestled over the question of whether to die as a loyal Jewish general or to surrender in order to preserve his life in the Roman camp (*War* 3:345–49, cf. 3:193–204, 137). The resolution to that struggle came when Josephus was able to give himself up to Vespasian as God's servant (*War* 3:354). He could continue his commitment to Judaism, but he would do it from the safety of the Roman side. Undoubtedly, Josephus' works contain much that is a rationale of self-justification for his action. Yet to see him as a rank opportunist is too harsh. And to depict his writings as an exercise of justification does not begin to do justice to the breadth of Josephus' self-understanding.

Josephus saw himself as part of a complex pattern of world history in which he himself was chosen herald of some crucial historical events. This point of view emerges most clearly in the passage which describes Josephus' awareness of his own prophetic mission. The passage occurs shortly before Josephus' description of his surrender to Vespasian at Jotapata.

> Suddenly there came back into his mind those nightly dreams, in which God had foretold to him the impending fate of the Jews and the destinies of the Roman sovereigns. He was an interpreter of dreams and skilled in divining the meaning of ambiguous utterances of the Deity; a priest himself and of priestly descent, he was not ignorant of the prophecies in the sacred books. At that hour he was inspired to read their meaning, and, recalling the dreadful images of his recent dreams, he offered up a silent prayer to God. "Since it pleases thee," so it ran, "who didst create the Jewish nation, to break thy work, since fortune has wholly passed to the Romans, and since thou hast made choice of my spirit to announce the things that are to come, I willingly surrender to the Romans and consent to life; but I take thee to witness that I go, not as a traitor, but as thy minister." (*War* 3:351–54)

Josephus thus claims to have foreseen by revelation the impending fate of the Jewish nation as well as the rise to power of the Roman sovereigns of the Flavian house in the person of Vespasian. The background for the moment of "insight" concerning the downfall of the Jewish state may have been Josephus' trip to Rome when he was overwhelmingly impressed by the might of the Roman Empire (*Life* 17–19). His subsequent efforts at the opening of the war to dissuade his fellow Jews from revolt may have been an expression of his sense of futility about the prospects of a Jewish victory (cf. 3:136). His own defeat as head of the Galilean army certainly must have reinforced that conviction and led directly to his prophetic certainty of the downfall of the entire nation (cf. *War* 4:388; 6:311).

The "revelation" of Josephus about the rise of Vespasian seems to be specifically related to the interpretation of a Jewish prophecy, illuminated by his recent dreams. In a later passage Josephus refers to this oracle, contrasting his own interpretation with that of the Jewish revolutionaries:

> But what more than all else incited them to the war was an ambiguous oracle, likewise found in their sacred scriptures, to the effect that at that time one from their country would become ruler of the world. This they understood to mean someone of their own race, and many of their wise men went astray in their interpretation of it. The oracle, however, in reality signified the sovereignty of Vespasian, who was proclaimed Emperor on Jewish soil. (*War* 6:312–13)

Two years after Josephus uttered this prophecy to the conquering Roman general, Vespasian was declared emperor.[5] The fact that Josephus was then released from chains and thereafter received favorable treatment at the hands of the Flavians supports the claim that he had actually made such a prophecy.

Josephus identified the roots of his prophetic capacity in his heritage and training as a priest (*War* 3:352). Although his dreams were the subject of the interpretation, it was Josephus' priestly knowledge of the scripture which enabled him to give them meaning. As such Josephus did not give a new prophecy, but was apparently "inspired" to apply to his contemporary situation sayings which had been spoken long before by the canonical prophets (*War* 3:353).[6] The historical content of his prophecy reveals his conviction that God acts in history. The fact that the temple in Jerusalem was destroyed by the Romans on the very day that the first temple was destroyed by Babylonians in the sixth century B.C.E. served in retrospect as a sign to Josephus that he had properly discerned God's plan in history (*War* 6:267–70; cf.

---

5. Abraham Schalit argues persuasively that Josephus made the prophecy to Vespasian as a captive in 69 C.E. when it was clearer that Vespasian might well become emperor. See Hildegard Temporini and Wolfgang Haase, eds., "Die Erhebung Vespasians nach Flavius Josephus, Talmud und Midrasch. Zur Geschichte einer messianischen Prophetie" in *Aufstieg und Niedergang der Römische Welt; Geschichte und Kultur Roms im Spiegel der Neueren Forschung* (Berlin: Walter de Gruyter, 1975), 2:208–327.

6. On this, see the careful analysis of J. Blinkensopp, "Prophecy and Priesthood in Josephus," *Journal of Jewish Studies* 25 (1974): 239–62.

2:457). He saw himself to be, at the right historic moment, a significant part of that plan.[7]

JOSEPHUS AS HISTORIAN

Given the pro-Roman nature of Josephus' prophetic role, it is little wonder that Titus commissioned him to write the official account of the Jewish War, signed it, and ordered its publication (*Life* 364). *The Jewish War*, first published in Aramaic within a decade after the war, was addressed to Jews living throughout the East who might be tempted to resist Rome in the aftermath of the Roman conquest of the Palestinian homeland. It thus served the pro-Roman purpose of seeking to avert further threat to the empire, especially from the Parthian Empire to the east where many Jews of the diaspora resided.[8] The author shows his readers how the outcome of the war demonstrated that God's favor is with the Roman Empire and that the great military power of the Romans makes any attempt at revolt senseless. Thus, while this work extols the Romans, the Palestinian Jews are portrayed as having been misguided in their rebellion, even though they themselves believed God to be their ally. Their only hope of survival had been, as it was now for Josephus' readers, in a policy of submission to Rome (*War* 3:108–109, 136). When they had insisted on war, the Roman army under Titus as an instrument of divine purging, defeated the nation and destroyed the city and temple (e.g., *War* 6:110; cf. 6:124; 4:412).

One should not interpret Josephus' pro-Roman point of view as an abandonment of Judaism. For it was the God of the Jews who had gone over to the Romans, and the world events which Josephus had foreseen were understood by him as fulfillment of Jewish prophecy. Josephus believed that God's fortune was for "now" resting with the Romans (*War* 5:367). Thus, he thought the Jewish revolt had been "untimely" (*War* 2:355).[9] And as a result of the inability and unwill-

---

7. With this treatment of Josephus compare the understanding of the apostle Paul in Johannes Munck, *Paul and the Salvation of Mankind,* trans. Frank Clark (Richmond: John Knox Press, 1959); and W. D. Davies, "A New View of Paul —J. Munck," *Christian Origins and Judaism* (Philadelphia: Westminster Press, 1962).

8. At the opening of the war, the Palestinian Jews had sent embassies to their "friends beyond the Euphrates" urging them to persuade Parthia to attack Rome from the east (*War* 6:341; cf. 2:388ff.).

9. Lindner, *Geschichtsauffassung,* pp. 22, 43.

ingness of the Jews to perceive and submit to the divine plan, God broke his work with the Jewish state, withdrew from the holy city and temple, and allowed "fortune" to pass wholly to the Romans (*War* 3:354; cf. 2:360–61; 5:366–67).[10]

Further, Josephus defended Judaism in *The Jewish War* by placing the blame for the war not on the whole nation but on those misguided revolutionaries among the Jews who had instigated the war and pressed it to its bitter end (*War* 1:27; 5:444; 6:251).[11] These he depicted as brigands and tyrants who had transgressed the Jewish laws (*War* 2:517–18) and defiled the holy temple (*War* 5:402, 412; 4:157, 323, cf. 6:126–27). According to Josephus, whatever religious motivations they had embraced were either misinterpretations of Jewish prophecies (*War* 2:651, 6:315) or innovations in their traditions (*Antiquities* 18:9; 20:218; *War* 2:414; 4:147), both of which led to the war. By contrast, he portrayed the general Jewish populace as moderate, peace-loving Jews who were at the mercy of the revolutionaries, unwilling victims of their tyranny, their greed and their factional conflicts (*War* 1:9; 4:397, 564; 5:27–28, 251, 265, 439). Nevertheless, Josephus states, all the people of Israel were condemned by God to undergo the catastrophe of judgment upon them at the hand of the Romans (*War* 5:442, 559, 566).

In this view of history, evident in the *War,* Josephus is seeking to interpret for his fellow Jews the cataclysmic event of 70 C.E. and to indicate that the survival of God's chosen people throughout the Roman Empire would come, as it had for Josephus personally, through acceptance of Roman power and authority.[12] If Josephus' readers could discern in retrospect the correct interpretation of the forewarnings in signs and oracles which God had given to avert the crisis (*War* 6:288–315; cf *Antiquities* 8:409, 418–20), then they would have learned the lesson from their disaster and discovered rightly God's will in history.[13] Josephus' historical writing goes beyond instruction

---

10. Ibid., p. 42. For Lindner's discussion of Josephus' use of the word fortune (*tyche*) see pp. 42–48, 89–94, 142–43.

11. Josephus depicts revolutionaries as a group or groups within Judaism responsible for the war. He also maligns their motives. Farmer and Hengel have clearly established religious motivations for the revolutionaries which are discernible in Josephus in spite of his prejudice against them: William Farmer, *Maccabees, Zealots, and Josephus* (New York: Columbia University Press, 1956); M. Hengel, *Die Zeloten* (Leiden: E. J. Brill, 1961).

12. Lindner, *Geschichtsauffassung*, pp. 50, 68.

13. Ibid., p. 144, elsewhere.

when he attempts to convert his readers by calling upon them to appeal to the very God who had devastated their holy city and temple (*War* 5:416). Josephus believed that if his readers would repent of their impulse to rebel, as the revolutionaries in their blindness had failed to do (*War* 5:355, 572), then there might be hope for a better day for Israel[14] (*War* 5:19; cf. *Antiquities* 10:37).

Josephus thus offered guidance and consolation (*War* 3:108; 6:267)[15] in regard to the response of his people to their vanquished homeland. And he himself became a model for that response. In his speech to John of Gischala before the walls of Jerusalem, Josephus states that he would never "become so abject a captive as to abjure my race or to forget the traditions of my forefathers" (*War* 6:107; cf. *Apion* 2:277). It is the Judaism which emerged from the historical crisis that the author wishes to champion, a Judaism which would maintain its loyalty to the traditions and adjust to the world situation in which Rome was the empire presently favored by God. Josephus defends the kind of enlightened, cosmopolitan, pro-Roman Judaism which appealed to Jews like himself.[16] In that sense, Josephus had great pride in his people.

All these observations alert us to the bias of Josephus' histories and cause us to question the accuracy and objectivity of his reports: (1) of the origins of the war—he believed it to be practically, historically, and theologically misguided on the part of the Jews; (2) of the revolutionaries—they were at odds with him, accused and threatened him, and they destroyed the traditional dominance of aristocratic Jews, of which Josephus was one; (3) of Judaism—he desired Judaism to survive and be at peace with Roman sovereignty, and he had ambitions about his own role in making Judaism palatable to the Hellenistic world; (4) and of Rome and her emperors—he saw himself as a prophetic herald of their God-given authority and a captive who found his fame and fortune by writing under Roman patronage.

However, as is often the case with apologists and propagandists,

14. Lindner's opinion is that the conversion of diaspora Jews to Josephus' world outlook is the main purpose of the *War*: Lindner, *Geschichtsauffassung*, pp. 131–32. Ibid., pp. 131–33.

15. Braun, "Prophet Who Became a Historian," pp. 56–57.

16. See Otto Michel and Otto Bauernfeind, eds. and trans., *De Bello Judaico. Der Jüdische Krieg*, 4 vols. (Darmstadt: Wissenschaftliche Buchgesellschaft, 1962), 1:xvii.

truth and accuracy are favorite themes with Josephus. He wrote *The Jewish War*, he claims, in order to correct other distorted accounts which had "either from flattery of the Romans or from hatred of the Jews, misrepresented the facts" (*War* 1:2; cf. *Antiquities* 20:157). By contrast Josephus occasionally praises the Jews as a whole (e.g., *War* 2:198) and frequently maligns the Romans (the procurators and earlier emperors, but not Titus and Vespasian or Rome in general; cf. *War* 2:352). Neither of these correctives is, however, contrary to his bias.

Also Josephus records a letter from Agrippa II attesting to the truth of his account (*Life* 365–66). However, Agrippa's bias would parallel that of Josephus. Thus, despite Josephus' ancient claim to objectivity, his descriptions of the events of the war and his depictions of the revolutionaries are shot through with his subjective bias, his distinctive perspective and his purpose for writing. Anyone who reads Josephus' works in order to reconstruct historical events must persistently keep in mind the person of the author and the point of view from which those events are described.[17]

THE SOURCES OF JOSEPHUS

The effort to discern Josephus' apologetic is further complicated by the difficulties in the source criticism in Josephus. Although he commonly named his sources in his later works, he did not do so in *The Jewish War*. The writings of Nicholas of Damascus, court historian and philosopher for the Jewish king Herod the Great (37–4 B.C.E.), were most likely Josephus' source for the Herodian period.[18] Thus, Nicholas' work, which is no longer extant, probably stands behind *War* 1:31–2:116. Another source, Jewish in nature, may lie behind the description of the Jewish sects in *War* 2:119–66.[19]

17. On Josephus in the context of ancient historiography, see Harold Attridge, *The Interpretation of Biblical History in the Antiquitates Judaicae*, Harvard Dissertation Series, no. 7 (Missoula, Montana: Scholars Press, 1976). For a careful analysis of the differing purposes of the *War*, the *Antiquities* and the *Life*, see Shaye Cohen, "Josephus in Galilee and Rome: His *Vita* and Development as a Historian" (Ph.D. dissertation, Columbia University, 1975).
18. See S. Safrai and M. Stern, eds., "The Jewish People in the First Century," *Compendia Rerum Judaicarum ad Novum Testamentum* (Assen: Van Gorcum and Co., 1974), 1:21ff.
19. Michel, *Bello*, p. 27; Morton Smith, "The Description of the Essenes in Josephus and the Philosophumena," *Hebrew Union College Annual* 29 (1958): 273–313. Contrast, however, Solomon Zeitlin, "The Account of the Essenes in Josephus and the Philosophumena," *Jewish Quarterly Review* 59 (1959): 292–99. See a parallel account in *Antiquities* 18:11–25.

For the period of the procurators, 6–66 C.E., it is difficult to discern a written source. There are probably no Roman sources for this material, since it is in general quite critical of the Roman procurators and sympathetic with the response of the Jewish populace to Roman offenses. It does, however, contain Josephus' typical maligning of the revolutionaries. It also contains more detail in the reports of events from the mid-forties to the war, a fact which coincides with Josephus' promise to give more information during the period of his own lifetime (*War* 1:18). For his account of the Jews from 6 to 66 C.E., in the *Antiquities* as well as in the *War*, Josephus depended upon his own recollections or perhaps those of Agrippa II (*Life* 364–66), along with oral reports or fragmentary written records of Jews.[20]

The source analysis for the war period is also problematic. Josephus was an eyewitness, first in Jerusalem at the opening of the war, then as the commander of Galilee, and finally as a prisoner of war with Titus during the siege of Jerusalem (*War* 1:1–3; *Apion* 1:47). However, the contradictions in the accounts of the Galilean period in the *War* and *Life* indicate that Josephus may be most unreliable historically when he himself has played an active role in the events being described, as, for example, in the accounts of his role as general in Galilee. He claims to have taken laborious notes during the siege, and yet one wonders if he really would have had any literary ambitions at this point in his life.[21] Josephus mentions deserters and other eyewitnesses who informed him about the happenings inside the city (*Apion* 1:49), and indeed those who deserted, especially the high priests and aristocracy, might well have sought out Josephus as one who could perhaps insure them protection from the Romans.

In addition to Josephus' own resources, there is evidence he drew upon written sources for the war period. The reference in *War* 2:345ff. to the exact location of Roman troops at the beginning of the war would imply the use of a Roman source,[22] perhaps the *Commentaries of Vespasian* mentioned in *Life* 342, 358 and *Apion* 1:56. And yet in one of these passages, Josephus' account seems to be in contrast with the *Commentaries* (*Apion* 1:56). Perhaps his Roman source was other than the *Commentaries of Vespasian*.

20. Bentwich, *Josephus*, p. 195. Also, see Safrai, *Compendia*, 1:28.
21. Bentwich, *Josephus*, p. 95.
22. Weber, *Josephus and Vespasian*; H. S. T. Thackeray, *Josephus: The Man and the Historian* (New York: Jewish Institute of Religion Press, 1929), p. 37. But contrast R. J. H. Shutt, *Studies in Josephus* (London: SPCK, 1961), p. 29.

A recent analysis of these narratives argues that Josephus drew on a Roman source for his description of the rise of Vespasian (4:440–663) and another source for the report on the siege of Jerusalem (4:659–6:322).[23] Neither of these appear to have been the *Commentaries* of Vespasian or Titus. This analysis indicates that Josephus has shaped these sources by transpositions and built them up with speeches, autobiographical information, and references to Jewish activity in Jerusalem.

The possible written sources which have been suggested for Josephus' account of the war period explain only the accounts about the military activity of Romans against the Jews and do not account for the origin of the information which Josephus offers regarding the internal condition of the city during the war or the dynamics of the conflicts among revolutionary factions. For this latter information, he may have depended primarily upon oral reports from deserters at the time of the siege.

Probably there was a Roman source for the triumphal entry of the returning army in Rome (*War* 7:125ff.).[24] Also, Josephus may have used Roman records for his reconstruction of the narrative concerning the capture of Masada by Flavius Silva in 74 C.E. (*War* 7:252ff.), although much of this episode may be a fabrication by Josephus.

Finally, Josephus' narrative may have been influenced by Greek authors, either through the style of the secretaries who assisted him with the Greek translation of the *War*[25] or from his own tendency to borrow phrases and descriptions from other historians to describe the people and events which were a part of the Jewish War.[26] However, these considerations are conjectural, since there is probably little by way of style in his history of this period which could not have originated with Josephus himself.

WRITINGS OTHER THAN JOSEPHUS'

This study is based on the writings of Josephus, the major source for the political history of this period. There are, of course, other fruitful

23. For a summary of this position, see Lindner, *Geschichtsauffassung*, pp. 147–48. For Lindner's suggestion that Josephus may have used a source for the signs section (6:288–315), which may have been written by Josephus himself shortly after the war, see Lindner, *Geschichtsauffassung*, p. 131.

24. Michel, *Bello*, 1:xxviii.

25. Thackeray, *Josephus, The Man and the Historian*, p. 160. Contrast Shutt, *Studies*, p. 33.

26. Y. Baer, "Jerusalem in the Times of the Great Revolt" (in Hebrew), *Zion* 36 (1971): 127–90.

sources for our knowledge of this period. Although this study does not attempt to treat these sources, we will on occasion refer to writings other than Josephus to supplement or correct the historical picture which emerges from his accounts. As a general introduction to these sources, brief reference will now be made to those most relevant to our study.[27]

Several authors have written historical accounts which parallel and supplement those of Josephus. Philo (20 B.C.E. to 45 C.E.), the Jewish philosopher from Alexandria in Egypt, relates some incidents which took place in Judea at the times of the procurator Pilate (27–37 C.E.) and Emperor Gaius (37–41 C.E.). Also, the works of some Roman historians, Tacitus (55–120 C.E.), Suetonius (69 C.E.–140 C.E.), and Dio Cassius (163/164—early third century), have brief sections which deal with events of Israel's relationship with Rome during the period under study, 6–74 C.E.[28]

The New Testament writings, especially the four Gospels and the Acts of the Apostles, contain historical material from the time of Pilate and subsequent procurators. These are Christian theological documents written over a period of thirty years or more after the war, and they often express antipathy toward Judaism. As such, they must be read with caution as historical sources. Some other early Christian writers, such as Hippolytus, have also preserved material relevant to our knowledge of the Judaism of this period.

The literature of the Apocrypha and Pseudepigrapha of the Hebrew Bible,[29] as well as the scrolls from the Qumran community on the

27. It is important for the reader to keep in mind the limitation of this study, the use of one author, Josephus, as a basis for reconstructing the political history of this period. For a general introduction to other sources for the study of the first century, including a bibliography of texts and translations, see Schürer, *History*, pp. 6–122; and S. Safrai, *Compendia* 1:1–77.

28. Philo, *Embassy to Gaius*, in *Philo*, 10 vols., with trans. F. H. Colson and G. H. Whitaker (Cambridge: Harvard University Press, 1950–62); Tacitus, in *The Histories*, 4 vols., with trans. Clifford Moore, and *The Annals*, with trans. John Jackson (Cambridge: Harvard University Press, 1962–63); Suetonius, in *Lives of the Emperors*, 2 vols., with trans. J. C. Rolfe (Cambridge: Harvard University Press, 1964–65); and Dio Cassius, *Roman History*, with trans. Earnest Cary (New York: Macmillan & Co., 1914–27). See also M. Stern, *Greek and Latin Authors on Jews and Judaism*, vol. 1 (Jerusalem: The Israel Academy of Sciences and Humanities, 1974).

29. R. H. Charles, *The Apocrypha and Pseudepigrapha of the Old Testament*, 2 vols. (Oxford: Clarendon Press, 1913). For aids in the study of this material, see the volume by James Charlesworth, *Tools for the Study of the Apocrypha, Pseudepigrapha, and Cognate Works* (Durham: Bowen, 1970), and James Charlesworth and P. Dykers, *The Pseudepigrapha and Modern Research* (Missoula, Montana: Scholars Press, 1976). See a forthcoming English edition of the *Pseudepigrapha* by Doubleday.

Dead Sea,[30] contain many works which are dated between the time of the Maccabees and the Roman-Jewish War. Although they have little historical narrative of first century events, they are rich sources for the life, beliefs, and practices of the Jews of that period.

The large body of Rabbinic literature, such as the *Mishnah*, the *Tosephta*, the *Jerusalem Talmud*, the *Babylonian Talmud*, and the midrash writings, contain legal and homiletical traditions from many centuries of Judaism.[31] Although written down several hundred years later, they contain oral traditions which predate the Roman-Jewish War of 66–74 C.E. These traditions are, however, very difficult to date. Furthermore, the branch of Pharisaism which survived the war to preserve these traditions was not in general sympathetic to the nation's cause against Rome.

Also, there are important archaeological sources. The coins minted by Israel during the revolt represent our only direct sources from the revolutionaries.[32] The inscriptions and symbols on these coins help to illuminate the purposes and hopes of Israel's war efforts. Archaeological work in Palestine in general, and Jerusalem in particular, is of growing importance in discerning the extent of Jewish resistance and the amount of Roman devastation.[33] The finds at the fortress Masada, where some rebels held out against the Romans until 74 C.E., enable us to gain a clearer picture of at least one of the revolutionary factions.[34]

30. Geza Vermes, *The Dead Sea Scrolls in English* (London, 1968). See also J. A. Fitzmyer, *The Dead Sea Scrolls: Major Publications and Tools for Study*, Sources for Biblical Study 8 (Missoula, Montana: Society of Biblical Literature and Scholars Press, 1975).

31. For an introduction to this material, see John Bowker, *The Targums and Rabbinic Literature* (Cambridge: University Press, 1969). See also Urbach, *The Sages*, 2 vols., trans. Israel Abrahams (Jerusalem: Magnes Press, 1975); and Jacob Neusner, *The Traditions about the Pharisees before 70*, 3 vols. (Leiden: E. J. Brill, 1971).

32. See especially Leo Kadman, *The Coins of the Jewish War of 66–73* (Tel Aviv: Schocken, 1960); and Y. Meshorer, *Jewish Coins of the Second Temple Period*, trans. I. H. Levine (Tel Aviv: Am Hassefer, 1967).

33. As examples of this, see M. Har-el, "The Zealots' Fortresses in Galilee," *Israel Exploration Journal* 22 (1972): 123–30; and Eric Meyers, "Galilaean Regionalism as a Factor in Historical Reconstruction" in the G. Ernest Wright Memorial issue of the *Bulletin of the American Society for Oriental Research*, 1976. Additional works on the archaeology for this period include M. Avi-Yonah, *The World History of the Jewish People: The Herodian Period* (Ramat Gan: Masada Publishing Company, 1975); *Jerusalem Revealed* (Jerusalem: Israel Exploration Society, 1975); and B. Mazar, D. Freedman, G. Kornfield, *The Mountain of the Lord* (New York: Doubleday, 1975).

34. Y. Yadin, *Masada: Herod's Fortress and the Zealots' Last Stand* (New York: Random House, 1966).

Throughout this work, we will mention or simply note relevant passages in these different writings. We do not, however, deal with them to any extent because the subject of this study is the writings of Josephus.

II

HISTORICAL BACKGROUND

We have chosen to consider 6 C.E. as the year which inaugurated the historical period culminating in the Roman-Jewish War. This was the year when the Roman province of Judea was established, an event which initiated a new era in Israel's relationship with Rome. Also, it is in this year that Judas the Galilean revolted, an event which Josephus describes as having "sowed the seed from which sprang" the later conflict (*Antiquities* 18:8). Thus we identify 6 C.E. as the beginning of the prewar period under study. However, Josephus began his history *The Jewish War* with events preceding this time. In the present chapter, we will summarize this background history and deal with other introductory matters important for our more detailed study of the period 6–74 C.E.

FORMATIVE EVENTS
FROM THE TIME OF THE MACCABEES

Josephus began his history of the Jewish War by referring to the Maccabean Revolt of 167–142 B.C.E. (*War* 1:1–53). This revolt inaugurated a period of almost eighty years of Israelite independence (142–63 B.C.E.) which came in the midst of centuries of control by successive foreign powers. For the most part, Israel had been willing to tolerate foreign domination. Except for the Babylonian Empire which had forced a majority of Israelites into exile (586 B.C.E.), the Persian (538–332 B.C.E.), Greek (332–323 B.C.E.), and Egyptian (323–198 B.C.E.) empires permitted the Jews to have relative autonomy to express their religious worship and traditions in their Israelite homeland. The Syrian overlords (198–142 B.C.E.) under Antiochus IV

Epiphanes (175–165 B.C.E.) attempted to control the Palestinian land by forcing the Hellenistic culture and religion upon the Jews, a move which resulted in a rebellious reaction on the part of many Jews (*War* 1:36–47; *Antiquities* 12:265ff.).

Ever since the rebuilding of the nation after the Babylonian Exile (589–539 B.C.E.), the legal traditions of the Torah and the worship in the temple had been the central distinguishing institutions of the Jewish nation. Now, however, the Syrian Empire began to force Jews to abandon their religious practices, such as circumcision and the avoidance of certain foods, in order to gain a firmer control over Palestine (*War* 1:34; *Antiquities* 12:253–56). Also, Antiochus IV had a statue of Olympian Zeus set in the holiest place within the temple, and he prohibited any further sacrifices to the God of the Jews (*Antiquities* 12:250–53).

The Jewish reaction to this foreign oppression resulted in a war for religious freedom which is known as the Maccabean Revolt (167–142 B.C.E.).[1] It was initiated by Mattathias, a Jew from Modein who refused to submit to the Syrian dictates and who called out, "Whoever is zealous for our country's laws and the worship of God, let him come with me!" (*Antiquities* 12:271). Operating out of caves and mountain places, Mattathias and his sons (who came to be known as the Maccabees) organized the guerrilla warfare which eventually led to their religious freedom. After Jewish worship in the temple was restored in 164 B.C.E., the movement continued as a struggle for complete political separation from the Syrian hegemony (*War* 1:40–53), which was achieved in 142 B.C.E. The family of the Maccabees, who had become the rulers in Israel during the revolt, reigned until 63 B.C.E. (*War* 1:54–151).

To the Jews, the Maccabean Revolt was more than a war to preserve local religious practices and worship. For centuries the Jews had believed that the one true God had chosen to reveal himself to them. They had come to know God's will in the law, or Torah; and the land on which they lived had been given by God to the Jews.[2] Therefore,

---

1. See also 1 and 2 Maccabees. For a recent discussion of the Maccabean Revolt including bibliography, see Emil Schürer, *The History of the Jewish People in the Age of Jesus Christ (175 B.C.–A.D. 135)*, ed. Geza Vermes and Fergus Millar (Edinburgh: T. and T. Clark, 1973), 1:125–242.
2. For the significance of the land in the Maccabean Revolt, see W. D. Davies *The Gospel and the Land* (Berkeley: University of California Press, 1974), pp. 99, 427.

they believed that it was not right that another nation with its laws should have dominion over them.

The Jews also understood themselves as the people chosen by God to reveal his ways to the other nations, to be a "light to the nations" (Isaiah 42:6). Many Jews therefore believed they were destined not only for freedom from foreign domination, but also ultimately to exercise world dominion in the justice and glory of their God (e.g., Daniel, chapter 7). Although there were many different views current among Jews about the means—historical and supernatural—by which world dominion might be attained, this eschatological hope was a formative dimension in the subsequent life of the Jewish nation.[3]

The historical memory of the Maccabean Revolt helped to keep this eschatological hope burning in later years. God had vindicated the cause of this small band of Maccabean warriors who had defended the law and temple against the foreign tyranny of the large Syrian Empire. Surely God would protect his people against any oppressors if they were loyal to him in this way.

Josephus viewed the Maccabean Revolt against Syrian domination as a righteous rebellion which had inaugurated a glorious period of independence for Israel. However, Josephus did not view the Maccabean Revolt as a justification for the later Jewish revolt against the Romans; on the contrary, he considered the latter revolt as an unwarranted attack by unlawful Jews against overlords who were basically sympathetic and tolerant. Other Jews, however, did see a parallel between the Maccabean Revolt and the Roman-Jewish War. The recollection of the revolt was part of the common heritage of first century Jews (*War* 7:255).[4] The people celebrated annual festivals in the temple commemorating the great events of that period which

---

3. On the rise of Jewish apocalyptic, see H. H. Rowley, *The Relevance of Apocalyptic* (London, 1963); D. S. Russell, *The Method and Message of Jewish Apocalyptic* (London, 1964); and Klaus Koch, *The Rediscovery of Apocalyptic* (Allenson: Naperville, 1972).

4. For a discussion of the impact of the Maccabean era upon the first century, see W. R. Farmer, *Maccabees, Zealots and Josephus* (New York: Columbia University, 1956). See the critical review by Sydney Hoenig, "Maccabees, Zealots and Josephus, Second Commonwealth Parallelisms," *Jewish Quarterly Review* 59 (1958): 75–80.

brought liberation.[5]   As such, the Maccabean Revolt would have served as a model and source of inspiration for many Jews in their struggle to secure liberation from the Romans.   Some people may have thought the Jews would be established as world rulers.[6]

The brief narrative about the Maccabees in Josephus' history is a prelude to his description of the loss of Israel's independence to the Romans.   At the time of a conflict between two Hasmonaean (Maccabean) descendants vying for the throne, each courted Pompey, the commander of Roman troops in the East (*War* 1:131–32).   Perhaps they courted Pompey because by the early half of the first century B.C.E., the Romans had gained such control of the Mediterranean world that some relation with the Romans was inevitable.[7]   With the support of one Hasmonaean faction and after a brief siege of the city against the other faction, Pompey gained control of Israel in 63 B.C.E. Hyrcanus II was the Hasmonaean who became the Jewish vassal high priest under the Romans from 63 to 40 B.C.E. (*War* 1:153–273).   In establishing his reign, the Romans diminished his territory and demanded an annual tax (*Antiquities* 14:74).   The return of foreign domination was beginning to be felt in Israel.   There was a brief respite from Roman domination when the Parthian Empire to the east succeeded in conquering Israel (40 B.C.E.) and freeing it from the Romans (*Antiquities* 14:330–64).   However, with the appearance of Herod the Great, Israel soon again became a Roman client state.

Herod was a half-Jew from Idumaea (south of Judea), who gained Rome's favor along with the authority to attempt to restore Israel to the Roman Empire.[8]   With the help of mercenary troops, he conquered

5. Especially the festival of Hanukkah which commemorated the rededication of the temple. See S. Zeitlin, "Hanukkah," *Jewish Quarterly Review* 29 (1938–39): 1–36; and T. H. Gaster, *Purim and Hanukkah in Custom and Tradition: Feast of Lots, Feast of Lights* (New York: Schuman, 1950).   The Megillath Taanith, a nationalistic calendar from the first century, includes some dates in which events from the Maccabean era were to be remembered and celebrated.   See H. Lichtenstein, "Die Fasten Scroll," *Hebrew Union College Annual* 8–9 (1931–32): 257–351.   For a discussion of this work, see Farmer, *Maccabees*, pp. 132–58, 205–9.

6. On the prophecy of a world ruler from Judea, see below pp. 171–72.

7. For treatment of the overall history of the Roman-Jewish relationship, see Michael Grant, *The Jews in the Roman World* (New York: Charles Scribner's Sons, 1973).

8. On Herod the Great, see Abraham Schalit, *König Herodes; Der Mann und Sein Werk* (Berlin: Walter de Gruyter, 1969).   In English, see M. Stern, "The Reign of Herod" in *The World History of the Jewish People*, First Series: Ancient Times, ed. Michael Avi-Yonah, et al. (Jerusalem: Masada Publishing Co., 1975), 7:71–123; and Schürer, *History*, pp. 287–329.

Jewish territory and succeeded in establishing himself as king of the Jews in 37 B.C.E. (*War* 1:343). Although Herod was a local Jewish ruler, he was clearly a vassal-king to the Romans. The needs of the country were secondary to his efforts to maintain a place for himself within the empire (*Antiquities* 15:328). Having forced his rule upon the nation, he reigned like a tyrant. During his reign the Jewish high council lost its power. The high priest, formerly an officer with a life term, was appointed and deposed at Herod's will (*Antiquities* 15:40–41). Herod also abolished some of the civil rights of the people (*Antiquities* 15:366). His brutality toward opposition, including his own family, was horrendous. He retained his control by fear and repression. It did not take long for the nation under Herod to feel the full weight of the oppressiveness of foreign rule.

Despite the fact that Herod gave the nation as a whole an unprecedented era of peace and productivity (*Antiquities* 15:383)[9] through agricultural development, work relief, and resettlement programs, he bled the populace poor with taxes (*War* 1:524; 2:85–86; *Antiquities* 16:149–59; 17:302–14). The tribute exacted by Rome was large in itself. Herod's revenues were huge, used primarily to maintain his own court and military troops as well as to support his extensive, luxurious building programs. Taxes were so high that twice Herod was able to remit sizable portions of the payment when he wished to ingratiate himself with the people (*Antiquities* 15:365; 16:64). In addition, he sometimes seized property (*Antiquities* 15:6) and extorted gifts in exchange for his favor. The impoverishment of the people was worsened greatly by the devastating earthquakes, pestilence, and famines which took place during Herod's reign (*Antiquities* 15:121, 299–302; *War* 1:370).

Herod's reign was also characterized by the promotion of the non-Jewish, Greek culture so popular throughout the empire at that time. He surrounded himself with so many non-Jewish advisers steeped in Greek culture that his reign practically amounted to direct gentile rule. The taxes he levied were used for the construction of Hellenistic cities and buildings—including temples—within Palestine, many of them dedicated to Caesar (e.g., *War* 1:401–21; *Antiquities* 16:136–45). The resettlement of new residents into these cities tipped the balance

9. On this point, see Grant, *Jews*, p. 73.

of population in Palestine in favor of non-Jewish residents.[10] Herod was also lavish with gifts in support of building projects, public works, and the establishment of games for nations outside Israel (e.g., *War* 1:422–28; *Antiquities* 16:146–55). To Herod's credit, he was responsible for the magnificent reconstruction of the Jewish temple in Jerusalem (*Antiquities* 15:380–425), yet it was typical of him that he placed a golden eagle, the symbol of the Roman Empire, above the entrance gate. In this way and many others, national Jewish laws and customs were disregarded (*Antiquities* 15:267; 16:1–5). In addition, the brutality of the Greek games he instituted in Israel offended the sensibilities of the people. Thus, during Herod's reign, gentile culture was imported and developed in a massive way.

Herod encountered opposition from the Jewish people throughout his reign. He was opposed by Pharisees and Essenes who refused to recognize an Idumaean as king (*Antiquities* 15:368–71); by Pharisees who declined to swear an oath of loyalty to the emperor (*Antiquities* 17:41–46); by armed opponents who resisted him like brigands from mountain hideouts (*War* 1:304–14; *Antiquities* 14:413–30); by ten men, apparently supported by the populace, who vowed to kill him for introducing foreign customs (*Antiquities* 15:267–91); and by two teachers in Jerusalem who persuaded some youths to tear down the image of the golden eagle which Herod had erected above the temple gate (*War* 1:648–55; *Antiquities* 17:149–67). Herod probably prevented a general outburst of the anger of the masses by intimidation and manipulation (*Antiquities* 14:267, 315; 15:326).[11]

This last statement is confirmed by the fact that many popular outbreaks occurred after Herod's death (4 B.C.E.). Masses in Jerusalem demanded reduction of taxes, abolition of duties, liberation of prisoners, and a new high priest (*War* 2:5–7; *Antiquities* 17:204–12). Herod's son, Archelaus, while waiting for confirmation from Rome to take over as king, at first made concessions to the crowd. But when demonstrators continued to demand satisfaction for Herod's recent execution of the two teachers involved in the golden eagle incident, Archelaus ordered his troops to attack the demonstrators. Three thousand people were killed (*War* 2:8–13; *Antiquities* 17:213–18).

10. So Stern, "Herod," p. 101. The tensions between Hellenistic and Jewish cultures in Palestine contributed significantly to the later conflicts with Rome.
11. See further Stern, "Herod," p. 112; and Schürer, *History*, p. 315.

25

Then Archelaus went to Rome to plead his case for the kingship. Troops under a Roman officer named Sabinus were left in Judea to keep order, and proceeded to institute a search for the royal treasures. The populace of Jews who subsequently gathered in Jerusalem for the Feast of Weeks attacked these Roman troops and after several battles were able to contain them in Herod's temple (*War* 2:39–54; *Antiquities* 17:250–68). These events were accompanied by revolts in the countryside. An armed uprising of some of Herod's veterans took place in Idumaea (*War* 2:55; *Antiquities* 17:267–70). Judas, son of Hezekiah, raised an army to attack the royal arsenal at Sepphoris in Galilee and sought to attain the kingship (*War* 2:56; *Antiquities* 17:271–72). In Perea, a slave of Herod by the name of Simon gathered a body of men to seize royal power (*War* 2:57–59; *Antiquities* 17:273–77). Athronges, a shepherd with imposing physical stature, attempted the same in Judea (*War* 2:60–65; *Antiquities* 17:278–84). In addition to being expressions of social and political dissatisfaction, some of these uprisings may have been distinctly religious, messianic movements, intensified by eschatological expectations. Thus, for an apparent variety of motives, there were outbreaks of rebellion after Herod's death in virtually every sector of the nation.

At this point, Varus, the legate of Syria, was notified of the crisis, and he brought two legions and four troops of cavalry to Palestine (*War* 2:66–79; *Antiquities* 17:286–98). Galilee was subdued first. Varus then encamped before Jerusalem, whereupon the Jewish troops which were stationed outside the city fled. Jewish leaders inside the city, blaming the rebellion on the crowd which had gathered for the festival, proceeded to open the gates to Varus. Although many Jews had taken arms against the Romans, the masses were pardoned. Those most guilty for the various revolts were pursued into the countryside and crucified. They numbered about two thousand. These events, which are referred to as the War of Varus, had a great impact on the Jews (*Testament of Moses* 6:9 and Tacitus, *Histories* 5:9). Josephus compared this war to the invasion of Israel by Antiochus IV of Syria (*Apion* 1:34). The Jews were directly confronted with the overwhelming might of Rome by which the various revolts had been easily crushed. They were fortunate that Varus did not take punitive action against the masses. Had they persisted in their rebellion, the Roman troops could have brought extensive destruction upon the city and temple.

After Varus restored stability in Palestine, Emperor Augustus made the final disposition of Herod's kingdom by dividing the territory among his three sons (*War* 2:93; *Antiquities* 17:317–20). Philip was given Iturea, Trachonitis, Batanaea, Autanitis, and other areas comprising the northeastern part of Herod's kingdom. He reigned there from 4 B.C.E. until 34 C.E. Herod Antipas governed the territories of Galilee and Peraea from 4 B.C.E. until 39 C.E. Archelaus, who was given the most important territory, ruled over Judea, Idumaea to the south, and Samaria.[12] After ten years of incompetent rule (4 B.C.E.–6 C.E.), Archelaus was deposed and then banished. The territory of Archelaus, centering in Judea and the capital city of Jerusalem, was then converted into a province of Rome (*War* 2:117).

THE NATURE OF THE ROMAN
PROVINCIAL RELATIONSHIP

The territory of Palestine was important to the Roman Empire, for Israel served as a buffer state between the Romans and the Parthian Empire to the east. The Parthian Empire was the only remaining formidable threat to the extensive dominance of the Roman Empire in the Mediterranean world. The Parthians had already conquered Israel for a brief period from 40–37 B.C.E. Since there were large Jewish communities in Parthia, remaining there since the Babylonian Exile, the Parthians looked to Israel as a potential ally in a war against the Romans. Conversely, when Israel revolted against Rome in 66 C.E., they looked to their Jewish friends in Parthia to pressure that empire into joining Israel's war efforts (*War* 6:343; 2:388ff.). For these reasons it was important for the Romans to maintain good relations or firm control of this Israelite buffer state. This was especially so in light of Israel's reputation for being an unruly territory (*War* 2:91).

Consequently, in 6 C.E., the Romans decided to make Judea and related territories into a province.[13] The Jewish populace had been dissatisfied under the rule of Herod; and the Romans had previously considered making Israel into a province at Herod's death (*War* 2:81).

12. On the geographical areas of Palestine and their relevance to the history of Israel, see Michael Avi-Yonah, *The Holy Land* (Grand Rapids: Baker Book House, 1966).
13. For further discussion of the institutions and principles of the provincial relationship, see S. Safrai and M. Stern, eds., "The Jewish People in the First Century," *Compendia Rerum Judaicarum ad Novum Testamentum* (Philadelphia: Fortress, 1974), 1:308–46; and Schürer, *History*, 1:357–82.

Their decision at that time to divide the kingdom under Herod's sons worked well in the case of Philip and Antipas who retained their territories in peace through most of their reigns. But in the case of Archelaus, Jewish dissatisfaction was as firm as it had been under his father (*Antiquities* 17:342–44). So, in 6 C.E., the Romans decided to give this territory provincial status.

When the province of Judea was established, it was placed under the aegis of the larger Syrian province of the Roman Empire just north of Palestine. The governor of the Syrian province, with four legions at his disposal, was responsible for the protection of the eastern front of the empire. As overseer of the Eastern Empire, he was also responsible to see that no disturbance or revolt took place in Judea. Josephus records numerous occasions when the governor of Syria intervened in Jewish affairs to keep the peace or ease the tension in Roman-Jewish relationships (e.g., *Antiquities* 18:90).

Many Jews welcomed the change to provincial status and in fact had argued in favor of it before the emperor (*War* 2:91; *Antiquities* 17:314), thinking perhaps that they would receive more equitable treatment from a Roman procurator than they had received from the tyrannical Herod and Archelaus (*Antiquities* 17:342). Besides, under the provincial relationship, the Roman procurator had limited functions and did not rule over the area like a king. Consequently, some Jews must have favored a provincial relationship, because it would bring more governmental autonomy into the hands of the Jewish people themselves (*War* 2:80; *Antiquities* 17:300).[14] This new autonomy was expressed through the office of the high priest and the Jewish high council.

The office of the high priest and the Jewish council had been nominal institutions under the vassal kings. But in 6 C.E. the high priest became the primary political head of state. Appointed by the procurator (*Antiquities* 18:26), he was chosen from a small number of families among whom the high priestly office was hereditary. These families together constituted the nucleus of the governing aristocracy in Israel. Since the nation was a "theocracy" (*Apion* 2:165–67), religious and political functions were united in the one office. The high priest not only supervised and officiated at temple rituals, he was also politically

---

14. See also Gedalyah Allon, "The Attitude of the Pharisees to the Roman Government and the House of Herod," *Scripta Hierosolymitana* 7 (1961): 53–78.

responsible to the Romans for the autonomous administration of Jewish affairs.

The high priest was also head of the Jewish high council, or Sanhedrin (*Antiquities* 20:200). The Sanhedrin, which was composed of seventy members, was the principal institution of self-government. Its participants included members of the high priestly families, scribes of the Pharisaic or Sadducean sect who were experts in legal traditions and interpretations, and also some wealthy upperclass Jewish aristocrats called elders. Appointment was for life. The responsibilities of the Sanhedrin included legislative and judicial authority as well as administrative power (*Antiquities* 20:200, 202, 216–17; *Life* 62). As all these matters were interwoven with the observance of the Torah, no distinction was made between religious affairs and civil matters of justice. These institutions represented the relatively autonomous Jewish government as a province of Rome.

With provincial status, the Jewish nation experienced the direct, permanent presence of Roman officials and troops in Palestine. The procurator to Judea was appointed by the emperor from the Roman Equestrian Order, which ranked lower than the Senatorial Order and whose members had military experience.[15] As the leading Roman officer in Judea, he was chiefly responsible to maintain order. His headquarters were not in Jerusalem, where his constant presence would have been a source of antagonism for the Jews, but in the city of Caesarea on the coast (*War* 2:170). Caesarea may also have been chosen as headquarters because it contained elements from both the Jewish and the gentile people living in Palestine for whom the procurator was responsible.[16] No legions were maintained in Judea, since auxiliary troops were considered to be adequate.[17] These were stationed in Caesarea, with one cohort of two hundred men permanently stationed at the fortress Antonia in Jerusalem (*War* 5:244). The procurator, with additional troops, joined them at feast time when masses of Jews would be present in Jerusalem to celebrate in the temple. Because national senti-

15. Most imperial provinces were governed by men of higher, senatorial rank. Men of equestrian rank were sent to a few provinces like Judea, where, "owing to a tenacious individual culture, or a lack of it, the strict implementation of ordinary regulations seemed impossible": Schürer, *History*, pp. 357–58.
16. Bo Reicke, *The New Testament Era*, trans. David Green (Philadelphia: Fortress Press, 1968), p. 138.
17. In the end, auxiliary troops proved to be inadequate to maintain order in this Jewish province. See *Compendia*, 1:315, 324–27.

ment ran especially high then, there was thought to be a special need to keep the peace.

The procurator left most Jewish affairs in the hands of the local government. However, in political matters which related specifically to Roman interests, the procurator had ultimate authority. For example, in cases where there was threat of revolt or disturbance of the peace, the Roman authorities moved to restore order and punish the offenders. The procurator really had ultimate legal authority in general; although it was seldom done, he could intervene in internal Jewish affairs at any time. He alone held the right to execute the death penalty (*War* 2:227; *Antiquities* 20:5). The Jewish responsibility was little more than to hand over the offender to the procurator (*War* 6:303). The one exception to this was the right of Jews to kill any non-Jew who entered, and thereby desecrated, the temple (*War* 6:125).

The procurator was also responsible for seeing that taxes were collected. Although no new taxes were imposed at the time Judea became a province, the census brought new methods for their collection.[18] Practically every area of Jewish life was subject to taxation by the Romans, and the presence of the procurator was a constant reminder of that fact.

As the Roman representative in Judea, the procurator was also expected to respect Jewish religious sensibilities. The Romans generally guaranteed the local customs of the people in the empire. As a result of the enlightened policies of Augustus, the Jews had been granted special considerations by the Romans regarding their religious freedom. These privileges, which were the most extensive given to any subject peoples in the empire, continued under the provincial relationship. The Romans did not require emperor worship from the Jews. They accepted Jewish allegiance in the form of two daily sacrifices in the temple on behalf of the emperor's welfare (*War* 2:197). They permitted the Jews to accumulate sacred monies for the temple treasury without interference (*Antiquities* 16:160–78). The Romans did not conscript Jewish men into the Roman army, since such service would have conflicted with the observance of the sabbath and other Jewish festivals (*Antiquities* 16:28). Also, they did not require that Jews appear in court on the sabbath (*Antiquities* 16:163). In addition, Rome was committed to respect such local customs as the prohibition

18. *Compendia*, 1:334.

against images in Jerusalem (*Antiquities* 18:55–56). In principle, the Jewish religion had the protection of the Roman Empire.

Although the principles of the provincial arrangement were tolerable to most Jews, what took place in practice was often less than satisfactory. It is not hard to imagine how the Roman officers in Palestine did not always comprehend or appreciate the religious practices of the Jews. It must have seemed strange to them that the Jews reacted so stubbornly and belligerently to matters which seemed to them so common and so inconsequential, such as the placing of image-bearing banners in Jerusalem (*War* 2:170).[19] The difficulties of understanding Jewish peculiarities sometimes led the procurators to side with the Hellenistic part of the population in Palestine. At other times, as we shall see, matters of religious concern to Jews were treated with indifference or disdain. Related disruptions were frequently handled by military suppression. Such an absence of diplomacy on the part of the procurators simply served to escalate Jewish indignation.

The procurator was, however, restrained from excessive ill-treatment of the Jews by the fear of trial in Rome for incompetency or mismanagement.[20] He needed to be cautious not to offend Jews who had friends or influence among governmental circles in Rome. And, of course, he was aware that his oppressive acts might incite rebellion on the part of the Jews (*War* 2:231). Several procurators were recalled to Rome for trial (*Antiquities* 18:88–89; *War* 2:244). Cumanus (48–52 C.E.), for example, was recalled to Rome for his mishandling of a conflict between Galileans and Samaritans (*War* 2:233–46). Unfortunately, the efforts to put controls on procuratorial activities from Rome were usually slow and difficult. Emperor Tiberius appointed procurators for long terms of office in order to protect the provinces from exploitation by ever new Roman officials (*Antiquities* 18:169–79). In the forties, fifties, and sixties, however, other emperors with different policies sent new procurators more frequently. Often the office was simply a stepping stone in the career of the equestrian officer.[21] All of these factors contributed to the deterioration of the relationship between Jews and Romans which was to take place in the next sixty years.

19. See Schürer, *History*, pp. 356–57.
20. See also *Compendia*, 1:322–23.
21. Ibid., p. 317.

THE MAJOR JEWISH SECTS

A study of the background of first century Judaism requires a discussion of the major Jewish sects: Pharisees, Sadducees, and Essenes. Josephus makes numerous references to the sects in his history from the time of the Maccabees, when the sectarian groups arose, up to the time when Judea became a province of Rome in 6 C.E. Appropriately enough for our study, it is at that point in his narrative that he describes the beliefs and practices of these sects, although Josephus makes few explicit references to these sects in his history of the period from 6 to 74 C.E. The brief, general introductions to the sects contained in this section serve as a basis for discussing their political role in Israel's subsequent history.

A small minority of the five hundred thousand or so Jewish residents in Palestine[22] belonged to the major sects, the Pharisees comprising "over six thousand" (*Antiquities* 17:42), the Essenes "more than four thousand" (*Antiquities* 18:20) and the Sadducees "but a few men" (*Antiquities* 18:17). Though minorities, the sects often had a wider influence among nonsectarian Jews. There was no such thing, however, as "normative" Judaism in the prewar period, and no one sect had a particularly powerful hold on the country.[23] This means that at the time of the war no one sect by itself had enough influence or support to be able either to force the nation to war or to ensure the peace.

Being a member of a sect was simply one of the many legitimate ways of being Jewish, often the way chosen by those who were in positions of leadership or those who devoted more time to the earnest pursuit of the study and practice of Judaism. Sadducees were found among the wealthy landowners and aristocratic high priestly families. Pharisees were made up primarily of artisans and merchants from the middle and lower urban classes. Essenes drew upon the disenchanted from both classes.[24]

---

22. This is the estimated population of Palestine by J. Jeremias, *Jerusalem in the Time of Jesus* (Philadelphia: Fortress Press, 1969), p. 205. Contrast A. Byatt, "Josephus and Population Numbers in First Century Palestine," *Palestine Exploration Quarterly* 56, who estimates two and one-half million inhabitants.

23. See especially Morton Smith, "Palestinian Judaism in the First Century," *Israel: Its Role in Civilization*, ed. Moshe Davis (New York: The Seminary Israel Institute, 1956). He points out that Josephus' apologetic for the Pharisees in the *Antiquities* has led Josephus to exaggerate the influence, and perhaps also the number, of the Pharisees (pp. 74–79).

24. Jacob Neusner, *A Life of Yohanan ben Zakkai*, 2d ed. (Leiden: E. J. Brill, 1970), p. 23.

The majority of Jews were the ordinary peasants of Israel, who were in general lukewarm about religion, yet who entertained a popular religious loyalty to the divinely ordained institutions of Israel—the temple, the law, the holy city, the holy land, and religio-national festivals. Among these common people were smaller groups exhibiting a variety of charismatic, communal, and political characteristics.[25] Thus, far from being monolithic, the Judaism of the first century was rich and vigorously varied and by no means limited to the three major sects. And although at the opening of the war the Jewish people may have been united in their desire for independence, the subsequent struggles for leadership and the conflicts among revolutionaries really reflected the heterogeneous nature of Palestinian Judaism that had been there all along.

We also note that being a sectarian may not have been a fulltime vocation. Adherents were first of all artisans or priests or aristocrats or council members, and secondarily members of a sect.[26] Sectarian matters would have been demanding for those who had their own social institutions, such as the Essenes, and less demanding for Pharisees who, though having fellowships, lived and worked within the society. Many Sadducees were national leaders. Their sectarian beliefs and practices may have primarily served the ends of their leadership roles. If it is correct that sectarian life was often a secondary pursuit, this might explain why the later divisions in Israel over the war issue did not run along sectarian lines. Although the role of the sects in this historical period was very important, the allegiance to or influence of social class, geographic origin, priestly affiliation, or vocational economic group may have been stronger than sectarian ties.

The major sects differed on points of belief and practice. All Jews were united in their commitment to monotheism. Beyond that, both among and within sects, there was room for a variety of theological, anthropological, and eschatological points of view. As we shall see, such conceptual differences are cited by Josephus. However, the factors which probably gave the greatest content to the Jewish allegiance to God had less to do with doctrinal beliefs than with ethical-religious practices. Jews believed that God gave Moses the law as the guide for

25. See further, Smith, "Palestinian Judaism," pp. 71ff., 81.
26. For example, *War* 3:11; *Antiquities* 20:199; and *Life* 191. See Jacob Neusner, *From Politics to Piety* (Englewood Cliffs, N.J.: Prentice-Hall, 1971), p. 8.

the life and conduct of his people. What primarily distinguished the sects from each other was their differing interpretations and applications of the law in matters of temple ritual, purity regulations, criminal judgments, daily piety, and political involvement.

PHARISEES[27]

The Pharisees, who are considered the most accurate interpreters of the laws, and hold the position of the leading sect, attribute everything to Fate and to God; they hold that to act rightly or otherwise rests, indeed, for the most part with men, but that in each action Fate cooperates. Every soul, they maintain, is imperishable, but the soul of the good alone passes into another body, while the souls of the wicked suffer eternal punishment. (*War* 2:162–63)

In describing the Pharisees as "the most accurate interpreters of the laws" (*War* 2:162), Josephus points to the essence of Pharisaism: the attempt to put the whole of life under the control of the law. For example, while the law prescribed cleansing rituals for the life of a priest functioning in the temple, the Pharisees urged all Jews to carry out these purity regulations in their daily lives because they viewed all Israel as a "kingdom of priests" (Exodus 19:6).

The Pharisees were open to innovation. They expanded the scope of written laws by means of oral traditions in order to draw out from the written word regulations for the guidance of daily living and in order to reinterpret them to apply to changing conditions (*Antiquities* 13:297). While all Pharisees accepted this elucidation of the written law by means of oral traditions, some were more open to innovation than others. We know from Rabbinic sources, for example, that Hillel the Elder was a liberalizing force in Pharisaism during Herod's time. In addition to the traditional method of citing oral traditions of former sages, Hillel employed logical argument as a basis for the exposition of the text. This innovative method enabled him to apply the law in a way which took account of the social conditions of his time. Hillel's wisdom and learning won him the position of the leading Pharisee of

27. For passages which refer to Pharisees, see *War* 1:110–14, 571; 2:119, 162–64, 166, 411; *Antiquities* 13:171–72, 288–89, 292, 401, 405, 408–10, 415, 423; 15:3, 370; 17:41, 44, 46; 18:4, 11–17, 23; *Life* 10–12, 21, 191, 197ff. For a history of the critical study of the Pharisees, see J. Neusner, *The Rabbinic Traditions about the Pharisees before 70*, 3 vols. (Leiden: E. J. Brill, 1971). On the popular level, see Neusner, *Politics*, and W. D. Davies, *Introduction to Pharisaism* (Philadelphia: Fortress Press, 1967).

his day.[28] Shammai, a leading Pharisaic contemporary, was generally stricter in his application of the law than Hillel. Thus, although Pharisees were open to legal innovation, there were differences among them.

Such openness toward innovation in matters of law was also reflected in the Pharisaic attitude toward doctrine. Josephus attributes to the Pharisees the belief that God (Fate) is active in human life and that there is a life after death. These beliefs point to the innovations in Jewish thought which came during the last several centuries B.C.E. and which were accepted by the Pharisees: a belief in resurrection and a final judgment. The Pharisees, no less than the apocalypticists, held the belief that God would intervene dramatically to right injustices against his people, and establish a community based fully on God's law.[29]

The name "Pharisee" probably means "separatist," implying that the Pharisees saw themselves and Israel as a people set apart for obedience to the Lord. Thus, they were a deeply religious sect. When we first meet them in Josephus' narrative, they are actively involved in the governmental intrigues of the Hasmonaean rulers (*War* 1:110–14; *Antiquities* 13:288–89, 292–96, 401, 405, 408–10, 415, 423). Traditionally, the Pharisees have been seen as a "nonpolitical" sect which concerned itself with the state only when it interfered with their religious practices.[30] This assumption would suggest that the Pharisees were active in the courts of the Hasmonaeans to protect their religious interests and perhaps also those of the populace. They would be seen as being indifferent to the type of government in Palestine, whether it be a monarchy or a province of Rome, as long as they were free to pursue the law of God. In this way, the Pharisees favored Roman rule in 63 B.C.E. because it better served that purpose than other alternatives.

The view that the Pharisees had primarily nonpolitical motives can, however, be challenged. It has been suggested that Pharisees opposed the Hasmonaeans not to prevent the excessive politicization of Israel, but to safeguard the authority of the Sanhedrin and the populace from

28. On Hillel, see especially Nahum Glatzer, *Hillel the Elder: The Emergence of Classical Judaism* (New York: Schocken Books, 1956).
29. See especially W. D. Davies, "Apocalyptic and Pharisaism," *Christian Origins and Judaism* (Philadelphia: Westminster Press, 1962).
30. See, for example, the first edition of Emil Schürer's *A History of the Jewish People in the Time of Jesus Christ*, second division (New York: Scribner's, 1890), 2:17ff. All other references are to the 1975 edition.

usurpation by the kings.[31]   According to this view, the Pharisees favored Roman rule in 63 B.C.E. (*Antiquities* 14:40) and the provisional arrangement in both 4 B.C.E. (*War* 2:80–91) and 6 C.E. (*War* 2:342–46) because they believed that they would achieve greater authority for the populace under a high priestly government than they had experienced under the Maccabean and Herodian monarchies. They functioned as a political party to protect the political power of the people.   The Pharisees are thereby interpreted as opposing gentile rule in principle; but, as political realists with regard to the Roman Empire, they worked for a provincial government to protect and enhance the political power of the people.   The fact that there were purges against Pharisees in the time of Alexander Jannaeus and Herod the Great supports the view that they functioned as a political party (*Antiquities* 14:175; 17:44).

Probably both motivations—protection of the power of the populace and the need for freedom of religious expression—were operative.   We have already noted the variety within Pharisaic interpretation of the law.   Presumably that same variety was evident in the responses to Herod's reign.

The portrait which has come down to us of Hillel the Elder, for example, is characterized by gentleness, humility, and patience.   He did not accept Herod's regime, probably because he opposed foreign oppression in principle, but also because Herod's tyrannical manner was such a contrast to the values Hillel pursued.   But Hillel did not actively oppose Herod by any threat or intimidation; rather, his resistance took the form of a choice to pursue peace and social justice (*Aboth* 1:12). His innovations in legal interpretation led him to two significant legal decisions which enabled the poor to have greater opportunities to obtain loans (*Shebiit* 10:3–4) and guaranteed to those forced to sell their homes the opportunity to recover them within the subsequent year (*Arakin* 9:4).   Both decisions protected the poor and boosted the economy during some of the extreme periods of impoverishment of Herod's time.[32]   Messianism and apocalyptic speculation are not to be found in Hillel's teaching, perhaps because he thought they would lead

31. Allon, "Attitude of the Pharisees," pp. 55–60.   He claims the Pharisees defended the point of view "that the king may do nothing without the consent of the high priest and the Sanhedrin" (*Antiquities* 4:224).

32. For the social significance of Hillel's life and teaching, see especially Judah Goldin, "Hillel the Elder," *Journal of Religion* 26 (1946): 263–77.

to political dissension. Rather he perceived the future hope to be already present in the pursuit of peace and the love of humanity, in that "he who has acquired for himself words of the Torah has acquired life in the coming world."[33] Whatever future apocalyptic event of liberation Hillel may have believed in, he left it in God's hands.

Shammai too, although he sought to preserve the strictness of the law, was a man who pursued peace. Both probably represented many Pharisees who were encouraged by the words of an earlier Pharisee, "love work, shun authority, and do not court the ruling powers" (*Aboth* 1:10). Yet Hillel and Shammai had schools of followers who may have been more politically involved than they themselves were. Other Pharisees may not have been strict followers of either one.

We have seen how large numbers of Pharisees twice refused to take the oath to Herod, partly because they were opposed to taking oaths, partly also perhaps because they were unwilling to take an oath to a gentile emperor (*Antiquities* 15:368–71; 17:41–46). In any case, they refused to cooperate. Earlier two Pharisaic leaders had admonished the people to open the gates of Jerusalem to the threat of Herod's conquest, but only to prevent the slaughter which might have ensued if they had resisted (*Antiquities* 15:3). Some, who were realistic enough to see the futility of opposition to Herod, became involved in the political process in a peaceful way to persuade the Romans to grant provincial status to Israel. Other Pharisees, like the two sages who advised their pupils to tear down the golden eagle, actually resisted Herod—but only near the end of his life when his power was weakened (*War* 1:648–55; *Antiquities* 17:149–67). Others became involved in a political conspiracy to undermine Herod's authority and were executed for it (*Antiquities* 17:41–46).

A variety of Pharisaic attitudes may lie behind these different responses to Herod's reign. Hillel interpreted the law in the pursuit of peace for the benefit of the community, leaving the determination of the state in God's hands. Some Pharisees may have felt constrained to endure foreign oppression in the belief that it was God's punishment for the sins of the nation. Others, while opposing it in principle, may have tolerated it only because they still had religious freedom. Some, perhaps sympathetic to Hillel, were probably politically involved in peaceful ways. Some Pharisees opposed Herod's rule in zeal for the law.

33. See Glatzer, *Hillel*, pp. 63–73.

Perhaps the Shammaite wing who guarded the strictness of the law were less prone to accept the encroachments of Herod's reign. Depending on how intensely some of these views were held, they led certain Pharisees to join the ranks of the revolutionaries in 6 C.E. and perhaps also in 4 B.C.E. Thus it is important to keep multiple possibilities for Pharisaic involvement in mind as we trace the political events of the first century.

Recently it has been argued that as a result of the politically hostile atmosphere of the Herodians, the Pharisees as a whole became depoliticized, perhaps under Hillel's influence, and by the first century had become a strictly religious sect.[34] There are several grounds for the argument that the Pharisees made such a change. First, Josephus has few references to the Pharisees as a party in his narrative history of the period after 6 C.E. Second, Josephus' claim that the Pharisees had political power over the Sadducees in the first century C.E. because of their influence with the masses (*Antiquities* 18:17) is probably an exaggeration due to his apologetic desire to commend the Pharisees to the Romans at the time the *Antiquities* was written. Third, and most impressive, is that virtually all the New Testament and Rabbinic sources show that the Pharisees were preoccupied with matters of personal and sectarian piety during the prewar period of the first century.[35] The conclusion is that in the first century the Pharisees functioned as a religious sect, not a political party. Individual members, such as Simon ben Gamaliel, would have participated in the political life of Israel as aristocratic, upper class leaders, but not as representatives of the Pharisaic sect.[36]

While the Pharisees undoubtedly functioned in the first century C.E. more as a religious sect than a political party, some evidence indicates they were not completely depoliticized. While it is true that the

34. See Neusner, *Politics*, p. 91. Neusner agrees that Pharisees functioned as a political party up to the beginning of Herod's reign, but for different reasons from those claimed by Allon. Neusner claims they used political power to force their views and practices upon the country (p. 50).
35. See Neusner, *The Rabbinic Traditions*. He claims that Pharisaic laws from this period deal not with the governance of the country, but with rules for table fellowship (*Politics*, p. 90).
36. Neusner, *Politics*, p. 66. See also Cecil Roth, "The Pharisees in the War of 66–73," *Journal of Semitic Studies* 7 (1962): 66–67. For an excellent analysis of the larger role the Pharisees could have played in the subsequent course of events, see A. Schalit "Palestine under the Seleucids and Romans" in A. Toynbee, *The Crucible of Christianity* (New York: World Publishing Company, 1969), pp. 65–76.

Antiquities as well as the *Life* probably exaggerate the political role of the Pharisees, this exaggeration should not overshadow the fact that in the *War*, where no pro-Pharisaic apologetic is evident, the Pharisees are cited as "the leading sect" and "the most accurate interpreters of the laws" (2:162). Second, the fact that there are few explicit references to the Pharisaic party in Josephus' political narrative of the first century is not surprising, since there are even fewer explicit references to the Sadducees, whom we know to have been actively involved in political affairs. Besides, it should be noted that in the *War*, Josephus does refer to some Pharisees functioning as a political party as late as the period just before Herod's death in 4 B.C.E. (*War* 1:571). This leads one to wonder: if the Pharisees were politically active as late as the end of Herod's reign, did this involvement continue into the first century? These considerations encourage us to be open to the evidence from Josephus' writings regarding the political involvement of Pharisees in the period under study, 6 to 74 C.E.

SADDUCEES[37]

[The Sadducees] do away with Fate altogether, and remove God beyond, not merely the commission, but the very sight, of evil. They maintain that man has the free choice of good or evil, and that it rests with each man's will whether he follows the one or the other. As for the persistence of the soul after death, penalties in the underworld, and rewards, they will have none of them. (*War* 2:164–65)

They own no observances of any sort apart from the laws; in fact, they reckon it a virtue to dispute with the teachers of the path of wisdom that they pursue. There are but few men to whom this doctrine has been made known, but these are men of the highest standing. (*Antiquities* 18:16–17)

The Sadducees[38] were primarily comprised of "men of the highest standing" (*Antiquities* 18:17; cf. 13:298): namely, the wealthy aristocratic, ruling class of Israel, including most of the high priestly families. The appellation "Sadducee" probably comes from Zaddok, a high priest in the time of Solomon whose descendants claimed to have the legitimate right to rule Israel. During the Maccabean Revolt, several different groups claimed to be the true "sons of Zaddok." One such

37. For passages which refer to the Sadducees, see *War* 2:119, 164–66; *Antiquities* 13:171, 173, 293, 296–98; 18:11, 16–17; 20:199; *Life* 10.
38. There is no extant writing which is acknowledged to be by a Sadducee. The New Testament, Rabbinic literature, and Josephus' works make reference to the Sadducees, but they are biased against them and must be read with caution.

group was ostracized and went to Qumran near the Dead Sea. Another group retained control in Jerusalem in cooperation with the Hasmonaeans and came to be called Sadducees. The Sadducees had the most to lose from a war with Rome, for they were risking their wealth as well as their social and political positions.

The Sadducees were the most conservative element in Judaism. Josephus writes that "they own no observance of any sort apart from the laws" (*Antiquities* 18:16; cf. 13:298–99). They stuck with the letter of the written text of the Torah and accepted none of the Pharisaic interpretations or elucidations of the law designed to extend it to daily life. Their legal judgments were generally more strict, since they did not accommodate the law to changing times and circumstances. They followed the criminal codes of the Torah in civil matters, and they saw to it that the priests observed strictly the ritual regulations for temple worship. The Sadducees had greater freedom than the Pharisees in pursuit of their own life-style, since decisions about matters not dealt with in the written law were left to the individual.[39] Although this freedom gave the Sadducees greater possibilities for accommodation to Roman or Hellenistic ways, most, as we shall see, maintained a basic commitment to the Jewish institutions of the law, the temple, and the state.

The Sadducees rejected the doctrinal innovations of the Pharisees: the survival of the soul after death (*Antiquities* 18:16; *War* 2:163), the concept of a resurrection of the dead, the notion of an apocalyptic intervention of God with a supernatural salvation and final judgment, and a belief in realms of angels and demons. None of these doctrinal ideas can be found by a strict reading of the Torah; consequently, they are rejected by the Sadducees.[40] The Sadducees did affirm a doctrine of human freedom and responsibility whereby rewards and punishments are given in this life. In this scheme, they "do away with Fate altogether" and "remove God beyond the sight of evil" (*War* 2:164). Thus, they acclaim the freedom of the will, "the free choice of Good or Evil" (2:165), without any cooperation or intervention of God in the affairs of men (cf. *Antiquities* 13:173).

What the Sadducees believed at the individual level also held true

---

39. Günther Baumbach, "Das Sadduzaerverständnis bei Josephus Flavius und im Neuen Testament," *Kairos* 13 (1971): 27.
40. Neusner, *Yohanan*, p. 24.

at the national level. With no concept of Fate or apocalyptic intervention, they embraced a this-worldly eschatology. By means of the applications of the Torah throughout the land and the proper worship in the temple, the Sadducees hoped to secure liberation for the nation, so that the Israelite kingdom might be free as it had once been under the rule of David.[41] In principle, this implied an exclusion of gentiles, that is, Romans, from the land. In practice, however, the Sadducees sought to bring about their eschatological vision of an independent temple-state by trying to achieve as much autonomy as possible within the Roman Empire by use of the realistic political and diplomatic means at their disposal.

The history of the Sadducees in the first century is difficult to trace from Josephus' narrative because there are so few explicit references to them. However, since we know that they were the party of the ruling class, it is possible for us to trace the history of the high priesthood, and to a lesser extent that of the aristocracy, and see it as representative of the history of the Sadducean party. From the time of Herod (37–4 B.C.E.), the high priests were appointed and deposed at will by the Roman representative in Palestine, either the Herodian king or the procurator. They quite naturally appointed people, usually from several leading families, who were sympathetic to the Roman presence in Palestine. This close association between high priests and Romans has led to the traditional characterization of the Sadducees as "collaborators" with the Romans.

Recently, some scholars have challenged the view that the high priests were "collaborators." It has been suggested that as early as Joazar (6 C.E.), the high priests manifested anti-Roman behavior.[42] Shortly after Joazar's success in persuading the Jews to accept the Roman census, he was deposed for being at odds with the Jewish people (*Antiquities* 18:26). It is unlikely, the argument goes, that the Romans would have deposed him because he had represented the Roman side in a difference with the people. The real cause, therefore, must have been anti-Roman behavior. This suggestion is supported by Josephus' assertion that Joazar had been deposed earlier from a brief stint as high priest in 4 B.C.E. by Archelaus "for having supported the

41. Rudolf Meyer, *"Saddoukaios" Theological Dictionary of the New Testament,* 9 vols., ed. Gerhard Kittel, trans. Geoffrey Bromiley (Grand Rapids: Eerdmans, 1964), 7:35–54.
42. Baumbach, "Sadduzaerverständnis," p. 21.

rebels" (*Antiquities* 17:339) who had been active after the death of Herod. Joazar would then presumably have been reappointed by the people at the end of Archelaus' reign, and subsequently deposed by the legate of Syria for some anti-Roman behavior unknown to us.

This attempt to depict Joazar as anti-Roman is, however, unconvincing. The Romans might well have deposed a pro-Roman high priest because he was at odds with the people. If Joazar was "overpowered by a popular faction" (*Antiquities* 18:26), he would no longer be an effective high priest. It would not be surprising if, after persuading the reluctant Jews to accept the Roman census of 6 C.E., Joazar was no longer influential with his fellow countrymen, even if he was pro-Roman. He would have been replaced by a neutral figure more acceptable to a broader majority of the people.[43] Also, it is unlikely that the people were responsible for elevating Joazar to the priesthood the second time, since they had requested his deposition when he was high priest the first time (*Antiquities* 17:207). Joazar probably never really cooperated with the revolutionaries in 4 B.C.E. In fact, he supported Archelaus in 4 B.C.E. and Roman provincial rule in C.E. 6. Archelaus, to save face amid the popular demand for Joazar's deposition, probably dismissed him on the false grounds that he had cooperated with revolutionaries.[44] Later Archelaus himself probably reappointed Joazar at a time near the end of his reign when he needed all the support he could get. Thus, there is little evidence for overt anti-Roman activity in the priesthood of Joazar.

As we trace the history of the Sadducees in our study of the first century, we will be following the active involvement of the high priests in the political life of Israel. Although the evidence for resistance to Rome is scant in the case of Joazar, we will see that the Sadducees played an important role in the national resistance against the Romans in subsequent years.

THE ESSENES[45]

The doctrine of the Essenes is wont to leave everything in the hands of God. They regard the soul as immortal and believe that they ought to strive especially to draw near to righteousness. They send votive

43. E. M. Smallwood, "High Priests and Politics in Roman Palestine," *Journal of Theological Studies* 13 (1962): 21.
44. Ibid., p. 20.
45. For references to the Essenes in Josephus' writings, see *War* 1:78; 2:119–61, 567; 3:11; 5:145; *Antiquities* 13:171, 298, 311; 15:371–73, 378; 17:346; 18:11, 18–22; *Life* 10–11.

offerings to the temple but perform their sacrifices employing a different ritual of purification. For this reason they are barred from those sacred precincts of the temple that are frequented by all the people and perform their rites by themselves. Otherwise they are of the highest character, devoting themselves solely to agricultural labour. . . . They hold their possessions in common. . . . They neither bring wives into the community nor do they own slaves. . . . Instead they live by themselves and perform menial tasks for one another. (*Antiquities* 18:18–19, 21)

The name "Essenes" may mean "the pious ones," suggesting that they may have originated from the "pious" Hasidaeans, strict Jews who had remained loyal to Jewish tradition in the face of forced Hellenization by Syrian overlords in the early second century B.C.E.[46] Like the other sects we have considered, the Essenes emerged as a distinct group in the struggles for leadership of the nation following the Maccabean revolt from Syria (165–64 B.C.E.). The Essenes were apparently a predominantly priestly group who opposed the attempt of the Maccabean rulers to usurp the high priestly office without priestly descent. The Maccabeans, supported by the Sadducees, succeeded in establishing their priestly authority. As a result of this, by the end of the second century B.C.E., the Essenes had separated themselves from the temple and from the mainstream of Jewish life. They probably withdrew because they regarded the temple authorities and worship as illegitimate (*Antiquities* 18:22), the masses of Jews as impure (*War* 2:143), and the Pharisees as not strict enough in their application of the Torah.[47] The Essenes considered themselves set apart for holiness and purity, perhaps thinking they were the true Israel.

The Essenes established their own social institutions, living in separate communes in towns and cities throughout the country (*War* 2:124), although it is not clear whether these communal groups were outposts of a central headquarters or diverse but related splinter groups of the same sect.[48] The Essenes devoted themselves primarily to agricultural labor (*Antiquities* 18:19, 22), carried out their own priestly rituals (*Antiquities* 18:18–19, 22), generally spurned marriage (*War* 2:120–21; cf. *War* 2:160–61 and *Antiquities* 18:21), and held their possessions in common (*War* 2:122, 124–27; *Antiquities* 18:20).

46. Marcel Simon, *Jewish Sects in the Time of Jesus*, trans. James H. Farley (Philadelphia: Fortress Press, 1967), pp. 49–50.
47. Ibid., pp. 47–48.
48. Matthew Black, "The Patristic Accounts of Jewish Sectarianism," *Bulletin of John Rylands Library* 41 (1958–59): 293.

They are portrayed by Josephus as a peaceful people, especially in their relations with one another (*War* 2:125, 135).[49]

The Essenes were very strict in their interpretation of the law (cf. *War* 2:128–34; *Antiquities* 18:18, 20), more so than the Pharisees. They applied it to govern their behavior in all matters except regarding acts of charity, which were left to the initiative of the individual (*War* 2:134). In doctrinal matters, they believed that fate determines everything and man has no choice (*Antiquities* 13:172). They were "wont to leave everything in the hands of God"; in other words, the Essenes, like the Pharisees, trusted God to bring about their vindication by apocalyptic intervention and final judgment.[50]

Because of their isolation from the mainstream of Jewish life, it is unlikely that the Essenes made any significant contribution to the political history of Israel. Some evidence indicates that they may have reentered Jewish daily life for a time when Israel was under Herod the Great (37–4 B.C.E.) (*Antiquities* 15:372, 378), but they probably retreated again after his death in 4 B.C.E.

Most of our knowledge of the Essenes comes from the Dead Sea Scrolls, which were first discovered in caves on the shore of the Dead Sea in 1948. The site of Qumran was excavated as the location of an ancient Jewish monastic community. Some of the scrolls discovered there were manuscripts of scriptural writings from the Hebrew Bible, but others were sectarian writings not known before. Although the name "Essenes" does not appear in the scrolls, most scholars agree that the Qumran community responsible for these scrolls was Essene.

Despite the generally accepted view that the Qumran sect was Essene, some authors have claimed that the Dead Sea group was not Essene, but was rather the sect of revolutionaries founded by Judas of Galilee, whose descendants made up the leadership of a group called "the Sicarii."[51] However, serious objections can be raised against this theory.

49. See also Philo, who explicitly portrays the Essenes as pacifists (*Every Good Man* in F. H. Colson and G. H. Whitaker, trans., *Philo*, 12:78).

50. For the attribution of these beliefs to the Essenes, see Hippolytus, *Refutation of All Heresies* in *The Ante-Nicene Fathers*, ed. A. Roberts and J. Donaldson (New York: Charles Scribner's Sons, 1926), 9:27. Josephus clothes Jewish eschatological beliefs in the garb of Greek thought (cf. *War* 2:154–58).

51. Cecil Roth, "The Jewish Revolt against the Romans in Light of the Dead Sea Scrolls," *Exploration Quarterly* 90 (1958): 104–21; idem, *The Dead Sea Scrolls* (New York: W. W. Norton and Company, 1965); G. R. Driver, *The Judaean Scrolls* (New York: Schocken Books, 1965); idem, "The Mythology of Qumran," *Jewish Quarterly Review* 61 (1971): 241–81.

First, given the way in which the procurators suppressed unarmed followers of prophetic figures and executed the two sons of Judas the Galilean, it is historically implausible that a sect of revolutionaries, whether they were Judas' followers or militant Essenes, could have maintained a center in Palestine without being destroyed by Roman troops.[52]

Second, the hypothesis that the Sicarii wrote the Dead Sea Scrolls requires us to equate events described cryptically in the scrolls with events surrounding the death of a revolutionary named Menahem in 66 C.E.[53] To do this, it is necessary to assume that the scrolls were written in the brief period between 66 and 73 C.E., 73 C.E. being the year these scholars date the destruction of Qumran by the Romans. However, the scrolls and the history of Menahem do not exactly correlate.[54] And most archaeologists date the fall of Qumran at 68 C.E., not 73 C.E.;[55] so there would have been little time between 66 and 68 C.E. for the scrolls to have been written and hidden. Besides, the paleographic evidence regarding the manuscripts of these works indicates an earlier dating.[56]

Third, the idea that there was some close connection between the residents of Qumran and the revolutionary group of Sicarii which we know to have been at the fortress Masada is rendered unlikely by the geographical barriers between the two locations.[57]

Finally, there is no reference in the Qumran literature to the doctrine "no Lord but God," which, according to Josephus, was so characteristic of the Sicarii. And the later terrorist acts of the Sicarii would seem to

---

52. H. H. Rowley, "The Qumran Sectaries and the Zealots," *Vetus Testamentum* 9 (1959): 385.

53. Roth, "Dead Sea Scrolls," pp. 7ff.; Driver, *Judaean Scrolls*, pp. 267ff. For an account of Menahem's activity, see below.

54. See Rowley, "Qumran Sectaries," pp. 187ff.; idem., "Qumran: The Essenes and the Zealots," *Von Ugarit nach Qumran: Beitrage zur alttestamentlichen und altorientalischen Forschung Festscrift*, ed. Johannes Hempel and Leonard Rost (Berlin: Alfred Töpelmann, 1958), pp. 187ff.; Matthew Black, "The Judaean Scrolls: The Scrolls and the New Testament," *New Testament Studies* 13 (1966): 83; and R. deVaux, "The Judaean Scrolls: Essenes or Zealots?", *New Testament Studies* 13 (1966): 98.

55. The latest coins are from 68 C.E. Also, Vespasian was active in that area at this time. See R. deVaux, "Essenes or Zealots?", p. 103.

56. See F. M. Cross, *The Ancient Library of Qumran* (Garden City, N.Y.: Anchor, 1961), p. 89.

57. So Roth, "Dead Sea Scrolls," pp. 28–29; and Driver, *Judaean Scrolls*, pp. 393ff.

be at odds with the admonition in the scrolls to leave vengeance in the hands of God.[58]

The formidable objections to the hypothesis that the Qumran community were Sicarii lead us to reaffirm the more commonly accepted view that they were a community of Essenes who had their historical origins in the second century B.C.E.[59] The sect continued at Qumran until 68 C.E. except for a period of time during Herod's reign (37–4 B.C.E.).

Various writings attest in an obscure way to the historical origins of the sect. This Essene community had separated themselves from other Jews as the true "sons of light," atoning for the whole land by strict obedience to the law in preparation for the final day of vengeance. Their *Manual of Discipline* indicates the strictness upon which their communal life was based. Their *War Scroll* is a description of the final battle which would take place at the end time. The community itself was organized under military discipline, ready for the war in which the oppressive enemy would be defeated.[60] Members were admonished to hate the sons of darkness but to take no vengeance until God himself initiated the final struggle. Thus, we have what may have been military visions of the future with actual quietism in the present.[61]

This position was probably maintained during most of the period under study, although the Essenes may have changed at the time of the Roman-Jewish War if they saw that conflict as the fulfillment of their military visions. We will evaluate the evidence for that possibility in connection with our study of the period of the war.

58. Cross, *Ancient Library* (Garden City, N.Y.: 1961), p. 75, n. 33.

59. Rowley, "Qumran Sectaries," p. 391.

60. Neusner, *Yohanan*, p. 21.

61. The *War Scroll* contains the procedures and rules which were to be followed when the final eschatological battle was to be fought. David Daube, *Civil Disobedience in Antiquity* (Edinburgh: Edinburgh University Press, 1972), argues that in apocalyptic, the dominant theme is that the final denouement will occur by an inevitable plan which has been revealed to the believers. As such, it is only for them to stand and wait (p. 85). Daube writes of the originators of the *War Scroll*, "My hunch is that the group that produced this work was far removed from any practical plotting against whatever overlords may have governed the country" (p. 87).

III

RESISTANCE WITHIN THE JEWISH PROVINCE: 6-66 C.E.

Josephus' narrative of the prewar period shows the progressive deterioration of the relationship between the Jewish nation and the Romans from relative peace and cooperation to the breakdown of law and order in the countryside and disorder in Jerusalem. During this era, there was a great variety in the means of resistance against Rome. Some forms of resistance were peaceful attempts to ease tensions and to stem the tide of the more radical revolution which followed.

Our study begins with an analysis of the brief revolt of Judas the Galilean which took place when Judea received provincial status. It is important to make a careful evaluation of Judas the Galilean and his revolt, for the assessment of Judas' activity and influence significantly affects one's understanding of the whole period leading up to and including the war.

JUDAS THE GALILEAN: 6 C.E.

THE REVOLT OF 6 C.E.

When the Jewish territory under Archelaus became a Roman province, Coponius was appointed procurator and a census of people and property was conducted (*Antiquities* 18:2); for the first time, Judea experienced direct Roman rule in its territory. It was at this time that Judas the Galilean incited the populace to revolt:

> The territory of Archelaus was now reduced to a province, and Coponius, a Roman of the equestrian order, was sent out as procurator, entrusted by Augustus with full powers, including the infliction of capital punishment. Under his administration, a Galilaean, named Judas, incited his countrymen to revolt, upbraiding them as cowards for con-

47

senting to pay tribute to the Romans and tolerating mortal masters, after having God for their Lord. This man was a sophist who founded a sect of his own, having nothing in common with the others. (*War* 2:118)

Despite his surname, "the Galilean," Judas led his revolt in Judea, the territory which became a province at this time and in which the census was conducted.[1] The fact that Judas probably would have received the surname "the Galilean" (*War* 2:433; *Antiquities* 18:23; 20:102; *Acts* 5:37) in a territory outside Galilee supports the hypothesis that his revolt took place in Judea.

It may seem strange that Judas is called "the Galilean," if he was, as Josephus writes, from the city of Gamala in Gaulanitis (*Antiquities* 18:3).[2] However, Gamala and other places east of the Sea of Galilee, though outside the geographical boundaries of Galilee, were probably identified with Galilee culturally in the popular mind. In the later war, Gamala was included with Upper and Lower Galilee under the generalship of Josephus (*War* 2:568). So it would not have been strange that Judas of Gamala was referred to as "the Galilean."

Judas and his followers were reacting in accordance with ancient Jewish traditions which opposed a census (2 Samuel 24: 1–17; 1 Chronicles 21), based on the notion that assessment implies ownership.[3] The Jews believed that God owned the land and had given it to the Israelites for their use as his people. The Roman census of persons and property represented to Judas a usurping of God's right and implied a slavery to Rome. Judas encouraged his fellow countrymen to refuse to cooperate with the Romans and to oppose their direct rule in Palestine.

Because Judas would not recognize any other than God as Lord over the land and people, he offered a radical interpretation of the first commandment, "Thou shalt have no other gods before Me"

1. So Martin Hengel, *Die Zeloten* (Leiden: E. J. Brill, 1961), p. 342; and Morton Smith, "Zealots and Sicarii, Their Origins and Relation," *Harvard Theological Review* 64 (1971): 15.

2. This incongruity led S. Zeitlin to argue that "the Galilean" was a sectarian designation: "Who were the Galilaeans?" *Jewish Quarterly Review* 64 (1974): 189–203. He supports this with the claim that "the Galileans" refers to a sect in the *Life* of Josephus. However, the term "Galileans" in the *Life* simply designates the village people of Galilee. Josephus sometimes contrasts these people with the inhabitants of one of the three chief cities in Galilee (*Life* 123)—Sepphoris, Tiberias, and Gabara—who are identified by their city of residence (*Life* 30, 39, 125, etc.).

3. See Hengel, *Zeloten*, p. 138; and Günther Baumbach, "Zeloten und Sicarier," *Theologische Literatürzeitung* 90 (1965): 731.

(Exodus 20:3). It may be that the teaching of Judas implied a rejection of all human authority whatsoever. However, the fact that he rebelled at the time Judea became a province (the Jews had been paying taxes to Rome since 63 B.C.E.) suggests he opposed only "illegitimate" human authority; that is, authority which did not submit itself exclusively to the sovereignty of God. Judas certainly objected in general to the emperor's claim to divinity in his use of the title "Lord." Probably it was the specific implementation of direct Roman rule in the land, with census and resident troops, which in Judas' view most clearly offended the lordship of God. Jewish leaders who cooperated with the Roman "overlords" would probably have been considered illegitimate authorities as well, and therefore viewed not only as cowards but idolators. The active suppression of idolatrous contact with foreigners was understood by some Jews as a valid human expression of God's "zealous" wrath, the classical prototype of which is Phineas' stabbing of Zimri for having intercourse with a heathen woman (Numbers 25).[4] Although Judas himself may not have engaged in such suppression of fellow Jews, his teaching certainly encouraged such actions among others.

Josephus also claims that Judas the Galilean urged his followers, "Heaven would be their zealous helper to no lesser end than the furthering of their enterprise until it succeeded" (*Antiquities* 18:5). Apparently Judas believed that if God's people insisted on God's rule alone in the land, then God would act to establish that rule on their behalf. Being ideologically motivated, the resistance took no account of the political realities or possibilities of the situation.[5] It was a call to radical obedience with the prophetic promise of God's vindication.

Judas' teaching of "no Lord but God," which Josephus refers to as "the fourth philosophy,"[6] gave a Jewish legal rationale for resistance to Rome. It is not known how popular his cause was or how long his revolt lasted. But most Jews were apparently able to accommodate themselves to the Roman presence as long as they were not required to worship the emperor as divine and as long as there was no specific inter-

4. Compare the zealous suppression of idolatrous Jews during the Maccabean Revolt (e.g., 1 Maccabees 2:23–28).

5. Menachem Stern, "The Zealots," *Encyclopedia Judaica,* ed. Cecil Roth et al. (Jerusalem: Macmillan, 1971), supplementary volume (1972), p. 140.

6. *Antiquities* 18:9, 23. It was called the "fourth philosophy" by Josephus to indicate that it was a distinct alternative to the three traditional philosophies or sects of the Pharisees, Sadducees, and Essenes.

ference in Jewish practices of worship and laws, which for them would not have included Judas' strict interpretation of the first commandment as applied to the land.

It is important to observe that Judas' revolt was preceded by a history of resistance to the dominion of the Romans and their vassal kings in Palestine. In fact, many have identified Judas the Galilean with Judas the brigand-chief, the son of Hezekiah. We have already noted how Judas, son of Hezekiah, instigated a revolt against the Romans near Sepphoris of Galilee after the death of Herod in 4 B.C.E. (*War* 2:56; *Antiquities* 17:271–72). Hezekiah had been active in political brigandage near the Syrian border at the time of the rise of Herod. His son, Judas, was apparently carrying on the tradition of resistance. Josephus tells us nothing of the fate of this Judas in the subsequent War of Varus. It may be that he went underground and emerged again in Judea in 6 C.E. at the time of the census when he came to be known as Judas "the Galilean" (*War* 2:56; *Antiquities* 17:271–72).[7]

It may be argued that these two could not have have been the same person since the "aspirations of kingship" on the part of Judas, son of Hezekiah, were incompatible with the philosophy of "no lord but God" espoused by Judas the Galilean. However, as we have indicated, the fourth philosophy may only have rejected "illegitimate" human authority.[8] In fact, one of the descendants of Judas the Galilean did put himself forth as a messianic pretender years later (*War* 2:444). If the two Judases mentioned in the sources were the same, then Judas the Galilean belonged to a family which over a long period of time claimed royal lineage. The connection would be strengthened by the fact that Judas the Galilean was originally from Gamala, a city near the Syrian border where Hezekiah had been active a half century before (*War* 1:204; *Antiquities* 14:159–60). The idea of a dynasty of resistance stemming from Hezekiah and his son Judas parallels the dynasty of Judas the Galilean and his descendants and, if contiguous, would form a family of resisters more than a century in duration.

However, Josephus does not identify these two men as the same person. Perhaps he failed to coordinate the different sources which lay

---

7. For a list of those scholars who take this position and those who oppose it, see Hengel, *Zeloten*, p. 337, n. 4.
8. J. Kennard, "Judas the Galilaean and His Clan," *Jewish Quarterly Review* 36 (1946): 281–86.

behind the reports of the two revolts.[9] That may be true of the *War*. However, Josephus' reference in the *Antiquities* to Judas the Galilean as a Gaulanite from a city named Gamala (*Antiquities* 18:4) implies that Josephus was self-consciously distinguishing him from Judas, the son of Hezekiah, whom he had just mentioned (*Antiquities* 17:271–72).[10] Surely if Josephus had known that Judas the Galilean was identical with the brigand-chief of 4 b.c.e., it would have been to his advantage, given his bias against revolutionaries, to make that explicit.

Also, the description of each Judas is distinctly different. Judas the Galilean is not identified as a brigand-chief, nor is any violent revolutionary activity directly attributed to him.[11] He is described as a teacher. His role may have been to incite revolutionary activity, much like the two teachers who had instigated others to tear down the golden eagle a decade earlier. Also, no messianic claims are ascribed to him as they are to Judas, the son of Hezekiah. Thus, it is not certain that the Judas who revolted in 6 c.e. is to be identified with Judas, the son of Hezekiah, who led an uprising in 4 b.c.e. The possibility remains that they may have been two different kinds of figures.

Some have speculated that Judas the Galilean provided a focal point around which various groups and concerns were united in 6 c.e., in contrast to the disparate nature of the revolts throughout Israel at the time of the War of Varus in 4 b.c.e.[12] There may be some truth to that observation, but certain factors suggest that Judas' revolt was not so significant as it is often portrayed. First, the revolt was probably limited to Judea. Second, the desire to revolt would have been dampened by the recent memories of the War of Varus. Third, there was a desire among Jews to accommodate themselves to the "equitable" officers they hoped to get in the provincial arrangement (*War* 2:92), and many people welcomed direct Roman rule with the idea it would give the Jews greater autonomy than they had had under the Herodian vassal kings (*War* 2:80; *Antiquities* 17:300). Therefore, it is unlikely that

---

9. Kennard "Judas and Clan," p. 281; cf. Hengel, *Zeloten*, p. 338.

10. See the careful treatment of the character of Judas by Frances Malinowski, "Galilaean Judaism in the Writings of Flavius Josephus" (Ph.D. dissertation, Duke University, 1973), pp. 220–32.

11. Frederick Foakes-Jackson and Kirsopp Lake, eds., *The Beginnings of Christianity*, 5 vols. (London: Macmillan, 1920), vol. 1, p. 424.

12. Hengel, *Zeloten*, p. 336; and Günther Baumbach, "Die Zeloten: ihre geschichtliche und religionspolitische Bedeutung," *Bibel und Liturgie* 41 (1968): 11.

Judas would have gained widespread support for a serious attempt at rebellion. Fourth, although Josephus does state that "the populace . . . responded gladly" to his call for revolt (*Antiquities* 18:6), this passage is so rife with Josephus' apologetic desire to blame the later war on the instigation and innovation of Judas that it is clear the "glad response" is a telescoping of the popular revolutionary spirit of the fifties and sixties to the time of Judas' revolt in 6 C.E.

These considerations suggest that Judas' revolt was neither large nor sustained and probably not widely supported by different factions of the Israelite nation. These conclusions are supported by the fact that the people were persuaded to accept the census, presumably without coercion, by "the arguments of the high priest Joazar" (*Antiquities* 18:3). And Josephus does not even find it necessary to say that the Romans quelled Judas' revolt. Some have suggested that Judas' revolt must have been of significant size since it is also mentioned in Acts (5:37), an account which does explain that Judas was killed and his followers scattered. But in that passage Judas' revolt is compared with the meager four hundred men of Theudas' revolt (Acts 5:36; cf. *Antiquities* 20:97–98) and with the earliest Christian movement. Nowhere else, even in Rabbinic literature, is Judas' revolt mentioned. Hence, there is little evidence that this revolt was as significant as it is often portrayed.

DID JUDAS FOUND A SECT?

Judas' attempt to incite his countrymen to revolt might seem like only one among many resistance efforts against the Roman overlords. But this one stands out because Josephus describes Judas as a teacher (sophist) and claims that he founded a sect (*War* 2:118). This is the only point in the prewar narrative (cf. the parallel passages in *Antiquities* 18:4, 23–25) in which Josephus explicitly identifies a sect of Jews who were devoted to resisting Roman authority. Since this passage is followed immediately by a description of the Essenes, Pharisees, and Sadducees, it would be natural to assume that Judas' sect functioned in a similar way and was identifiable as a sect in the same way as the others. We might tend to assume that, like the other sects, it continued throughout the first century into the war period. However, these conclusions—that Judas founded a sect and that it continued throughout the prewar period of the first century—can be questioned, even on the basis of Josephus' own testimony.

In the first place there is no name given to this sect either in this account of its origin or in the parallel account in the *Antiquities* (18:4–10; 23–25). Most commentators assume they were called "Zealots." Although they may have been "zealous" for God's cause, there is no evidence that this term functioned as the name of a sect before 66 C.E.[13] Others have claimed that Judas' sect would have been called "Sicarii" (assassins), but by Josephus' testimony this term arose in the fifties as a nonsectarian designation on the part of Romans to describe an innovative method of resistance. It would not have been a title that this group would ever have used as a self-designation. No satisfactory explanation has been given for the contradiction between Josephus' claim that a sect was established in 6 C.E. and his failure to give it a name.[14]

Second, after Josephus mentions this sect in the *War*, he asserts that "Jewish philosophy in fact takes three forms," and then describes the Pharisees, Sadducees, and Essenes without including Judas' sect in the discussion (cf. *Antiquities* 18:10; *Life* 10). Moreover, there is no further mention of this sect in the subsequent narrative, either in the *War* or *Antiquities*. As we shall see, there are later individuals and groups who are said to have their origins with Judas, but at no point is there any mention of the term "sect." Even in the later references to Judas, he is identified only as the one who had incited Jews to revolt at the time of the census, but there is no mention in those passages of his having founded a sect (*War* 2:433; 7:253; *Antiquities* 20:102).

Finally, there is a contradiction in Josephus' description of the ideology of Judas' supposed sect. In the *War*, the sect is said to have nothing in common with any of the other sects, whereas in the *Antiquities* it is said that:

> This school agrees in all other respects with the opinions of the Pharisees, except that they have a passion for liberty that is almost uncon-

13. See especially Marc Borg, "The Currency of the Term 'Zealot,'" *Journal of Theological Studies* 19 (1973): 205–18.
14. Hengel argues that Josephus would have avoided the honorific title "Zealots" for "ruthless" and "irreligious" characters (Hengel, *Zeloten*, pp. 91–92; cf. S. G. F. Brandon, *Jesus and the Zealots* [Manchester: Manchester University Press, 1967], pp. 41ff.). However, Josephus does not hesitate to use the term for the faction of the "Zealots" active in the war period, along with his biased explanation that it described their "zeal for every vice" (*War* 4:161; 7:268–69).

querable, since they are convinced that God alone is their leader and master. (*Antiquities* 18:23)

This contradiction may be due to the apologetic purposes in Josephus' works. His dissociation of Judas' sect from the Pharisees in the earlier *War* may be due to his apologetic desire to separate the revolutionaries from traditional Judaism.[15] The connection made in the later *Antiquities* between Judas' sect and the Pharisees may be due to his later apologetic tendency to exaggerate the historical significance of the Pharisees.[16] Taken together, these observations leave one with less than decisive conclusions about a relationship between Judas' sect and the Pharisees. In the *Antiquities* (18:4, 9), Josephus writes that Saddok, a Pharisee, joined Judas in leading the revolt and founding a sect. Apparently some Pharisees, perhaps from the Shammaite wing of that party, joined Judas in advocating revolt. But to distinguish Saddok as a Pharisee may indicate that Judas himself was not one. There is no other specific information of Pharisaic cooperation with Judas. In any case, the evidence is ambiguous, and the origins of such a sect and its relationship to other Jewish sects remain unclear.

These considerations raise significant doubts about the accuracy of Josephus' reports. Did Judas found a sect? If he did, what was it like and how active was it? What was the nature of his influence on first century Judaism?

There is evidence in Josephus that there was a connection between Judas and certain later revolutionaries. Judas' descendants are mentioned by Josephus. His sons, James and Simon, were brought to trial and crucified under Tiberius Alexander who was procurator from 46–48 c.e. (*Antiquities* 20:102). Menahem, who took over the siege of the palace in Jerusalem at the opening of the war in 66 c.e. and who was subsequently killed by Eleazar, son of Ananias, was a son or grandson of Judas (*War* 2:433). Eleazar, son of Jairus, who fled to Masada after Menahem's death and who became commander at Masada, was also a descendant of Judas (*War* 7:253). The implication seems to be

---

15. Brandon, *Jesus*, pp. 38, 54. See William R. Farmer, *Maccabees, Zealots, and Josephus* (New York: Columbia University Press, 1956), pp. 33–34, n. 23; and Hengel, *Zeloten*, pp. 91–150. Baumbach, "Zeloten," p. 21, has a list of those who support a connection between Judas and the Pharisaic sect.

16. Baumbach argues that Josephus exaggerates the role of the Pharisees "in order to emphasize that their claim to leadership (in postwar Judaism) has already been justified on the basis of history": Baumbach, "Zeloten," p. 6. As such, he dismisses the *Antiquities* account of the supposed connection between Judas and the Pharisees as unhistorical.

that there was a dynasty of family leaders who engaged in revolutionary activities, although we know little of the nature or extent of these activities before the war period. During the war years they emerged in connection with the faction of revolutionaries on Masada whom Josephus calls "Sicarii."

In addition to a genealogical connection between Judas and some later revolutionaries, there is also an ideological relationship. Judas is called a "teacher" (*War* 2:118, 433), as is his son Menahem (*War* 2:445), indicating that they self-consciously passed their teaching on to others. Josephus later refers to Judas' radical view of the first commandment as a motivation for revolt among those whom Josephus calls "Sicarii." In the suicide speech of Eleazar to the Sicarii on Masada (*War* 7:323) and in the message of the Sicarii at Alexandria in Egypt after the war (*War* 7:410–19), there is the admonition "to esteem God alone as their Lord" (*War* 7:410). Thus, even after the war, some Sicarii were dying for the same doctrine of "no lord but God," which Josephus says originated with Judas. Such commitment and fortitude evident among families who espoused this teaching would seem to imply that they were part of a community with a tradition of devotion to this point of view. Thus, both historically by way of family descent and ideologically with regard to the radical view of the first commandment, there is a connection between Judas the Galilean and the later Sicarii.

The conclusion might be, in Josephus' words, that

> Judas and Saddok started among us an intrusive fourth school of philosophy; and when they had won an abundance of devotees, they filled the body politic immediately with tumult, also planting the seeds of those troubles which subsequently overtook it, all because of the novelty of this hitherto unknown philosophy. (*Antiquities* 18:9)

On the basis of this information, the picture emerges of a sect founded in 6 C.E. which gradually grew in influence and effectiveness and which in some fundamental way was responsible for the later downfall of the state.[17]

However, this picture cannot be accepted at face value. For along with Josephus' explicit statements about Judas' sect, we are confronted

---

17. Hengel best represents the traditionally accepted view when he argues that "Judas the Galilean founded the so-called fourth sect, an actual party with quite definite points of view . . . , a firm organization and unified leadership, which decisively determined the fate of the Jewish people during the next two generations and which formed the stable center-point of the growing Jewish freedom movement": Hengel, *Zeloten*, p. 89 (my translation).

with a puzzling fact. Nowhere in Josephus' narrative of the period between 6 and 66 C.E. is there any clear reference to this sect: there is no mention of any conspiratorial revolutionary activity in Josephus' account of political events from 6 to 44 C.E.; nor is there explicit mention of a sect or group motivated by Judas' ideology in the narrative for the period 44–66 C.E., although a great deal of revolutionary activity is described.

Josephus does apply to some of the revolutionaries of the fifties and sixties the term *sicarii*, the same term (Sicarii) later used to designate the sect of Judas' descendants in the war period. However, in his accounts of prewar revolutionaries Josephus employs the term *sicarii*, as he does "brigands," in a functional way, not as a sectarian appellation.[18] Josephus observes that during the procuratorship of Felix (52–60 C.E.) "a new (different) species of banditti was springing up in Jerusalem, the so-called *sicarii*, who committed murders in broad daylight in the heart of the city" (*War* 2:254).[19] They got their name, Josephus tells us elsewhere (*Antiquities* 20:186), from their use of a dagger or *sica* for assassinations. The group led by Judas' descendants who are designated during the war period as "Sicarii" were probably among the revolutionaries of the fifties and sixties, but Josephus' functional use of *sicarii* and "brigands" in his narrative of the prewar period does not reveal the connection explicitly. Only in one passage is the sectarian designation of "Sicarii" applied to the prewar period. After Josephus' entire narrative of the prewar and war periods, a summary passage describing the different revolutionary groups says that the Sicarii were active in 6 C.E. in response to Judas' preaching. But this is clearly an anachronistic use of a term which arose fifty years later to describe assassins using a *sica*.[20] This silence in Josephus' narrative regarding the activity of Judas' sect in the prewar period is surprising, especially in light of his apologetic desire to blame the war on a small group within Israel. If this sect had been active and Josephus had known about it, then we might assume he would have written about it.

18. Greek texts from this period have no means to distinguish between formal and common uses of a noun. We will translate this term in italics to designate the nonsectarian meaning of *sicarii*. We will capitalize "Sicarii" when it refers to the distinct faction of the war years.

19. In the *Antiquities* (20:185–86), Josephus does not mention the *sicarii* until the time of the procurator Festus (60–62 C.E.).

20. Malinowski cites the following passages as examples where Josephus describes past events with allusions to the present situation: *Antiquities* 18:2–10; 8:111–29; 4:180–91; *Apion* 2:157–61 ("Galilaean Judaism," p. 228).

If we take seriously this surprising silence in Josephus' narrative, we might be led to conclude that Judas did not really found a sect. After his revolt was crushed in 6 C.E. and his followers scattered, his family may have retreated to Galilee or Gamala where, under one of the sons of Herod, they did not have to live directly with the offensive presence of Rome. We do not hear of his sons, James and Simon, who may have been quite young in 6 C.E., until forty years later in 46 C.E. Perhaps they were just emerging to initiate resistance at the time shortly after Galilee and the Transjordan areas had become part of the Roman province. James and Simon were seized and executed apparently without a major incident; Josephus' failure to note the presence of a sect at this time suggests that none existed. It may be that only in the turmoil of the fifties and sixties were there enough followers motivated by Judas' teaching to have merited their recognition as a sect.[21] Even then, Judas' ideology would have been embraced only by some of those who engaged in revolutionary activity. This fact is obvious because, when the Sicarii do emerge as a distinct sect in Josephus' narrative of the war period (66–74 C.E.), they are only one, and indeed the smallest, of five revolutionary groups active in the war period.

If we follow this line of thinking, namely, that Judas did not in fact found a sect, then Josephus may have deliberately retrojected the existence of the later sect of Sicarii back to the time of Judas for apologetic purposes. To ascribe to Judas' teaching the beginning of a new sect is to emphasize its distinctiveness and novelty. To claim that it had nothing to do with other sects would serve to dissociate revolutionary teachings from the traditions and beliefs of most Jews. By retrojecting the sect to the time of Judas, Josephus could give greater scope to this "innovation" as a cause of the later war.[22] All these considerations fit

21. See also Lake, *Beginnings*, p. 492; and Salo Baron who writes, "Despite the physical continuity of leadership in Judas' family for over sixty years, it had little sectarian cohesiveness in more quiescent periods": Baron, *A Social and Religious History of the Jews*, 2d ed., 15 vols. (Philadelphia: The Jewish Publication Society of America, 1952), 2:48. See also Malinowski, "Galilaean Judaism," pp. 226–29.

22. Hengel considers it crucial that Josephus "makes the movement going out from Judas responsible for the later catastrophe": Hengel, *Zeloten*, p. 86. But he does not take account of Josephus' apologetic interests. Besides, this point of view is only found in the later *Antiquities*. Contrast Guignebert who argued that it was typical of classical authors to make a single individual responsible for a collective movement: Charles Guignebert, *The Jewish World in the Time of Jesus*, trans. S. H. Hooke (London: K. Paul, Trench, Trubner, 1939), p. 170. Also, Josephus holds other people and events responsible for the war (e.g., *War* 2:276).

well Josephus' biased attempts to blame the war on a small, separate group of revolutionaries, whose religious point of view was an innovation in traditional Judaism.

However, we need not suppose that Josephus deliberately retrojected the sect's existence to Judas' time. The silence of his narrative may simply betray a lack of knowledge on Josephus' part about whether a sect existed in the early period. In ignorance, he may have made a false inference that the later sect of Sicarii, which had ideological and genealogical roots in Judas of Galilee, had existed since Judas' time. This may be a typical example of attributing anachronistically the existence of an organization or group to the time of its predecessors.

In these considerations, we have used an argument based on the silence of Josephus' narrative to conclude that Judas may not have founded a sect. This conclusion, however, is probably too much to infer safely from Josephus' silence. After all, he does assert in the *War* and the *Antiquities* that Judas started a sect, and these explicit statements should perhaps not be outweighed by the later silence in the narrative of events, no matter how surprising. What Josephus' silence does easily explain is that, although Judas may have founded a sect, it was not active until the middle of the century. Given the disposition of the early procurators and the reluctant mood of the nation, it is unlikely that an active sect of revolutionaries would have survived the first forty years of provincial rule in Judea. Therefore the sect had no conspicuous successes or, for that matter, failures. As such, Josephus knew little about the early period of its history, and so he has nothing to tell of its activities.[23]

On the basis of Josephus' silence about conspiratorial revolutionary activity from 6–44 C.E., we have concluded that Judas' sect was inactive during this period. One might object that even this is too much to conclude from Josephus' silence, since he is also silent about the rise of the Christian movement or the important schools of the Pharisees.[24] However, Josephus was not writing a religious history; his failure to mention these matters is not surprising. But he was writing a political

---

23. So also Morton Smith in private correspondence, 1974.
24. Martin Hengel argues (private correspondence, 1974) that little can be made of Josephus' silence about revolutionary activities in this period since he is also silent about other important matters. In support of his view is the fact that Josephus states he will give less detailed information about events preceding his lifetime (*War* 1:18).

history, with special reference to the events which led to the war. He would not have failed to include revolutionary activities had he known of them. Thus, Josephus' silence suggests the probability that Judas' sect, if it existed in this early period, was quiescent until the mid-forties.[25]

THE SIGNIFICANCE OF JUDAS THE GALILEAN

Our evaluation of the evidence suggests that the revolt of Judas the Galilean in Judea in 6 C.E. was relatively small and ineffective. The sect which Judas founded was inactive during most of the first half of the first century. There is the reference to Judas' sons, but the presence of the sect is not explicitly mentioned in Josephus' description of the widespread revolutionary activity of the late forties, the fifties, and the sixties; no more can be inferred from the narrative than that it was probably one of the more important groups of brigands and *sicarii* active in this period. The rise to fame of Judas' sect, which probably took place at this time, may have been due to a change of leadership or methods, but in no way did they organize or control other revolutionary groups. We do not know the self-designation of this sect. Josephus, in his narrative of the war years, refers to them as the Sicarii. These Sicarii are identified as only one of five revolutionary factions active in the war. In general, it cannot be said that Judas' sect had the influence or importance which Josephus in some passages seems to attach to it.

The question still remains whether Judas the Galilean had a more general influence beyond the sect which he founded. Judas may have helped to bring to the fore an emphasis on "freedom from foreign masters," which became one of the rallying cries of the later revolution.[26] The wartime speeches related by Josephus contain frequent references to freedom, and some coins of the revolt bear the inscription,

25. It has been pointed out that since this point of view is based primarily on "an argument from silence," it may be important to "keep an open mind about the possibility of an 'underground' revolutionary sect operating with limited success in this period [which] contributed by various guerilla methods and propaganda to the politico-religious consciousness of the Jewish people which was a necessary pre-requisite for the sporadic and spontaneous popular revolts which followed" (William Telford, Cambridge University, in private correspondence, 1974).

26. For the extent of the theme of freedom and its relation to Judas the Galilean, see Hengel, *Zeloten*, pp. 114–27 and Günther Baumbach, "Das Freitheitverständnis der Zelotischen Bewegung," *Das Ferne und Nahe Wort*, no. 105 in *Beihefte zur Zeitschrift für die Alttestamentliche Wissenschaft* (Berlin: Alfred Töpelmann, 1967).

"Freedom of Zion."[27] The concept of freedom and the desire for liberation from foreign oppressors were not new for Israel, but it was a predominant emphasis of this revolt. Certainly many revolutionaries apart from Judas called for "freedom," and with different meanings—political, religious, and otherwise. Others, although they might not have accepted Judas' radical interpretation of the first commandment, may have picked up the general cry for freedom from Judas' example. By the time of the war, national interest in freedom was widespread and sustained independently of the specific teaching or sect of Judas and his descendants. Yet Judas' teaching was one of the important influences in that process leading up to the war for liberation.

It has been suggested that Judas had an indirect influence upon the Zealots, one of the other revolutionary groups of the war period.[28] The Zealot party, which was formed during the war period, emerged in part from among the priestly groups in Jerusalem. It may be that Saddok, the Pharisee who cooperated in Judas' revolt in 6 c.e., was a forefather of this later sect, for Saddok is a priestly name and many of the lower priests were Pharisees. Some of the later Zealots, like the Sicarii, endured torture and perhaps even committed suicide (*Dio Cassius* 66:6, 3). Although there is no evidence that these Zealots embraced the fourth philosophy or were connected with Judas' sect, they may have shared a heritage of determined resistance reaching back to the time of Judas' revolt. This suggestion is, however, hypothetical and is not explicit in Josephus' narrative.

Our general conclusion might be that in a limited sense Judas the Galilean was one of the formulators of the later national call for freedom from the Romans. This was perhaps the basis on which Josephus claimed that Judas' teaching was a major cause of the later war.[29] However, our understanding of Josephus' biases and our evaluation of his narrative caution us against overestimating the importance of Judas' activity or the extent of his later influence. This estimate of the significance of Judas the Galilean will be kept in mind as we analyze the events of the subsequent period and the causes of the war.

---

27. See Leo Kadman, *The Coins of the Roman Jewish War of 66–73* (Tel Aviv: Schocken, 1960).
28. See Stern, "Zealots," p. 144.
29. This was suggested by Menachem Stern in conversation, 1975.

FROM JUDAS TO THE DEATH OF AGRIPPA: 6–44 C.E.

The procurators who were assigned to Judea during this period were for the most part of Italian origin:[30] Coponius (6–9 C.E.), Marcus Ambibilus (9–12 C.E.), Annius Rufus (12–15 C.E.), Valerius Gratus (15–26 C.E.), Pontius Pilate (26–36 C.E.), Marcellus (36 or 37 C.E.), and Marullus (37–41 C.E.). Josephus reports no instances of conflict between Jews and Romans from 6 to 26 C.E. The fact that four different high priests were appointed by Gratus (15–26 C.E.) in the first three years of his procuratorship may indicate tensions of some kind,[31] but there is no evidence of revolutionary activity or national disturbances.

When Pilate arrived as procurator in 26 C.E., he brought into Jerusalem under the cover of night Roman troops who carried army standards bearing Roman images (*War* 2:169–74; *Antiquities* 18:55–59). The prohibition of images was an important part of Jewish law and had been respected by previous procurators. These particular image-bearing standards were especially offensive to Jews in that they were used in the pagan religious practices of the Roman army (*War* 6:316).[32] Crowds of indignant Jews followed Pilate to his headquarters at Caesarea in order to protest his action. They remained there for many days, even baring their necks to the Roman sword at the threat of execution. They claimed that "they were ready rather to die than to transgress the law (*War* 2:174). Pilate, fearing a larger Jewish reaction if he were to harm the protesters, was constrained to remove the offensive standards from Jerusalem.

Shortly thereafter, Pilate confiscated funds from the temple treasury to finance his construction of an aqueduct (*War* 2:175–77; *Antiquities* 18:60–62). The temple treasury kept annual dues from Jews all over the world. The money was used for the rebuilding and the maintaining of the temple. Naturally, the Jews were irate at this interference in their internal affairs and the idea of a gentile using sacred money. A disturbance took place when they protested to Pilate on his next visit to Jerusalem. This time his soldiers attacked the unarmed Jews, killed some, dispersed others, and, as a result, suppressed the Jewish protest against Pilate's action.

30. *Compendia*, 1:318.
31. Cf. E. M. Smallwood, "High Priests and Politics in Roman Palestine," *Journal of Theological Studies* 13 (1962): 22.
32. Concerning this incident, see Carl H. Kraeling, "The Episode of the Roman Standards at Jerusalem," *Harvard Theological Review* 35 (1942): 263–89.

In 36 C.E., a group of Samaritans gathered to follow a prophet onto Mount Gerizim where they were to see some sacred vessels that had been buried by Moses. Pilate attacked this group and had their leaders put to death. The Samaritans subsequently protested to Vitellius, the Roman governor of Syria, that they had been attacked unjustly, claiming they had gathered not as rebels against the Romans but as refugees from the persecutions of Pilate. As a result of this charge, Pilate was recalled to Rome (*Antiquities* 18:85–89).

Josephus tells us that after Pilate was removed, Vitellius came to inspect the Jewish province, visited Jerusalem, was warmly received, and found the city at peace (*Antiquities* 18:90ff., 120ff.). As a reward for his welcome, Vitellius remitted to the inhabitants of the city all taxes on the sale of agricultural produce, and he restored the high priestly vestments from the custody of the procurators into the hands of the high priests themselves. He also, without incident, administered to the people the oath of loyalty to the new emperor Gaius (*Antiquities* 18:124). The apparent diplomatic manner of this senatorial governor from the important province of Syria contrasts sharply with the harshness frequently evident among the procurators of the smaller province of Judea, who were drawn from the Equestrian Order. The cooperative response to Vitellius indicates the stability of the nation and the desire for a peaceful relationship with the Romans (Philo, *Embassy* 231).

During the procuratorship of Marullus (37–41 C.E.), the emperor Gaius, who was a proponent of Hellenistic culture and took worship of the emperor more seriously than his predecessors, decided to remove the religious privileges of the Jews by forcing emperor worship upon them. He sent Petronius, the new legate of Syria, to put a statue of him in the temple at Jerusalem (*War* 2:184–203; *Antiquities* 18:261–309). This was the most abhorrent act imaginable to the Jews, for it would have desecrated the center of their religious and national life and undermined their entire culture. Masses of Jews and their leaders assembled with their families, first in the plain of Ptolemais and subsequently at Tiberias in Galilee, to insist that no such action be taken. When the Jews simply refused to accept Petronius' orders, he asked them if they would be willing to go to war with Rome over the issue:

> The Jews replied that they offered sacrifice twice daily for Caesar and the Roman people, but that if he wished to set up these statues, he

must first sacrifice the entire Jewish nation; and that they presented themselves, their wives and their children, ready for the slaughter. (*War* 2:197; cf. *Antiquities* 18:271)

Josephus does indicate that the Jews would have gone to war over this issue (*Antiquities* 18:270),[33] although it is clear that they were certainly not bent upon revolt if the matter could be handled otherwise (see *Antiquities* 18:302).[34] The demonstrations were quite restrained. The people came unarmed, expressing a willingness to die for their traditions (Philo, *Embassy* 115, 209, 229–33). And there is no indication of lawless disturbances (*Embassy* 190).

Petronius did respond to their protest by appealing to Gaius to rescind his order. However, this threat to the temple was only resolved by the emperor's death in 41 C.E. (*War* 2:203).[35] Yet the memory of the incident and the fear of its recurrence must have been a strain on Roman-Jewish relations.

In 41 C.E., Judea was changed back into a kingdom and, along with the rest of Palestine, was placed under King Herod Agrippa I. This was done as a result of the favor which Herod Agrippa I had with the new emperor Claudius (*War* 2:206–13). Agrippa pursued a fairly nationalistic course. His efforts to rebuild the walls of Jerusalem (*War* 2:218–19; *Antiquities* 19:326–27) and his attempt to initiate a conference of the Roman vassal kings of the eastern part of the empire (*Antiquities* 19:338–42) were, however, both halted by Marsus, the next governor of Syria. Perhaps because Agrippa I was somewhat independent of Rome, there is little evidence of resistance or disturbances in Israel under his kingship. The pro-Jewish emphasis of his reign was evident from the strong reaction by gentile residents of Palestine which occurred against him after his death in 44 C.E. (*Antiquities* 18:356–57).

In each of the disturbances which Josephus relates in the period from 26 to 44 C.E., the Jewish protest was a spontaneous response to offen-

33. See also Philo, *Embassy to Gaius*, 208, 215; and Tacitus, *Histories*, 5:9. Philo implies that Jews throughout the empire and Parthia might have joined the nation's cause (*Embassy* 215–16). Certainly the statue and any conflict resulting from it would have meant suffering for all Jews (*Embassy* 184, 194). At the time of this incident, Philo was leading an embassy to Gaius regarding a conflict between the Jewish and Greek populations of Alexandria in Egypt. He notes that the status of Jews in the whole empire would be affected by the Roman decision in this matter also (*Embassy* 370–71).
34. See also Brandon, *Jesus*, p. 88, n. 1.
35. In *Antiquities* 18:289ff., there is a separate tradition that Agrippa I had the order of Gaius rescinded by special appeal to the emperor before his death.

sive Roman activity in Palestine. Jewish outrage was expressed non-violently, and when it appeared that there may have been potential for violence (*War* 2:175–77), it was a matter of the tumult of an angry crowd rather than any kind of armed uprising. The people as a whole, including elements from all major groups in Israel, reacted to these disturbances;[36] and there is no evidence of a small group or sect urging the nation to revolt. When the offenses were removed, there is every indication that the Jews returned to a peaceful acceptance of Roman rule. Only one passage in the entire narrative hints at the possibility of brigandage, and it is expressed only as a fear of what might have happened had the incident with Gaius not been resolved. This possibility of brigandage is mentioned only in the *Antiquities* and is clearly related to economic motives: "Let him [Petronius] point out [to Gaius] that since the land was unsown [cf. *War* 2:200], there would be a harvest of banditry, because the requirement of tribute could not be met" (*Antiquities* 18:274).

In contrast to his repeated references to brigandage and to revolutionaries in his narrative of the later period, the absence of evidence for conspiratorial revolutionary activity in Josephus' account of the period from 6 to 44 C.E. is striking. The suggestion that Josephus was somehow trying to emphasize the vicious nature of Pilate and to point up the forbearance of the Jews is unlikely.[37] Nor is it likely that Josephus was ignorant of such revolutionary activity or unwilling to draw attention to it.[38] It has been suggested that a revolutionary group, such as the followers of Judas, would have been an underground organization. Those who refused to recognize Rome's authority might have lived in the mountains or the desert in order to avoid paying taxes and been forced to support themselves by brigandage, much like the "brigands" in the time of Herod.[39] Some later references by Josephus imply that brigandage was an ongoing problem in Israel (*Antiquities* 20:5;

36. For an excellent discussion of the way in which resistance to Rome was expressed by a cross-section of the Israelite nation, see M. Borg, "Conflict as a Context for Interpreting the Teachings of Jesus" (Ph.D. dissertation, Oxford University, 1972), pp. 36–62.

37. Against Brandon, *Jesus*, p. 79; cf. idem, "The Zealots: The Jewish Resistance against Rome, A.D. 6–73," *History Today* 15 (1965): 640.

38. Against Hengel, *Zeloten*, pp. 88, 344, n. 1.

39. See William R. Farmer, "Zealots," *Interpreters Dictionary of the Bible*, 4 vols. (New York: Abingdon, 1962), 4:936–39.

War 2:253),[40] but the evidence suggests a lull in such activity during this period. Certainly if revolutionaries had been very active, their efforts would have been no secret, and Josephus would have taken the opportunity to blame most of the trouble on them[41] as he does so pervasively in other parts of his works. Thus, given his bias, Josephus' silence points to the relative lack of conspiratorial revolutionary activity during this period from 6 to 44 C.E.

Other sources support this picture. Tacitus, in his discussion of Jewish-Roman relations in the first century, writes that "under Tiberius all was quiet" (*Histories* 5:9). Philo records an incident in which Pilate placed in Jerusalem shields bearing the emperor's name (not his image). Requests for removal of the shields were made to Pilate by the populace along with Jewish aristocrats and the four sons of Herod, but were denied. Only when a petition was sent to Emperor Tiberius did Pilate take the shields out of the city. This episode is similar to those recorded by Josephus, and gives no hint of conspiratorial revolutionary activity among Jews.[42]

In the New Testament narratives which relate to the time of Pilate, there are several references to "brigands," but it is not certain whether they were political brigands or highway robbers (Mark 15:27; Matthew 27:38). The "brigands" who were crucified with Jesus may have been executed for political reasons,[43] but there is no indication they were part of any sect or movement. A certain Barabbas was in prison with men who had committed murder during a riot in Jerusalem (Mark 15:6–15 and parallels).[44] These murders, however, may have occurred in a popular riot like that which followed Pilate's confiscation of the

40. Josephus says that when a brigand-chief named Eleazar was seized by the procurator Felix (52–60 C.E.), he had been ravaging the countryside for twenty years.
41. M. Smith, "Zealots and Sicarii, Their Origins and Relation," *Harvard Theological Review* 64 (1971): 12.
42. Philo, *Embassy to Gaius*, 38; 209–306. See P. L. Maier, "The Episode of the Golden Roman Shields at Jerusalem," *Harvard Theological Review* 62 (1969): 109–21.
43. The death penalty was applied to both mercenary and political brigands. See Bernard Jackson, *Theft in Early Jewish Law* (Oxford: Clarendon Press, 1972), pp. 252–53.
44. The whole episode in which Barabbas figures is rife with historical difficulties, especially the lack of any ancient support for the custom of releasing a prisoner at feast time (Mark 15:6). See P. Winter, *On the Trial of Jesus* (Berlin: Walter de Gruyter, 1961), pp. 89ff. This story "may be a late Christian creation to contrast Jesus, the true Messiah whom the Jews rejected, with an imaginary specimen of the false Messiahs, the would-be revolutionary murderers, whom they later followed" (Morton Smith, in private correspondence).

65

temple treasury, rather than a revolt instigated by revolutionaries. Mention is also made of an incident in which Pilate had some Galileans put to death while they were offering sacrifices in the temple at Jerusalem, but there is no indication of what provoked his action (Luke 13:1-2).[45] The actual offenses committed by these various persons are uncertain, partly because Pilate was known for his harshness and may have killed some innocent people as revolutionaries (Philo, *Embassy* 302). The pious Samaritans, whom he attacked and whose leaders he put to death, claimed that they had been forced to defend themselves because of his persecutions (*Antiquities* 18:85-89). In fact, it was for this that Pilate was recalled to Rome.

Many factors may have contributed to the relatively peaceful period from 6 to 44 C.E. The memory of the War of Varus in 4 B.C.E. and the failure of Judas' revolt in 6 C.E. must have discouraged revolutionary activity. The earlier harsh rule of Herod and Archelaus apparently made the people willing to cooperate with "equitable rulers" (*War* 2:91; *Antiquities* 17:314). The emperors Augustus (27 B.C.E.–14 C.E.) and Tiberius (14–37 C.E.) were favorable toward Jews.[46] Tiberius encouraged responsibility among procurators by increasing the length of their appointment (*Antiquities* 18:172-78). The procurators in Judea from 6 to 44 C.E., being of Italian origin, were not particularly biased in favor of the Hellenistic element of the population in Palestine. The high priests of this period were almost all from the family of Ananus, a ruling house which provided stable leadership.[47] Also, Herod Antipas in Galilee (4 B.C.E.–39 C.E.), Philip in the Transjordan (4 B.C.E.–33/34 C.E.), and then Agrippa I over the whole country (41–44 C.E.) gained general respect among Jews and ruled in peace.[48] If these leaders were "equitable rulers," then the Jews showed that they could accommodate themselves to Roman rule.

Even when the Roman officials did act offensively, as in the cases of

45. Concerning this incident, see J. Blinzler, "Die Niedermetzelung von Galilaern durch Pilatus," *Novum Testamentum* 2 (1957): 24–49.

46. Although Pontius Pilate was procurator under Tiberius, he was appointed and supervised by Sejanus, the prefect of the guard in Rome, whose strong anti-Jewish bias was well known (Philo, *Flaccus* 1). At Sejanus' death, Tiberius reaffirmed his commitment to the Jewish rights guaranteed by Augustus (Philo, *Embassy* 159–61).

47. On this point, see P. W. Barnett, "Under Tiberius All Was Quiet," *New Testament Studies* 21 (1975): 569. See the entire article (pp. 564–71) for a recent treatment of this peaceful period in Judea.

48. On Antipas, see H. W. Hoehner, *Herod Antipas* (Cambridge: University Press, 1972).

Pilate and the emperor Gaius, the record shows that the Jews pursued nonrevolutionary ways to deal with the matter. The sit-in before Pilate at Caesarea won the removal of the offensive standards from Jerusalem. The demonstration in Jerusalem over Pilate's confiscation of the temple treasury was a similar public protest, although it ended in suppression by Roman troops. The masses of people who flocked to Petronius won his support by their willingness to die rather than tolerate Gaius' statue in the temple. And their refusal to tend their fields at this time was a nonviolent economic protest which would have prevented the Judean tribute to Rome from being met and would have deprived the empire of a source of grain (*Life* 71; Philo, *Embassy to Gaius* 248–53, 257). And the aristocracy, including Herodians and Sadducean high priests, succeeded in solving at least one crisis diplomatically by petitioning Rome (Philo, *Embassy to Gaius* 38:209–306).

We know from other sources that the followers of Hillel, under the leadership of Gamaliel, continued to pursue peaceful solutions in the life of the nation (Acts 5:33–39). Also during this period, the redactor[49] of the *Testament of Moses* was admonishing Jews to accept willingly innocent martyrdom at the hands of the Romans in order to guarantee that God would take revenge on the unjust enemy (*Testament of Moses* 9:7). John the Baptist called his fellow Israelites to repent in face of a coming judgment (Mark 1:1–12 and parallels). Jesus taught the love of enemy and the willingness to cooperate with someone (presumably a Roman soldier) who might be pressing a Jew into temporary service (Matthew 5:38–48).[50]

All of these are examples of nonrevolutionary ways to deal with the presence of foreign occupation in Israel. The demonstrations of passive resistance continued into the late forties; the diplomatic efforts were to be repeated often; and the prophetic call to hope in God's apocalyptic judgment continued into the fifties and early sixties. By then, however, the revolutionary spirit had been enlivened and would eventually lead to war. But it can be inferred from Josephus' account

---

49. Although the Testament was probably written about Maccabean times, it was interpreted, updated, and given an anti-militant character in Herodian times, probably between 4 B.C.E. and 30 C.E. See *Studies on the Testament of Moses,* ed. George Nickelsburg, Jr. (Society of Biblical Literature, 1973).

50. See K. Stendahl, "Hate. Non-Retaliation, and Love," *Harvard Theological Review* 55 (1962): 343–55. Recently, S. G. F. Brandon has depicted Jesus as a revolutionary in *Jesus and the Zealots,* cited above. For a critique of this work, see Walter Wink, "Jesus and Revolution," *Union Seminary Quarterly Review* 25 (1969): 37–59.

that in this early period of accommodation the Jews were seeking non-violent means to protest and to oppose the occupying power, Rome.[51]

FROM THE DEATH OF AGRIPPA I TO THE OPENING OF THE WAR: 44–66 C.E.

After the death of Agrippa I, advisers counseled the emperor against passing the Jewish kingship to Agrippa II partly due perhaps to the nationalistic tendencies of Agrippa I and partly because Agrippa II was only seventeen years of age. Therefore, the kingdom of Agrippa, which included Judea, as well as Galilee, Peraea, and Samaria, became a province of Rome. One might have expected a revolt in 44 C.E., as there had been in 6 C.E. when Judea alone became a province of Rome. It would seem that there might have been a strong Jewish reaction to provincial status following the negative experience Jews had encountered under Pilate and the period of relative peace and independence under Agrippa I. That, however, was not the case. Some Peraeans did attempt to settle a dispute over the borders of the village of Zia without waiting for Fadus (44–46 C.E.), the new procurator, to arrive from Rome (*Antiquities* 20:2–4). In another instance, when Fadus tried to control the Jews by taking charge of the high priestly vestments so essential to their high festivals, the Jews appealed to the emperor. They succeeded in having the authority over temple matters given to Herod of Chalcis[52] (*Antiquities* 20:6–16). Longinus, the new governor of Syria, feared that Fadus' action might force the Jewish people into rebellion (*Antiquities* 20:7). However, there is no indication of any disturbance.

According to Josephus, Fadus kept Judea clear of robber bands:

> Not long afterwards Tholomaeus the arch-brigand, who had inflicted very severe mischief upon Idumaea and upon the Arabs, was brought before him in chains and put to death. From then on the whole of Judaea was purged of robber-bands, thanks to the prudent concern displayed by Fadus. (*Antiquities* 20:5)

---

51. For another treatment of this point of view, see D. Rhoads, "The Assumption of Moses and Jewish History: 4 B.C.–A.D. 48," *Studies in the Testament of Moses*, Septuagint and Cognate Studies, no. 4, ed. G. W. E. Nickelsburg (Society of Biblical Literature, 1973), pp. 53–58. See also the relevant article by David Flusser, "A New Sensitivity in Judaism and the Christian Message," *Harvard Theological Review* 61 (1968): 107–27.

52. Herod of Chalcis was the brother of Agrippa I. Upon his death in 48 C.E., the territory of Chalcis as well as the responsibility for temple affairs was given to Agrippa II.

We know nothing about Tholomaeus or his motives, whether he was a political brigand who defended Jewish territory against the Arabs or a robber chieftain who attacked caravans and lived by plunder. It is not even clear that Tholomaeus was a Jew.[53] The robber bands of Judea may have been ordinary robbers; or they may have been men who resisted Roman or Herodian rule and were thus forced to live by brigandage, operating from their homes in the mountains. But it is likely that Josephus' account simply means that the conscientious rule of Fadus prevented any robber bands from arising.

Whatever national hopes surfaced at this point must have clustered around the figure of Theudas (*Antiquities* 20:97–99), a prophetic figure who led some Jews to take up their possessions and cross the Jordan, which he claimed would be parted to provide them easy passage. There is no mention that these Jews were armed or that they were organizing a revolt. Nevertheless, Fadus pursued them, captured and later killed Theudas, and slew many of his followers (cf. Acts 5:36).

. We have the following brief notice from the procuratorship of Tiberius Alexander (46–48 C.E.):

> Besides this James and Simon, the sons of Judas the Galilaean, were brought up for trial and, at the order of Alexander, were crucified. This was the Judas who, as I have explained above, had aroused the people to revolt against the Romans while Quirinius was taking the census in Judaea. (*Antiquities* 20:102)

This reference indicates the continued presence of the family of Judas. We know nothing of their activity. No mention is made of any sect or following. No hint of any disturbance or attempt at revolt is recorded; and if there was a revolt, it was obviously of no consequence, for Josephus would have been aware of it and found it useful to mention.

Thus the reestablishment of provincial status after the brief reign of Agrippa I did not cause the furor one might have expected. The favorable judgment which kept the control of the high priestly vestments out of Roman hands must have given some assurances of religious autonomy.[54] The Jewish following of the prophet Theudas probably expressed more a longing for national freedom than a willingness to participate in armed revolt. And the quick and overwhelming way in

53. *Compendia*, 1:361.
54. Smallwood, "High Priests," p. 22.

which Fadus dealt with Theudas and his followers must have discouraged resistance against the Romans. The other incidents of this four-year period (44–48 C.E.) are treated by Josephus as rather isolated events of no national consequence, involving no disturbances. Indeed none of the occurrences mentioned here are even recorded in the *War*, where Josephus refers favorably to the procurators of this period, Fadus and Tiberius Alexander, as those "who by abstaining from all interference with the customs of the country kept the nation at peace" (*War* 2:221).[55] Surely this absence of Roman offenses and interference in Jewish life contributed to the relative peace of this period and helped relieve Jewish apprehensions about the renewal of direct Roman rule.

However, the peace did not last. The worst fears of the Jews were realized during the procuratorship of Cumanus (48–52 C.E.) when a series of events led to an armed clash between Jews and Romans. The initial incident occurred in Jerusalem at feast time when one of the Roman soldiers on the roof of the portico of the temple made an obscene gesture (*War* 2:223–27; *Antiquities* 20:105–12), expressing the insensitivity and hostility of the soldiers toward the Jewish religion. The Jews worshiping below were highly offended at this blasphemy against God (*Antiquities* 20:108). The crowd demanded that Cumanus punish the soldier. Then, some "seditious persons" (*War* 2:225) threw stones at the troops, whereupon Cumanus, fearing a riot, called up reinforcements. Although the troops never attacked, many Jews were crushed in the panic of mass flight from the temple area.

The national mourning over these deaths had hardly ceased when other seditious Jews attacked and plundered the caravan of a slave-official of Caesar on the road to Jerusalem near Beth-horon in Judea (*War* 2:228; *Antiquities* 20:113–14). The Romans apparently assumed that the Jewish "brigands" responsible for the attack came from the neighboring villages and acted with the knowledge and consent of the local leaders; for Cumanus' troops thereupon plundered the nearby Judean villages and arrested the local Jewish officials who had failed to pursue those responsible for the attack (*War* 2:229–30; *Antiquities*

---

55. Tiberius Alexander was a former Jew from an illustrious family in Alexandria, and nephew of Philo the well-known Jewish philosopher. He had been a Roman administrative officer in Egypt and in 63 C.E. was conducting war against the Parthians under Corbolo. Later he became the prefect of Egypt. See *Compendia*, 1:362; and Emil Schürer, *History of the Jewish People in the Time of Jesus Christ,* ed. Geza Vermes and Fergus Millar (Edinburgh: T. & T. Clark, 1973), 1:456–57.

20:114–17). In these raids, a Roman soldier tore and burned a copy of the Torah. The Jews, "as though it were their whole country which had been consumed in the flames," rushed to Cumanus at Caesarea to demand the soldier's punishment. This is the last act of passive resistance in the narrative of Josephus, and from the language of the account one might think it bordered on a riot. Only when the protesters would not relent did the procurator, perhaps in a fear of a rebellion, have the offending soldier beheaded.

Although the official Roman policy of religious toleration toward the Jews was one of noninterference, there was often a vast difference between the official policy and the actual irritations despite this policy. The incompetent handling of these matters by Cumanus was an expression both of his inability as a state administrator and of his insensitivity to Jewish customs and concerns. The deaths of the Jews and the penal activity of Roman troops plundering the villages of Judea must have intensified the frustration of the Jews, creating the volatile atmosphere in which the following incident occurred sometime later: some Galileans on their way to a Jerusalem festival with a large number of other Jews were attacked by Samaritans at a village called Gema and one of them was killed.[56] The Galilean leaders went to Cumanus entreating him to punish the murderers at once. Cumanus, busy with other matters, neglected their petitions. When the masses of Jews at the festival —tired of Roman ineptness and insensitivity—heard of it, they took the matter into their own hands. Enlisting a local brigand-chief named Eleazar ben Dinai and one Alexander as their leaders, they went to avenge the murder by burning several Samaritan villages and killing the inhabitants. At this, Cumanus went with his troops, armed the Samaritans, and in an encounter with the Jews slew some and took others prisoners.

> As for the rest of the party who had rushed to war with the Samaritans, the magistrates of Jerusalem hastened after them, clad in sackcloth and with ashes strewn upon their heads, and implored them to return home and not, by their desire for reprisals on the Samaritans, to bring down the wrath of the Romans on Jerusalem, but to take pity on their country and sanctuary, on their own wives and children; all these were threatened with destruction merely for the object of aveng-

---

56. For a discussion of contradictions in the accounts of this incident in *War* 2:233–46 and *Antiquities* 20:118–36, see Moses Aberbach, "The Conflicting Accounts of Josephus and Tacitus Concerning Cumanus' and Felix's Terms of Office," *Jewish Quarterly Review* 40 (1949): 1–14; and *Compendia*, 1:374ff.

ing the blood of a single Galilaean. Yielding to these remonstrances the Jews dispersed. (*War* 2:237–38)

It seems obvious from the accounts, both in the *War* and the *Antiquities* that the impetus for Jewish outrage was directed against the Samaritans. Yet in the *Antiquities*, Josephus reports that the Jewish masses were urged "to resort to arms and to assert their liberty" (*Antiquities* 20:120), which might indicate that it was directed against Rome. Later in the report, several men are accused of having "instigated the mob to revolt against the Romans" (*Antiquities* 20:130–31). This seems, however, to refer to the fact that they took the matter into their own hands, avenging the Samaritans themselves instead of waiting for the Romans to handle the matter, which is just what the Jews were formally accused of doing by the Samaritans before the tribunal of Quadratus, the governor of Syria (*Antiquities* 20:126). This in itself was an assertion of liberty, tantamount to an act of war which involved a failure to recognize the existing Roman authorities. Once the Jews were armed and active, they were apparently willing to fight against the Romans—and direct rebellion was at hand. The seriousness of the matter was indicated both by the desperate pleas of the Jerusalem magistrates and the fact that the case was considered in the Imperial Court.

DISSENSION IN THE COUNTRYSIDE

Although the Imperial Court decided in favor of the Jews, punishing both the Samaritan and Jewish leaders of the revolt and banishing Cumanus for his negligence in the affair, the Jews had once again been confronted with the insolence of Roman rule in Israel (*Antiquities* 20:120). And this incident, which took place around 51 C.E., was a turning point in the Jewish relationship with Rome, for the assertion of liberty and the direct clash with Roman soldiers in Judea stirred up all the dissatisfied elements throughout the countryside.[57]

It is at this point in his history of first century Judaism that Josephus gives evidence of widespread active dissension against the Romans. He attests to this in both accounts:

Many of them, however, emboldened by impunity, had recourse to

---

57. Jewish dissatisfaction in Palestine was further aggravated by the expulsion of Jews from Rome in 50 C.E. Claudius expelled them because of "di:turbances at the instigation of Chrestus" (Suetonius, *Claudius* 25:4).

robbery, and raids and insurrections, fostered by the more reckless, broke out all over the country. (*War* 2:239)

From that time the whole of Judaea was infested with bands of brigands. (*Antiquities* 20:124)

The assertion of freedom in the Jewish-Samaritan conflict was not an organized ideological revolt, but an expression of frustration at the failure of Roman responsibility in the province. And the fact that these brigands were "emboldened by impunity" indicates a fundamental breakdown of law and order in the countryside. Cumanus had not been willing to act on the matter until it came to the brink of revolt.

There followed an interim period while Cumanus was in Rome and the next procurator, Felix, had not arrived. The dissidents, already stirred up by these events, did not at this time return to peace and order but continued to express their dissension.

This disorder in the countryside went from bad to worse during the tenure of the next procurator, Felix (52–60 C.E.). He was not of the Equestrian Order, but was a freedman who gained this post by influence in the Imperial Court. To confer a procuratorship with a military command upon such a person was unprecedented.[58] He was ill-prepared for the position and the corruption of his public and private life was offensive to the Jews (Tacitus, *Histories* 5:9). He did succeed in capturing Eleazar ben Dinai and he executed some other brigands. Yet by the end of his term in 60 C.E., the country was again infested with brigands. It was during his time in Judea that the *sicarii* arose and apocalyptic prophets increased.[59]

The next two procurators, Festus (60–62 C.E.) and Albinus (62–64 C.E.), initiated action against the brigands when they first took office, but by then the brigandage which had begun under Cumanus had a firm foothold in the country. Albinus' corruption only worsened the situation, plundering private and public funds, accepting bribes to release brigands, and at the end of his term emptying the prisons of all but the worst criminals.

---

58. Schürer, *History*, 1: 460–61.
59. In 54 C.E., the sixteen-year-old Nero succeeded Claudius as emperor. The avid pro-Hellenistic policies and the poor administration of Nero's reign were a significant factor in the increase of general unrest indicated by the activities of the *sicarii* and the apocalyptic prophets. See Reicke, *Era*, pp. 206–207.

The wicked extremities of the last procurator, Florus (64–66 C.E.), are amply described by Josephus.[60] The utter absence of authority in the land and the offensive actions by Romans which so outraged ordinary Jews gave the brigands impunity for their exploits from either Jew or Roman. Josephus writes that it seemed "throughout the countryside that all were at liberty to practice brigandage" (*War* 2:278).

The revolutionary activity which was manifest in the countryside during these last two decades before the war seems to have been disparate and unorganized. Social and economic conditions favored the development of local robber bands, not the growth of a single resistance organization.[61] Josephus' use of the word "brigand" to describe the activity implies this.[62] The references to *sicarii* also imply more a method of resistance than an organized group. When disorders were reduced in one place, they broke out elsewhere (*War* 2:264). Several times Josephus remarks that the land was cleared of brigands (*War* 2:254, 271), but then they sprang up again (*War* 2:254–55), further evidence of the absence of an organized or continuous movement. These reports of local brigandage and resistance give no evidence of a sect or sects around which the dissenters clustered.[63] Had Josephus known of one, he certainly would have referred to it in order to blame the resistance on it. Hence, the widespread movement in the countryside was probably a spontaneous and disparate expression of dissatisfaction, and it was without central organization or leadership.[64]

---

60. In 62, the youthful Nero's advisers were ousted. Apparently, the appointments of Albinus and Florus as procurators of Judea were representative of the harshness of Nero's new advisers. See Reicke, *Era*, pp. 209–10. The deterioration of the situation in Palestine reflected the larger unrest within the empire.

61. So Smith, "Zealots," p. 14.

62. See K. H. Rengstorf, *"Lēstēs," Theological Dictionary of the New Testament,* 9 vols., ed. Gerhard Kittel, trans. Geoffrey Bromiley (Grand Rapids: Eerdmans, 1964), 4:257–62. For an analysis of Josephus' use of the term "brigand" see below pp. 159–62 and appendix I.

63. Hengel argues that the sect of Judas the Galilean's followers provided the focal point for this unrest through the line of Judas' sons James and Simon, then Eleazar ben Dinai, and Menahem, a son of Judas. (*Zeloten*, pp. 356, 369). But James and Simon are not significant figures. Nor is there a known relation between Eleazar and the family of Judas. And if Menahem (who emerges at the opening of the war) had been the central figure in the prewar period, the fact probably would have been mentioned by Josephus.

64. See also Kaufmann Kohler, "Wer waren die Zeloten oder Kannaim?" Festschrift zu Ehren des Dr. Harkavy, ed., D. von Günzburg (St. Petersburg, 1908), p. 15; Guignebert, *The Jewish World*, p. 170; Borge Salomonsen, "Some Remarks on the Zealots with Special Reference to the Term 'Qannaim' in Rabbinic Literature," *New Testament Studies* 12 (1965–66): 167–68.

The sporadic nature of these expressions of dissatisfaction and rebellion in the countryside in this period from 44–66 C.E. is also apparent from the fact that the individual figures who are mentioned seem to be unrelated to each other. The prophet Theudas led some Jews to cross the Jordan in Fadus' time (*Antiquities* 20:97–99). James and Simon, sons of Judas, were crucified under Tiberius Alexander (*Antiquities* 20:102). Eleazar ben Dinai, along with Alexander, was enlisted to lead the resistance during the brief revolt at the time of Cumanus. Shortly thereafter Eleazar was captured and sent to Rome by Felix (*War* 2:253; *Antiquities* 20:161). Later, several different prophetic figures persuaded some Jews to gather in the desert, promising that they would see there signs of deliverance (*War* 2:259). An Egyptian prophet led a multitude from the Mount of Olives, avowing that divine help would enable them to take over the city from the Romans. He was stopped by the Romans under Felix (*War* 2:261–63; *Antiquities* 20:169–71). Another Jewish prophet, who led a group into the wilderness for salvation and rest from troubles, was cut down by the procurator Festus (60–62 C.E.). Josephus makes no attempt to see any pattern or relation among these figures; he records their activity as isolated incidents.

In all of this, there is only one indication of a united front of resistance in the countryside. Late in the procuratorship of Felix (52–60 C.E.),

> The imposters and brigands, banding together, incited numbers to revolt, exhorting them to assert their independence, and threatening to kill any who submitted to Roman domination and forcibly to suppress those who voluntarily accepted servitude. Distributing themselves in companies throughout the country, they looted the houses of the wealthy, murdered their owners, and set the villages on fire. The effects of their frenzy were thus felt throughout all Judaea, and every day saw this war being fanned into fiercer flame. (*War* 2:264–65)

The reference to "banding together" can be taken to mean that there was a widespread organized cooperation of revolutionaries.[65] However, no united effort in the prewar period is reported anywhere else in the *War* or the *Antiquities*. And parallel passages in the *Antiquities* do not refer to such cooperation (*Antiquities* 20:160, 172). If there was cooperation among these groups, it appears to have been an isolated incident. Elsewhere Josephus clearly describes the "imposters" as

65. So Hengel, *Zeloten*, p. 239.

prophetic pretenders who did not participate in the terrorist tactics of the brigands (*War* 2:258).

Also, this passage does not refer to any central leader or group, nor is there any obvious connection with a particular ideology, such as the fourth philosophy. No common economic or social or religious motive is cited for their active suppression of Jewish cooperation with the Romans. In this passage, as elsewhere in Josephus' writings, the Greek is not altogether clear. The word translated "banding together" literally means "having been brought together," but may merely mean "acting during the same period." Perhaps, then, the passage can best be taken to mean not that there was a widespread cooperation but that there were local groups whose resistance in this period had a common effect; namely, their activities throughout the countryside stirred up the people and constrained Jewish officials and the wealthy to cease their cooperation with Rome.[66] This interpretation accords best with the overall evidence of revolutionary activity in the prewar period.

DISSENSION IN JERUSALEM

The unrest and disorder in the countryside of Judea, which began late in the procuratorship of Cumanus (48–52 C.E.) became manifest somewhat later in the city of Jerusalem. Some of the seeds of it were sown in the decade of the fifties. The repeated assassinations by *sicarii* in the mid-fifties created an atmosphere of fear and distrust in the city. In the late fifties, during the time of the procurator Felix (52–60 C.E.), there was a conflict between some high priests and the lower priests along with the leaders of the Jerusalem populace. It is not clear what the conflict was about, but the two groups would clash with stones and abusive language.[67] Josephus remarks that "it was as if there were no one in charge of the city, so that they acted as they did with full licence," (*Antiquities* 20:181). Other conflicts arose among Jerusalem leaders during the procuratorship of Festus (60–62 C.E.).[68]

Also during the time of Festus, the atmosphere in Jerusalem was indirectly affected by a conflict between the Syrian and Jewish inhabit-

---

66. Smith, "Zealots," pp. 1–19, and in private correspondence.
67. This coalition of lower priests and leaders of the populace may have fore-shadowed the later coalition of priests "supported by the stalwarts of the revolutionary party" (*War* 2:410) who were instrumental in the cessation of sacrifices for the emperor and the subsequent division in the city at the beginning of the war.
68. Some prophetic figures also stirred up the populace of the city (*War* 2:258).

ants of Caesarea as to who controlled that city. The emperor Nero decided the matter in favor of the Greeks, and the Jews lost their equal rights in the city. This was undoubtedly perceived as a setback for Jewish rights in Palestine generally and must have contributed to the instability of the Jewish leadership in Jerusalem.

During the time of the procurator Albinus (62–64 C.E.) the stability of the city was fundamentally undermined. The feud between those factions which had clashed in the late fifties was renewed (*Antiquities* 20:205–207). Then a more violent struggle followed involving various factions in the city. Josephus writes, "Each ruffian, with his own band of followers grouped around him, towered above his company like a brigand chief or tyrant, employing his bodyguard to plunder peaceable citizens" (*War* 2:275). In the *War* account, Josephus attributes these conflicts to the revolutionary faction within the city (*War* 2:274). However, the report from *Antiquities* reveals the specific context of the dissension which came as a result of the appointment by the procurator of a new high priest.

> And now the king deposed Jesus the son of Damnaeus from the high priesthood and appointed as his successor Jesus the son of Gamaliel. In consequence, a feud arose between the latter and his predecessor. They each collected a band of the most reckless sort and it frequently happened that after exchanging insults they went further and hurled stones. Ananias, however, kept the upper hand by using his wealth to attract those who were willing to receive bribes. Costobar and Saul also on their own part collected gangs of villains. They themselves were of royal lineage and found favour because of their kinship with Agrippa, but were lawless and quick to plunder the property of those weaker than themselves. From that moment particularly, sickness fell upon our city, and everything went steadily from bad to worse. (*Antiquities* 20:213–14)

The *Antiquities* account makes it clear that at this time there was a struggle for leadership and power in the city among various factions.[69] Even here the dispute was among Jews and not directed against the Romans. Nor is there mention of a revolutionary sect or organized resistance to Rome. Rather the parties concerned were trying to bribe the procurator (*War* 2:274) and Agrippa II (*Antiquities* 20:213–14) to grant them authority. But the corruption of the procurator Albinus provided the context for such a struggle to take place. The result was a breakdown of order in the city which contributed to the later outbreak

69. Smallwood, "High Priests," p. 27.

of the revolt. For this reason, Josephus marks this as the point at which the city was susceptible to rebellion and war. As the parallel account in the *War* confirms, "from this date were sown in the city the seeds of its impending fall" (*War* 2:276).

The corruption of Albinus which was a root cause of the disorder in the city (*War* 2:271) was surpassed by the violence and robbery of the last procurator, Florus (64–66 C.E.) (*War* 2:277–79; *Antiquities* 20:252–57). His wickedness and lawlessness were so excessive that Josephus refers to him as the one who "constrained us to go to war with the Romans, for we preferred to perish together rather than by degrees" (*Antiquities* 20:257). As we shall see, it was his offensive behavior which led to the clashes between Jews and Romans in Jerusalem that opened the war.

THE *sicarii*

Josephus informs us that the *sicarii* arose early in the time of Felix (52–60 C.E.):

> But while the country was thus cleared of these pests, a new species of banditti was springing up in Jerusalem, the so-called *sicarii*, who committed murders in broad daylight in the heart of the city. The festivals were their special seasons, when they would mingle with the crowd, carrying short daggers concealed under their clothing, with which they stabbed their enemies. Then, when they fell, the murderers joined in the cries of indignation and, through this plausible behaviour, were never discovered. The first to be assassinated by them was Jonathan the high-priest; after his death there were numerous daily murders. (*War* 2:254–56)

We would assume from this description and from what is known of the brigands elsewhere (*War* 2:264–65) that *sicarii* assassinated Jews who were cooperating with Rome, such as Jonathan the high priest, for political or religious reasons. The *Antiquities* account of the assassination of Jonathan contradicts this idea by claiming that the procurator Felix bribed certain brigands to murder Jonathan because of a personal feud between them (*Antiquities* 20:162–66). This latter account may be due to Josephus' desire to malign the motives of the revolutionaries by giving bribery as their reason for killing and to blame the procurators for Judea's troubles by attributing the rise of the *sicarii* to Roman misrule. However, it is not impossible that some revolutionaries may have been spurred by the procurator's bribe to get rid of one who was their own enemy. Whatever the cause of the initial assassination of Jonathan, this terrorist method of resistance came to be used regularly with impunity by the revolutionaries (*Antiquities* 20: 165).

From the accounts of the *sicarii* in Felix' time we learn that they are generally classified among those whom Josephus calls "brigands." They were from the countryside, entering the city with the crowds at feast times to avoid recognition. Their use of daggers made it difficult to detect and capture them. We do not get the impression of one sect or group, but a method of resistance and revenge which came to be successfully used by different individuals. A later reference to the *sicarii* in the time of Festus (60–62 C.E.) associates the assassinations in the city with the plundering done by brigands in the countryside (*Antiquities* 20:185–87). Here also the two terms "brigands" and *sicarii* function to depict the various types of terrorist resistance taking place in the nation at this time, without reference to any sect or organized group.

However, later activities of the *sicarii* may indicate the presence of an organized group. In *Antiquities* 20:208–10, Josephus describes how the *sicarii* entered Jerusalem by night during a festival to kidnap the secretary of the temple captain. The secretary was used as a hostage for the release of others of their number who had been imprisoned by the Romans. The high priest Ananias, who happened to be the father of the temple captain, was in a position to negotiate with the procurator Albinus.

> This was the beginning of greater troubles; for the brigands contrived by one means or another to kidnap some of Ananias' staff and would hold them until they had received in exchange some of the *sicarii*. When they had once more become not inconsiderable in number, they grew bold again and proceeded to harass every part of the land. (*Antiquities* 20:208–10)

In this passage the term *sicarii* may have come to refer to a particular group. There is no functional reason to apply the term *sicarii* to them —that is, they are not here employing *sicae,* or daggers, for assassination. Kidnapping for the release of some of their number indicates that they were a familiar close-knit group of resisters who would take risks for the release of others of their number. Their success with the release of prisoners does not necessarily mean that their numbers were large, but rather that their methods were successful. In fact, the use of terrorist methods in itself may imply that they were a small group. Also, it was necessary for them to have several groups of prisoners released before they would be able to replenish their ranks sufficiently to resume the plundering and burning of pro-Roman villages in the countryside. There is, then, evidence of a prewar organized group of resisters who were active in the city and the countryside. This organized group, however, is nowhere described as the focal point for the nation's revolutionaries. Nor is there any attempt to depict them as a sect or to connect them with the later faction of Sicarii on Masada, although that may be implied simply by the continuity of the use of the term *sicarii* both here and for the later group on Masada.[70]

MOTIVATIONS OF THE RESISTANCE

A summary of the motives and rationale for the revolutionary activities we have discussed would help to put the prewar period into clearer focus. It would also serve to reinforce the notion of the varied nature of the unrest and expressions of dissent taking place throughout Israel at this time.

Economic, Social, and Political Motivations

As we have indicated, social and political conditions in Palestine favored the kind of disparate, local, and spontaneous expressions of dissatisfaction that we find in Josephus' accounts of the brigandage in this period.[71]

Taxes were high and covered every sector of Jewish life. These included not only the Roman taxes, customs and frontier duties, but also the Jewish tithes and dues that went for the support of the priestly

70. In the prewar period, Josephus never clearly uses the term *sicarii* to refer to a distinct group. However, Josephus does use the term to designate a particular sect when he refers to the revolutionaries on Masada during the war and the revolutionaries active in Alexandria and Cyrene after the war. The distinction we have made between Josephus' use of *sicarii* as a technical term and his use of "Sicarii" as a sectarian designation reflects Thackeray's translations. Up to and including *War* 2:425, which refers to those who entered the temple to join Eleazar, son of Ananias, in the civil war in Jerusalem, Thackeray translates *sicarii*. The next reference (*War* 4:400), which refers to those who were in possession of Masada, and each subsequent occurrence he translates as a proper title, "Sicarii."

71. For an excellent discussion of the social causes of the war, see Moses Aberbach, *The Roman-Jewish War* (London: R. Golub and Company, 1966); see also Heinz Kreissig, "Die Sozialen Zusammenhange des Jüdischen Krieges" (Ph.D. dissertation, Humboldt University, 1965).

hierarchy and temple worship.[72]   Matters became even worse when Roman taxes were increased during the procuratorship of Albinus (*War* 2:273).   Of course, the poor were always in danger of being exploited by the tax collectors.

Besides, the land was unproductive and there were few natural resources.   Those who rented land stood the risk in an unproductive year of losing to the landowners their goods or, if it became necessary to indenture themselves, their freedom.   Small farmers were threatened with the expropriation of their land by the Romans if they were unable to pay the tribute.[73] The result was an abundance of fugitive slaves and miserable free working men.   This often led to brigandage.   Perhaps the most severe threat which initiated much of the widespread brigandage of the late forties and early fifties was the famine of 48 C.E. (*Antiquities* 20:51).

Much of the unrest in this period was directed against the wealthy Jews.   Upper-class Jews preserved the lucrative positions such as tax collector for themselves often by bribery of the Roman officials.   As we have seen, the high priests exploited the lower orders of the priesthood in order to maintain their income (*Antiquities* 20:206–207).   And there was oppression in Jerusalem by the lay aristocracy (*Antiquities* 20:214).   This may account for some of the terrorism against high priests and aristocracy which took place in Jerusalem.   In the countryside, landowners exploited the peasants in order to meet their tax obligation to the Romans.   Terrorism and brigandage against them by the lower classes were intended to suppress their cooperation with the Romans and to gain remuneration for their own losses.   Since the wealthy had the most to lose by a war with Rome, the revolutionary cause was quite popular among lower classes who saw rebellion not only as a struggle against the Romans but also as an opportunity to gain revenge against the oppressive Jews of the upper class.[74]

Of course, all of this unrest was encouraged by the breakdown of law and order in the province.   Cumanus' indifference to the murder of a Galilean pilgrim was typical (*War* 2:233–46; *Antiquities* 20:118–36).   After that, as we have indicated, brigands operated in the countryside with relative impunity (*War* 2:239).   Occasionally, a procura-

---

72. For a list of taxes and financial dues, see Frederick C. Grant, *The Economic Background of the Gospels* (London: Oxford University Press, 1926).
73. Hengel, *Zeloten*, p. 341.
74. Aberbach, *The Roman-Jewish War*, p. 30.

tor would attempt to clear the country of brigands, but the efforts were neither adequate nor sustained (*War* 2:254, 271). The failure of Felix to punish the assassins of the high priest Jonathan led to subsequent terrorism in Jerusalem (*Antiquities* 20:165). In the sixties, prisoners were released by the procurators for bribes or in response to terrorist demands (e.g., *War* 2:273). Albinus emptied the prisons of offenders to gain favor at the time of his removal from office (*Antiquities* 20:215). This political failure to deal with Jewish unrest only encouraged illegal activities among those who were in poverty or who were affected by political and religious disillusionment or who operated from strictly mercenary motives as ordinary robbers. The political ineptitude and corruption of the procurators must have given the Jewish leaders a longing to govern their own affairs.

The situation was exacerbated by the economic impact of the completion of the temple in the mid-sixties (*Antiquities* 20:219–22). Eighteen thousand workers, who had been employed for this task, were now without work. These workers had been paid out of the temple treasury which was regularly replenished by the annual dues from each male Jew in Israel and the diaspora. These funds were always in danger of confiscation by the procurators, as Pilate had done in order to build an aqueduct (*War* 2:175–77; *Antiquities* 18:60–62). Such confiscation would affect the course of construction and the fate of the workers. When the temple was completed, the Jewish leaders decided that the funds should be used to hire some of the unemployed workers to pave the streets of Jerusalem in white stone (*Antiquities* 20:222). But Florus had other ideas for the surplus monies. He attempted to confiscate the temple treasury for his own needs (*War* 2:331), but he was opposed by those who knew that they were defending the economic well-being of themselves and their city. This opposition brought about the first clash of the war, and much of the impetus for it came from the economic instability which had by this time affected, in one way or another, every part of the nation's populace.

Religious Motivations

It seems quite clear that, in general, Josephus suppressed the religious motivations of the revolutionaries by ascribing to them evil and dishonorable intentions. Therefore, it is necessary to infer from descriptions of their actions what honorific motives, if any, may have impelled

them.   First, we will look briefly at Josephus' descriptions of the
prophetic figures, about whose religious motives he is fairly explicit.

The popularity of the prophetic figures who arose and gained a following in this period attests to what a growing burden the Roman
occupation of Israel had become.[75] Promises for "signs of their deliverance" and "salvation and rest from their troubles" offered a hopeful way for many ordinary Jews to find relief from the oppression of
their economic and social conditions.

The promises of Theudas and others had great religious, national
significance.   Theudas' promise to part the waters of the Jordan is
reminiscent of Israel's escape from the bondage of the Egyptians (*Antiquities* 20:97–99).   As such, Theudas may have called Jews from
the Roman bondage to a new beginning, inaugurating a redemption on
the analogy of the exodus[76] and trusting God to bring their actions to
a hopeful conclusion.

Among the prophetic figures, the "wilderness" motif is prominent, a
motif which recalls that the signs of God's presence were evident in the
wilderness journey from Egypt to the promised land.   Josephus tells of
those who led a following into the wilderness where the signs of deliverance would be manifest (*War* 2:259; see *Antiquities* 20:167–68).
The Egyptian prophet led his group through the wilderness before approaching Jerusalem (*War* 2:261–63; *Antiquities* 20:169–71; Acts
20:38).   Another Jewish prophet claimed that the wilderness would
be the place where "salvation and rest from troubles" were to be found
(*Antiquities* 20:188).   This motif emerges again at the end of the war
period, when the defeated Jews requested Titus to give them egress
from the city to go into the wilderness (*War* 6:351).   Perhaps it is an
indication of their despair of gaining freedom from the Romans that
many Jews looked to the wilderness as the place where God's activity
of liberation would be initiated.

As far as we know, all of the prewar prophetic movements were nonviolent, except perhaps that of the Egyptian prophet.   This does not
mean, however, that they were not a significant part of anti-Roman
resistance.   Their eschatological behavior had as its object the destruc-

75. The several references in the New Testament to such prophetic figures affirm
their popularity.   See especially Mark 13:5–8, 21–23; Matthew 24:4–7, 24–25;
Luke 21:8–9; Acts 5:36; 20:38.
76. W. D. Davies, *The Setting of the Sermon on the Mount* (Cambridge: Cambridge University Press, 1963), p. 116.   See also pp. 25–94 for a discussion of
the exodus typology.

tion of the present order and its replacement by a divinely ordained one.   The apocalyptic promises of God's saving action may have provided an alternative to violent revolution for some who despaired of the efficacy of human revolutionary efforts against the Romans.   If they would act in faith to follow the word of God's agent, the Almighty would surely bless their obedience with his act of deliverance.   These movements certainly had the effect of stirring up the people (*War* 2:258).   And although most may not have been violent movements, they fed the atmosphere in which revolutionary activity took place.   The fact that the Romans dealt with them by prompt military suppression indicates that they viewed them as anti-Roman and a threat to the established order.[77]

If the hope of God's deliverance inspired these prophetic figures who took nonviolent actions of faith, perhaps the same hopes inspired those who were moved to violent revolutionary actions.   It is on this basis that we may attribute honorific intentions to the actions of many revolutionaries.   Some Jews may have reasoned that if they were willing to take revolutionary actions against the Romans or their Jewish collaborators in defense of their nation and law, then God would surely cooperate to bring their actions to success.   Reasoning in this way, one is led to look at the Jewish understanding of "zeal," for much of the religious commitment to resist or oppose Rome can reasonably be accounted for under the concept of "zeal."

The word "zealot" has often been misused to refer only to those, and to all of those, who were committed to rebellion against Rome.   And it is usually capitalized and made a proper name as if it designated a sect to which all such persons belonged.   However, a study of "zeal" in Jewish literature indicates that there was a variety of meanings and associations attached to this term.   (1) "Zeal" was often understood as the devotion which one had toward keeping the Jewish law and being willing to suffer for that commitment.   In this regard, those Jews in the time of Pilate who were willing to die rather than transgress the law would be depicted as zealous (*War* 2:169–74).[78]   (2) In other uses,

77. See R. MacMullen *Enemies of the Roman Order* (Cambridge, Mass.: Harvard University Press, 1966), especially pp. 128–62.
78. Although the term "zeal" does not occur in this passage, it is very typical of the cases where it does appear.   See 1 Maccabees 2:28, 50; 2 Maccabees 4:2; Testament of Ashur 4:2–5; 4 Maccabees 18:12; Galatians 1:13; Acts 25:3; Romans 10:2; and *Dead Sea Scrolls*, Manual of Discipline 4:4 and 9:23.

"zeal" refers to Jews who were willing to punish other Jews who had disobeyed the law, either as a form of vengeance or as a means of defending and preserving the law of Israel. The apostle Paul's reference to himself as a "zealot," who as a Jew had persecuted Christians, is probably to be understood in this way (Galatians 1:13–14).[79] (3) "Zeal" was also connected with killing or punishing offenders as a means of destroying that which pollutes or defiles the land, temple, or hereditary purity of the people of Israel. The killing of any gentile who entered the sanctuary of the temple was viewed as a zealous act preserving the holiness of God's temple (Acts 21:28–31).[80] (4) Finally, another portrayal of "zeal" was the act of killing legal offenders, especially idolators, as a sacrifice to atone for the presence of sin and to appease God's wrath. The classic model was Phineas, the Old Testament priest, who took the law into his own hands and killed Zimri for having intercourse with a Midianite woman (Numbers 25:1–15).[81]

Some of these meanings of zeal may overlap in certain passages, but none is necessarily to be associated with revolutionary activity. In fact, not one of the examples given above, by itself, would have been considered revolutionary in first century Palestine. However, one can see how "zealous" motivations might have been operative among Jewish dissidents of this period. They might have opposed the Romans and those Jews who associated with them in order to cleanse the nation of defiling gentiles. Those who adhered to the fourth philosophy may have viewed those Jews who cooperated with the occupying power as idolators who needed to be killed before God's wrath would be removed from the land. Jonathan the high priest may have been killed for this reason. Or his assassins may have considered him to be an illegitimate occupant of the high priestly office and thus a defiler of the temple. Some wealthy Jews may have been terrorized because they were neglecting the Jewish law and embracing Hellenistic practices. The zealous defense of Jewish institutions from the Roman threat may have impelled others to revolutionary actions.

79. Cf. also 1 Maccabees 48:1–2; Jubilees 30:17–19; Testament of Levi 5:3; Philippians 3:5–6; Acts 21:20, 28; 22:3–5; Philo, *Embassy to Gaius* 2:253. In the *Dead Sea Scrolls*, Psalms of Thanksgiving 2:15 and 14:4 refer to a zealous hatred for offenders without reference to killing them.
80. See also Judith 9:4; Jubilees 3:8, 15; 2 Baruch 66:1–6; John 2:17; perhaps also Testament of Ashur 4:2–5.
81. Cf. also Testament of Levi 5:6; *Babylonian Talmud*, Sanhedrin 82a; *Sifre on Numbers* 25:1–15.

It is not possible for us to recover accurately the religious motivations of the Jewish dissidents, because Josephus is silent on that score. But our inferences enable us to understand that much of Jewish opposition to Rome may have issued from a zealous mentality. They also enable us to clarify the reasons for zealous activity against fellow Jews. It was necessary to cleanse the people or the land of "apostate" Jews, as well as gentiles, in order for God to favor them, support their cause, and remove the foreign oppression from the land.

Again we must be cautious not to assume that a "zealot" was necessarily a "revolutionary." In Jewish and Christian literature, there are a variety of offenses about which Jews were zealous: intercourse with heathen women (which leads to idolatry);[82] idolatry;[83] the presence of uncircumcised in the land;[84] the defilement of the sanctuary;[85] profaning God's name;[86] and other offenses against the Jewish legal traditions.[87] Other such transgressions may have been associated with zeal but are not directly related to zeal in the literature. The variety of these offenses and the cross-section of literature in which these references occur imply that zeal was not the exclusive characteristic of any one group or sect.[88]

Although some zealous Jews may have persecuted those who were guilty of all of the offenses mentioned here, it is probable that many were zealous about some offenses and not others. For example, Jewish zealots may have agreed that the presence of a gentile in the sanctuary merited immediate death (Acts 21:28–31), but many would not have initiated action to cleanse the temple by refusing to offer the sacrifices on behalf of the Roman emperor, which was a revolutionary action (*War* 2:408). Others may have put to death the Jews who had intercourse with heathen women (Mishnah Sanhedrin 9:6), but would

82. Numbers 25:1–25; Judith 9:4; Jubilees 30; Testament of Levi 6:3; Mishnah Sanhedrin 9:6.

83. Numbers 25:1–15; 1 Kings 19:10–14; 1 Maccabees 2:23–28; 2 Baruch 6:4–5.

84. 1 Maccabees 2:44–46; 2 Baruch 66:5; Hippolytus, *Refutation of All Heresies* 9:22.

85. Jubilees 30:11, 14; John 2:15; Acts 21:28; Mishnah Sanhedrin 9:6.

86. Jubilees 30:15; 2 Baruch 6:2, 4; Mishnah Sanhedrin 9:6; Philo, *Embassy to Gaius* 212.

87. 1 Maccabees 2:44–46; Galatians 1:13–14; Acts 22:3–5; 21:28; *Dead Sea Scrolls*, Psalms of Thanksgiving 14:14.

88. Although the literature cited above extends over a span of several centuries, it probably reflects the various associations of the concept "zeal" in the first century before it became so closely identified with revolutionaries during the war years, 66–74 C.E.

not have suppressed as idolators those who paid taxes to Rome, as Judas the Galilean may have done.

Thus, in the prewar period, whether a zealot was a revolutionary depended on the nature of the offense about which he was zealous, not simply on the fact that he had zeal. What would make a zealot a revolutionary were zealous actions carried out directly against the Roman occupation of Israel and against those Jews who cooperated with them. Thus, not all zealots were revolutionaries, just as not all revolutionaries were zealots.

Josephus' history of the war implies that it was only when the war issue came into sharp critical focus in Jerusalem in the winter of 68 C.E. that the term "zealot" came to refer distinctly to revolutionaries, as distinct from the "moderates." It was then that one of the factions of revolutionaries in Jerusalem came to be called the "Zealots." There is no evidence in any of the literature for the use of "zealot" as a party name before that time.[89] Thus in regard to the prewar period, it is necessary for us to attempt to distinguish in each case, such as Paul the zealot or the *sicarii* or Simon the zealot, just what kind of zeal was involved and the nature of the offense. When we do that, we find that "zeal" had to do with a way of being Jewish and was not limited to any one sect or faction. And we find it likely that many of the revolutionary acts of "terrorism" or "brigandage" were motivated, at least in part, by this religious zeal.

ALTERNATIVE EXPRESSIONS OF RESISTANCE

In this section, we will discuss what other options for resistance against the Romans were being pursued during the turmoil of the late prewar period. We have indicated that there is little evidence for resistance among high priests, or Sadducees, in the early part of the century. The short-term appointments of high priests in the first decade of the provincial relationship may have been done by the Romans to prevent an entrenchment of political power in that office.[90] Caiaphas

89. Foakes-Jackson and Kirsopp Lake, eds., *Beginnings of Christianity*, p. 426; and Marcus Borg, "The Currency of the Term 'Zealot,'" *Journal of Theological Studies* 22 (1971): 504–12. The fact that Paul refers to himself in the fifties as a "zealot" with no indication that the term had anything to do with revolution vis-à-vis the Romans counts in favor of the argument that there was no Jewish sect called Zealots at that time.
90. Günther Baumbach, "Das Sadduzaerverständnis bei Josephus Flavius und im Neuen Testament," p. 20.

served an extensive term as high priest (18–37 C.E.), but was probably deposed in 37 C.E. for his ineffectiveness after the removal of the procurator Pilate (26–36 C.E.) with whom he had had a close association. We have noted that some Sadducean aristocrats may have joined with those initiating an appeal to Tiberius for the removal of offensive shields from Jerusalem. And some high priests took part in the negotiations with Petronius over the attempt to put Gaius' statue in the temple. Apart from these instances, there is little evidence of strong anti-Roman sentiment on the part of high priests from 6 to 44 C.E.

However, the subsequent period shows a good deal of strife. The high priesthoods of Jonathan, Ananias, Ishmael, and Ananus are four examples of the worsening relationship between high priests and procurators in the years from 44 to 66 C.E.

Jonathan, son of Ananus, served as high priest for a brief period in 37 C.E. (*Antiquities* 18:95). Later, when he was offered the high priesthood by Agrippa I (*Antiquities* 19:313–16), he refused to accept the appointment, perhaps because he felt he could exercise more influence on behalf of his people outside the high priestly office.[91] Later, he went with a delegation to Rome in order to defend Jewish actions at the time of the uprising of Eleazar ben Dinai and to accuse the procurator Cumanus (48–52 C.E.) of delinquency in the affair (*War* 2:240, 242). While there, he was apparently influential in obtaining the assignment of Felix (52–60 C.E.) as procurator in Palestine (*Antiquities* 20:162). However, when Felix proved to be an incompetent official, Jonathan repeatedly criticized him. He may even have threatened to use his influence to have him recalled to Rome. Later, Jonathan was killed by *sicarii* (*War* 2:256). In one version of the story of Jonathan's death, as we have seen, Felix supposedly bribed the revolutionary assassins to rid him of this nagging critic (*Antiquities* 20:162–64).

Ananias, son of Nedebaeus, was the high priest (48–59 C.E.: cf. *Antiquities* 20:103) at the time of the revolt of Eleazar ben Dinai and was sent to Rome to answer for the actions of the Jewish people (*War* 2:243; *Antiquities* 20:131). When the Jews were exonerated, Ananias returned to Israel. Later in his term as high priest, some of his underlings were kidnapped by *sicarii,* and he intervened on their behalf by bribing the procurator to release some captured revolutionaries from imprisonment (*Antiquities* 20:208–10). One might well suspect collu-

91. Smallwood, "High Priests," p. 24.

sion between Ananias and the *sicarii*. However, this is unlikely. Assassinations by *sicarii* had created an atmosphere of great fear in Jerusalem. The high priest Jonathan had recently been killed, and the terrorist tactics of the revolutionaries were proving to be effective. Thus, fear may have been Ananias' motive for cooperating with the revolutionaries. And he was not unjustified, for a few years later, at the opening of the war, his house was burned (*War* 2:426), and he was assassinated (*War* 2:429). Although Ananias' cooperation with the kidnappers may not have been anti-Roman in intent,[92] he did seek to manipulate the procurator, and he did have an association with revolutionaries. Also, Ananias was the father of Eleazar, the temple captain who officially opened the war by persuading the lower priests to abolish the sacrifices for the emperor (*War* 2:409).

During the time that Ishmael, son of Phabi, was high priest (59–61 C.E.), King Agrippa II built a wall onto his palace adjoining the temple in Jerusalem (*Antiquities* 20:194ff.). The wall was high enough so that the Roman guards on the wall could oversee the activities inside the temple area. Ishmael, taking this to be an intrusion upon national religious practices of the Jews, proceeded to have the walls of the temple raised to block any view of the temple activities. When the procurator Festus became irate at this act of independence and ordered the Jews to remove their wall, Ishmael appealed the matter to Rome for adjudication. The Jews were vindicated in the matter, although Ishmael was retained in Rome as a hostage (*Antiquities* 20:195).

Ananus was high priest for a brief period in 62 C.E. (*Antiquities* 20:197, 199). During an interim period after Festus was recalled to Rome and Albinus had not yet arrived to take up his duties as procurator, Ananus convened the Sanhedrin, which in turn condemned and then executed James the brother of Jesus (*Antiquities* 20:200–202). His actions were outside the Roman agreement with Israel: the procurator had to be consulted in order for the Sanhedrin to be convened, and the procurator alone was responsible for the use of the death penalty. Ananus was deposed upon Albinus' arrival after being a high priest for only three months. Ananus was the high priest later put in charge of military training and the fortification of Jerusalem in the war years.

Two main reasons can be given for this deteriorating relationship be-

---

92. Against Smallwood, "High Priests," p. 28, who suspects collusion between Ananias and the *sicarii*.

tween high priest and procurator in these two decades before the war. First, in 44 C.E. the right to appoint the high priest was taken from the procurators and granted to Herodian representatives, Herod of Chalcis and later Agrippa II (*Antiquities* 20:15–16). As a result, the high priest had a certain independence of the procurator. Also, any high priest and procurator who served side by side at any given time might not have been on the best of terms. Second, the high priest must have shared the anger and disgust of the people at the increasing incompetence, insensitivity, and corruption of the later procurators. As the resulting anarchy in Israel worsened, the high priests did little to reassert civil authority. Indeed, if they had, it is likely that such a move would have been met with disfavor from the Jewish populace.

The efforts which the high priests did make to restore order in Israel were by means of delegations of protest to Rome. The repeated success of these efforts must have given to the high priests the confidence that Jewish acts of defiance against an incompetent procurator would ultimately be vindicated. The priestly rulers of Israel must have been convinced that the relative autonomy promised under the provincial relationship with Rome could be attained by such diplomatic means. Unfortunately the increasing offenses of the procurators and the lengthy delay involved in the appeals to Rome nullified the positive effects of these diplomatic successes.

If the actions of the four high priests mentioned above are representative of Sadducean attitudes, then Sadducees would hardly fit neatly into the category of "collaborators." They probably resented the foreign occupation, were angered by the maladministration of the procurators, and desired to govern Jewish affairs their own way. Realistically aware of the awesome military power of the Romans, they seem to have tried every means—defiance, diplomacy, delegation, and bribery —to achieve freedom for their people within the context of the empire. Yet the accumulative frustration of the Jewish people at the failure of their leaders to provide any permanent solution led many Jews to believe that such autonomy could not be gained by these political means.

The power struggle among the high priestly families in Jerusalem during the late prewar years may indicate that some Sadducees thought they could restore order by a change of leadership (*Antiquities* 20: 213). The supporters of the Herodian family may have thought it was time for a resurgence of kingship (*Antiquities* 20:214). These efforts by Herodians and high priests were possibly motivated by the conviction that they could cooperate better with the Romans in an orderly governance of the nation than the high priests presently in office.

There is little direct evidence for the involvement of Pharisees in resistance against Rome in this period. It seems likely that in the earlier period (6–44 C.E.) Pharisees were involved in acts of passive resistance, such as the sit-in before Pilate at Casarea. Sadducees probably would not have risked their power and wealth to hold such demonstrations before the Romans. And a trip to Caesarea might have seemed strange and futile to most ordinary peasants. In fact, if Pilate had not feared a larger revolt, he might have suppressed such a group. His reluctance to suppress the protesters may have been because they were persons who were broadly influential with the populace. The commitment "to die rather than transgress the law" was certainly typical of Pharisaic devotion to the Torah. It is likely then that many of those who put their life on the line before Pilate on behalf of their people were Pharisees. They may also have been prominent in subsequent acts of civil protest which, for at least two decades, helped to control the occupying forces and to satisfy the discontented populace, thus preventing them from taking more drastic, revolutionary activities. Only one such act of passive resistance occurred in the later period (44–66 C.E.) when a group of irate Jews protested the burning of the Torah by a Roman soldier in the late forties (*War* 2:229–30; *Antiquities* 20:114–17). Although the demonstration resulted in the punishment of the soldier, the whole atmosphere of the country was changing in such a way as to make such civil action ineffective in stemming the tide of revolutionary activity.

Many Pharisees, especially the more conservative ones who saw themselves as zealous guardians of the law and advocates of separation from foreign influence, must have been disturbed at the growing disregard of Jewish customs by the procurators and Roman soldiers. That such acts of passive resistance did not continue into the fifties and sixties may mean that some dissatisfied Pharisees became one of the sources from which later revolution sprang. At the same time, we have every reason to think that the Pharisees of the house of Hillel continued to urge ways of peace and to warn the nation about the consequences of its revolutionary activity. However, as the breakdown of law and order continued in the prewar period, less and less attention was paid to these voices of caution.

We hear nothing of the Essenes in this period. From their monastic community at Qumran, they may well have disapproved of the revolutionary activity throughout the land as a sign of the failure to wait upon God to initiate the final struggle.

It has been argued that the Christian sect in Israel during this time identified with its nation's cause against Rome.[93] However, it seems likely that the Christian leadership in Jerusalem was not so zealously devoted to Jewish institutions.[94] The approval of a gentile expression of Christianity is an example of this (Acts 15:1–9; Galatians 2:1–10). Also, the execution of James, the brother of Jesus and the leader of the Jerusalem church, must have been triggered by some breach of Judaism (*Antiquities* 20:200–202). These Christians may have shared some similarities with liberal Pharisaism of the period. In fact, it was probably a group of Pharisees, "strict in the observance of the law," who appealed to the Roman procurator to depose Ananus for his unauthorized execution of James, perhaps in fear that a more general purge might ensue which would affect themselves. On the other hand, there is some evidence that a minority of the Christian community in Jerusalem was at odds with the leadership (Acts 15:5; 21:20–24; Galatians 2:4–5) and might well have supported the general resistance of the nation against the increasing offenses of the Romans.

It is difficult to know the mind of the general populace. Certainly there was division as to the proper extent resistance should take against the Romans. Many feared war (*War* 2:237–38). Yet the populace as a whole did not suppress those engaged in revolutionary activities. As such, they may have given tacit support (e.g., *War* 2:229–30; *Antiquities* 20:114–17). We have seen that, with the breakdown of order in the fifties and sixties, the tide was turned in favor of open rebellion against Rome. It is difficult to know what might have been able to reverse that tide, for our analysis shows that some form or another of resistance against the Romans came to characterize almost every segment of Jewish society.

93. S. G. F. Brandon, *The Fall of Jerusalem and the Christian Church* (London: SPCK, 1968).
94. See, for example, Walter Schmithals, "Paul and James," *Studies in Biblical Theology*, no. 46 (Naperville: Allenson, 1965).

Many factors in the Roman relationship with the Jewish province contributed to this movement toward revolution. Claudius (41–54 C.E.) and Nero (54–68 C.E.) appointed procurators for shorter terms than Tiberius had done, an arrangement not conducive to responsibility in office. Many of the procurators sent to Judea were ill-prepared for the post. Some of these later procurators were of Greek origin, perhaps thereby less tolerant of Jewish customs and more sympathetic to the Syro-Greek population in Palestine.[95] Also, during this period, the Roman troops under the procurator were drawn from the non-Jewish population within Palestine.[96] The offensive behavior of these soldiers and the several Jewish clashes with Roman troops in this period were part of the general Jewish-gentile conflict in Palestine as a whole. The stability of the high priestly leadership was undermined in the fifties and sixties when they came to be chosen from different families and appointed with greater frequency. In addition, Herod of Chalcis and Agrippa II had neither the widespread support of Jews nor the influence with the Romans which characterized the Herodians of the earlier period. Thus, the leadership of the province in the late prewar period (44–66 C.E.) was not so stable or "equitable" as it had been in the earlier period. Under these circumstances, the Jews came more and more to be "unruly" subjects.

The decision of Nero in 60 C.E. to deny to the Jews of Caesarea equal rights with the Syrian population there must have generally undermined confidence in the fundamental Roman attitudes toward Jews[97] and increased the tension between Jews and gentiles throughout Palestine. Josephus writes that this decision led directly to the war, since the Jewish population continued their conflict with the Syrians until "at last they kindled the flames of war" (*Antiquities* 20:184). The conflicts in Caesarea broke into the open in 66 C.E. when the Greeks succeeded in receiving official approval from Nero to take over the government of that city. The hostility and fear created throughout the nation by this situation contributed greatly to the atmosphere in Jerusalem where a clash beween Jews and Roman troops opened the war.

---

95. *Compendia*, 1:319.
96. Ibid., 1:327–29.
97. On the significance of this event and Nero's negligence toward the Jews (*War* 6:337), see Barnett, "Under Tiberius," pp. 565, 569–70.

IV

REVOLUTIONARIES OF THE WAR
PERIOD: 66-74 C.E.

We turn now to a consideration of Josephus' description of the revolutionaries during the war period. Here our major concern is to stress the complexities of the revolutionary groups and their interrelations.

It is erroneous to argue that the Jewish revolt was caused by a monolithic group of revolutionaries who incited the Jews and their leaders to war with Rome. It is true that in his narrative of the actual siege of Jerusalem, Josephus himself lumps the revolutionaries together and sees them as pitted against peaceful Jewish citizens and the Roman army. However, they were united at this point because they were confronted by a common enemy, the Romans. In the early war period, before and during the early stages of the siege, the revolutionaries were certainly not unified. Rather, Josephus traces a number of significant revolutionary groups and describes constant conflicts among these groups. In a summary passage in the *War,* Josephus lists these groups:

(1) The Sicarii were the first to set the example of this lawlessness and cruelty of their kinsmen, leaving no word unspoken to insult, no deed untried to ruin the victims of their conspiracy. Yet even they were shown by (2) John of Gischala to be more moderate than himself. For not only did he put to death all who proposed just and salutary measures, treating such persons as his bitterest enemies among all the citizens, but he also in his public capacity loaded his country with evils innumerable, such as one might expect would be inflicted upon men by one who had already dared to practice impiety even towards God. For he had unlawful food served at his table and abandoned the established rules of purity of our forefathers; so that it could no longer excite surprise, that one guilty of such mad impiety

towards God failed to observe towards men the offices of gentleness and charity. Again, there was (3) Simon, son of Gioras: what crime did not he commit: Or what outrage did he refrain from inflicting upon the persons of those very freemen who had created him a despot? What ties of friendship or of kindred but rendered these men more audacious in their daily murders? For to do injury to a foreigner they considered an act of petty malice, but thought they cut a splendid figure by maltreating their nearest relations. Yet even their infatuation was outdone by the madness of the (4) Idumaeans. For those most abominable wretches, after butchering the chief priests, so that no particle of religious worship might continue, proceeded to extirpate whatever relics were left of our civil polity, introducing into every department perfect lawlessness. In this (5) the so-called Zealots excelled, a class which justified their name by their actions; for they copied every deed of ill, nor was there any previous villainy recorded in history that they failed zealously to emulate. And yet they took their title from their professed zeal for virtue, either in mockery of those they wronged, so brutal was their nature, or reckoning the greatest of evils good. (*War* 7:262–70)

All of these groups—the Sicarii, the followers of John of Gischala, the followers of Simon bar Giora, the Idumaeans, and the Zealots—can be identified in Josephus' earlier narrative of the war years. However, this summary quotation suggests some of the difficulties in evaluating those groups. How did they arise? Did the Sicarii, who supposedly came first, influence any other groups to revolt? If these groups arose independently, what were the conditions and convictions from which they originated? Two of the groups are identified by their leaders—John and Simon. Does the fact that these figures stand out as war leaders suggest the possibility of messianic claims made by these or other revolutionaries? One group, the Sicarii, is identified by its method of assassination. Does this suggest that groups differed in their revolutionary methods? The Idumaeans and Zealots are condemned for overthrowing the traditional Jewish government and causing civil chaos. What does that suggest about the goals and hopes of the revolutionaries? John is chastised for eating sacred food, which urges us to consider the degree of religious sensibility and motivation of the various groups and leaders. The Idumaeans are identified by their geographical origin. Is it possible to know the geographical origin of the other groups, and if so, what significance must this have for their revolutionary concerns and expectations? The Zealots are the only group with a title which was self-designated. What does that suggest about what this group thought of itself? Who made up these groups—priests, ordinary citizens, the aristocracy, country folk, city people, Pharisees or other sectarians, lower-class citizens, slaves, refugees? And how does this knowledge inform us about the similarities and differences among these revolutionary groups who led the revolt against Rome?

The answers to all the above questions are crucial for an understanding of the revolt against Rome, especially in light of Josephus' belief that it was internal faction and sedition which caused the downfall of the Jewish state even more than the actual clash with Rome (*War* 5:257). It is clearly a part of Josephus' bias to blame the war upon the internal faction and infighting among the revolutionary groups. Josephus has probably exaggerated the division, but the conflicts among the revolutionaries are so pervasive and integral to his entire narrative that they could not be regarded as fabrications without throwing out the whole of his history of the war.

It is important to note that at some point in Josephus' narrative each of these groups is engaged in battle against other revolutionary groups: Eleazar, son of Ananias, against Menahem (*War* 2:444); the Zealots against John's party (*War* 5:5); the Idumaeans against John's party (*War* 4:570); the Zealots against Simon (*War* 4:514); John's party against Simon's party (*War* 4:557). In other passages, expressed differences separate the groups although they are not engaged in armed conflict with one another: Zealots and the Idumaeans (*War* 4:353); Simon and the Sicarii on Masada (*War* 4:508).

The only occasion on which these various groups cooperated with each other was in fear of, or in battle against, a common enemy: Eleazar, son of Ananias, and Menahem against the traditional government of high priests (*War* 2:425, 434); Simon bar Giora and the Sicarii in refuge from Ananus and the provisional government (*War* 4:505); Zealots and John of Gischala and the Idumaeans against the provisional government and the Jerusalem populace (*War* 4:228, 310); John and the Zealots against the Idumaeans (*War* 4:570); the Idumaeans and Simon against John and the Zealots (*War* 4:573); all forces in Jerusalem against the Romans (*War* 5:279). In every case, these coalitions broke up when the threat of the common enemy was removed. That enemy was, in most instances, a group of fellow Jews— either moderates or another revolutionary faction.

This division continued, Josephus tells us, until the Romans began the siege of Jerusalem in the spring of 70 C.E. We are told that the infighting continued even when there was a lull in the battles with the Romans (*War* 5:98, 252). Even at the point of greatest Jewish unity, Josephus lists four different groups in the city—Zealots, Idumaeans, Simon, and John—and reports the outstanding warriors from each group (*War* 6:92, 148; cf. Tacitus *Histories* 5:12). In another passage, he records the relative strength of these factions:

> The strength of the combatants and insurgents within the city was as follows. Simon had an army exclusive of the Idumaeans, of ten thousand men; over these were fifty officers, Simon himself being commander-in-chief. His Idumaean contingent numbered five thousand and had ten chiefs, among whom James, son of Sosas, and Simon, son of Cathlas, ranked hghest. John, at the time when he seized the temple, had an army of six thousand men, commanded by twenty officers; but now the Zealots also had joined him having abandoned their quarrel, to the number of two thousand four hundred, led by Eleazar, their former chief, and Simon, son of Arinus. (*War* 5:248–50)

In addition to these groups, the Sicarii were at this time occupying Masada. Thus it is clear that there were five distinct parties of revolutionaries during the war period—the Sicarii, Zealots, Idumaeans, John's following, and Simon's forces.

It is obvious that the differences among these revolutionary groups must be taken seriously. One cannot simply characterize one group, such as the Zealots, and then submerge the other groups under the same umbrella of outlook and ideas. The life of each group must be traced out in its history on its own terms. We cannot validly speak of first century Zealots (either capitalized or not) as if we were somehow describing all Jewish revolutionaries of the first century. Rather, it is necessary to attempt to delineate the history and origins of the various groups and to seek to discover the beliefs, motivations, methods, and constituency of each individual group and to discern their particular importance in shaping the events of the war.

THE ZEALOTS

In order to understand the nature and make-up of the Zealots, it is first of all necessary to trace their origins and predecessors through the early part of the war. The origins of the Zealot party, which was not formed until the winter of 67–68 C.E., can be traced back to the initial clash between the citizens of Jerusalem and Roman troops under the

97

procurator Florus in the summer of 66 C.E. This conflict followed
many abuses by Florus, including his extraction of seventeen talents
from the temple treasury (*War* 2:293), the plunder of the city by his
forces (2:305), and his attempt to capture and control the temple
(2:328–31). His offensiveness to the populace made it dangerous for
him to remain in the city (*War* 2:332). After his departure, Agrippa
II arrived in order to persuade the people to return to a submissive relationship to Rome (*War* 2:342–404).[1] Josephus relates to us that
when Agrippa's speech was concluded, the people "began to cry out
that they were not taking up arms against the Romans, but against
Florus, because of all he had done them" (*War* 2:402). Then, on
Agrippa's advice, they agreed to rectify their acts of war by collecting
the tribute which they had refused to pay and by repairing the porticoes
between the temple and the Antonia Fortress which had been torn
down in battle with Florus. However, when Agrippa tried to persuade
the citizens to submit to Florus until a new procurator arrived, the
Jews "heaped abuse upon the king and formally proclaimed his [the
king's] banishment from the city" (*War* 2:406). Thus, the main motivation for this opening battle with Roman troops in the city was
Jewish outrage over the abuses of Florus and his interference in the
affairs of temple and state.

In this context—with the populace in a rebellious mood, the control
of the city left in the hands of the high priests supported by a Roman
garrison, and Agrippa banished from the city—the lower priests took
an action which was tantamount to a declaration of war. Led by the
temple captain, Eleazar, son of Ananias, and supported by the revolutionary leaders of the populace, they decided to refuse any further
gifts or offerings from gentiles—including the sacrifices offered twice
daily on behalf of the Roman empire and emperor:

> Eleazar, son of Ananias the high-priest, a very daring youth, then hold-
> ing the position of captain, persuaded those who officiated in the
> Temple services to accept no gift or sacrifice from a foreigner. This
> action laid the foundation of the war with the Romans; for the sacri-
> fices offered on behalf of that nation and the emperor were in conse-
> quence rejected. The chief priests and the notables earnestly besought
> them not to abandon the customary offering for their rulers, but the
> priests remained obdurate. Their numbers gave them great confidence,
> supported as they were by the stalwarts of the revolutionary party; but

1. Agrippa II was a descendant of Herod. For the identity of this Herodian
king, see above p. 68. Throughout the war Agrippa II was pro-Roman.

they relied above all on the authority of the captain Eleazar. (*War* 2:409-10).

This coalition of lower priests and leaders of the populace in opposition to the traditional high priestly authorities goes back to conflicts in the time of Felix and Albinus (*Antiquities* 20:180-81; 205-207). Those conflicts were characterized by the oppression of lower priests by the traditional chief priests. The refusal to accept sacrifices of gentiles may thus have been a way for the oppressed lower priests to assert some control over the temple cultus. It is interesting to note that, in the civil war which followed the cessation of sacrifices, Eleazar's group, who occupied the temple and the lower city, excluded their high priestly opponents from temple worship (*War* 2:425). Thus, the conflict between these groups may in part have been a class struggle.[2]

The refusal of sacrifices was also a nationalistic act equivalent to a declaration of war. The offer of two sacrifices daily on behalf of the emperor had been part of the agreement with Rome which expressed Jewish loyalty to Rome in place of worship of the emperor. As such, the cessation of sacrifies for gentiles broke the mutual treaty with Rome, and Israel was now officially outside the empire (*War* 2:415). Also, the cessation of these sacrifices may have been intended to prevent the gentiles, including Romans, from receiving the supernatural benefits these offerings were supposed to bring.[3] The revolutionaries may have believed that in this way Roman attempts to reconquer Israel would be thwarted by their lack of divine support.

The refusal of gifts and sacrifices from gentiles may also have been a zealous act of cleansing the temple. The Jews already had a law which demanded capital punishment for any gentile who entered the inner court of the temple, an ordinance based on the law of purification (*War* 6:125; *Antiquities* 15:417).[4] Similarly, the cessation of gentile sacrifices might have been a religious renewal of the temple cult based on a radical understanding of the prohibition of gentiles, which excluded also their gifts and sacrifices.[5] And the subsequent exclusion

2. Cf. S. G. F. Brandon, *Jesus and the Zealots* (Manchester: Manchester University Press, 1967), p. 131.
3. So Morton Smith, in private correspondence, 1975.
4. See Kaufman Kohler, "Wer waren die Zeloten oder Kannaim," *Festschrift zu Ehren des Dr. Harkavy*, ed. D. von Günzberg (St. Petersburg, 1908), p. 13, n. 1.
5. So Baumbach, who says this group was bringing about a cleansing of the temple from all impurity and therefore the complete sanctification of this house of God: Günther Baumbach, "Die Zeloten: ihre geschichtliche und religionspolitische Bedeutung," *Bibel und Liturgie* 41 (1968): 8.

of the traditional pro-Roman high priests from temple worship may have been part of such a purification of the temple.[6]

Eleazar, as the son of a high priest, was likely a Sadducee. However, it is not impossible that a member of the high priestly family would be a Pharisee. It has been argued that, in the last years before the revolt, the temple captain was a Pharisaic priest, appointed by pressure from Pharisees in order to ensure that temple worship was carried out according to their beliefs.[7] Also, some of the lower priests may have been conservative Pharisees of the house of Shammai. If this is so, then there were sectarian issues at stake in the cessation of sacrifices by this priestly group.

In all of these considerations it is important to recognize the extreme difficulty of separating the religious, political, and social motives of the revolutionaries.

When the chief priests and leading Pharisees were unable to dissuade the priests from this "strange innovation" in their religion (*War* 2:414) which was provoking war with Rome, the control of the city began to slip from their hands (*War* 2:418). Civil war broke out. Eleazar and his followers occupied the temple area and the lower city, while the chief priests, having sent to Florus and Agrippa for reinforcements, occupied the upper city (2:422)—each battling the other for control of Jerusalem and the state. During this time, a temple festival was held under Eleazar, and his opponents were excluded (*War* 2:426). The followers of Eleazar, composed of Jerusalemites, were then joined by *sicarii* (*War* 2:425) from Judea, who enabled them to make a successful siege against the chief priests in the upper city. Then a certain Menahem and his armed brigands entered the city, took over leadership of the revolt from Eleazar, and successfully conducted the siege of Herod's palace in the Upper City. Menahem's "tyranny" was stopped, however, when the partisans of Eleazar, rejecting Menahem's messianic claims to absolute authority, assassinated him and compelled his followers to flee to Masada (*War* 2:442–48).

---

6. So Baumbach, who adds that their exclusion may have been based on the reproach of the high priests in Ezekiel 5:11; 22:26; 44:4–5: Baumbach, "Zeloten," p. 8. See also M. Hengel, *Die Zeloten* (Leiden: E. J. Brill, 1961), pp. 211–29 for a general discussion of Jewish zeal for the sanctuary. These actions were not based on the "no Lord but God" philosophy of the Sicarii.

7. See S. Safrai, "The High Priesthood and the Sanhedrin in the Time of the Second Temple," *The World History of the Jewish People*, first series, vol. 7 (Jerusalem: Masada Publishing Company, 1975), p. 273, who follows A. Buchler, *Die Priester und Der Cultus* (Vienna, 1895), p. 106.

The *sicarii* and Menahem had enabled the Jerusalem insurgents to carry out their siege successfully against the traditional authorities and the royalist troops of Agrippa. Eleazar now resumed charge of the revolt. The Roman garrison, which had taken refuge in the towers, finally requested a safe exit in return for surrender. This was accepted and the appropriate oaths were taken. However, once the Romans had laid down their arms, Eleazar's party attacked and killed them. Only the Roman commander Metilius, who promised to become a Jew and be circumcised, was spared. This event, Josephus tells us, took place on the sabbath (*War* 2:449–56), which, if correct, throws some doubt upon the religious motivations of these revolutionaries.

It is not clear who was in charge of Jerusalem between the massacre of the Romans in August of 66 and the approach of Cestius, the governor of Syria, with Roman forces in October. It was the insurgents, however, who led the fight against him. During the battles, they killed Cestius' envoys because they feared that a promise of amnesty would be accepted by the populace (*War* 2:523–26). They also discovered and thwarted a plot by some leading citizens to open the gates to Cestius (*War* 2:533–35). Unexpectedly, Cestius then abandoned the siege of Jerusalem, probably because of the approaching winter and because his troops were threatened from behind by brigands who had gathered in the hills around Jerusalem (*War* 2:523). When he retreated he was pursued by the insurgents and brigands, and probably much of the populace, into the countryside of Judea beyond Bethhoron, and great damage was done to his rear columns (*War* 2:540–54). Then, with the weapons and booty seized in their attacks on Cestius, the Jewish victors returned to Jerusalem with songs of triumph (*War* 2:554).

After this victory, most pro-Roman Jews were brought to the side of the rebels and the whole city united to form the provisional government of war with Ananus the high priest at its head. The traditional high priests thus resumed their leadership of the government, and Eleazar, son of Ananias, joined with them as their general to Idumaea (*War* 2:566).

After listing the appointments of responsibility in this government, Josephus makes mention of another Eleazar, the son of Simon:

> As for Eleazar, son of Simon, notwithstanding that he had in his hands the Roman spoils, the money taken from Cestius, and a great part of

101

the public treasure, they did not entrust him with office, because they observed his despotic nature, and that his subservient admirers[8] conducted themselves like his bodyguard. Gradually, however, financial needs and the intrigues of Eleazar had such influence with the people that they ended by yielding the supreme command to him. (*War* 2:564–65)

We know little about Eleazar, son of Simon. Josephus asserts that he was influential with the people in Jerusalem, which may mean that he was a native of that city.[9] And he was a priest. These observations suggest that Eleazar may have been in the city at the opening of the war and participated in the priestly-lay coalition under Eleazar, son of Ananias, which cut off the sacrifices from gentiles. He must have emerged as a revolutionary leader during the defense of the city against Cestius, since he subsequently controlled the spoils from the rout of Cestius. No other leader of the rebels is mentioned by Josephus at this time. If these conjectures are correct, then Eleazar, son of Simon, may have been a link between the earlier priestly-lay group and the Zealot party which formed a year later in the winter of 67–68 C.E. At that time a group of revolutionaries, including Eleazar, son of Simon, seized the temple and formed a new government by choosing a high priest by lot. It is this group which Josephus calls "Zealots." Josephus specifically cites Eleazar as the one who "caused the Zealots to break with the populace and withdraw into the sacred precincts" (*War* 5:5). And he is referred to as "the most influential man of the party [Zealots], from his ability both to conceive measures and in carrying them into effect" (*War* 4:225). He was therefore probably responsible for the decision to choose a new high priest by lot. Eleazar may also have been involved in training the new high priest (*War* 4:157), since he himself was a priest and shared the leadership of the party with

8. This verse contains the word *zelotas*, which Thackeray, following the Latin translation (sectari), renders "admirers." Kingdon argues for the translation "Zealots": "Who Were the Zealots and Their Leaders in A.D. 66?," *New Testament Studies* 17 (1970): 70, n. 1. But since the Zealot party was not formed until the next year, perhaps it means, "those who came to be Zealots." Smith argues for "zealots" as if the presence of zealots (small z) in the city preceded the formation of the Zealot party: Morton Smith, "Zealots and Sicarii, Their Origins and Relations," *Harvard Theological Review* 64 (1971): 16. Cf. also *War* 2:651. Menachem Stern thinks that this reference is a party designation. implying that the Zealot party had already formed in the city: "The Zealots," *Encyclopedia Judaica*, ed. Cecil Roth et al. (Jerusalem: The Macmillan Company, 1971), supplementary volume (1972): 141.

9. Eleazar may have been from Judea, as many priests were. If, however, he was a revolutionary brigand who had terrorized the countryside, Josephus probably would have referred to him as a "brigand," which he does not. See below, pp. 159–62.

another priest (*War* 4:225), a certain Zacharias, son of Amphicalleus.[10]

These references indicate that there was a continuity of priestly leadership from the time sacrifices from gentiles were stopped under Eleazar, son of Ananias, to the rise of the Zealot party under Eleazar, son of Simon. There may also have been some continuity in the make-up of their followers. The earlier group under Eleazar, son of Ananias, included lower priests from both Judea and Jerusalem. These were supported by the stalwarts of the revolutionary party, probably Jerusalemites who most favored war. Apparently, these two groups comprised a fairly sizable number. Although we cannot be certain that this priestly-led coalition continued to be a revolutionary force in the city after the defeat of Cestius, that possibility is suggested by the continuity of concerns about ritual in the temple and opposition to the traditional government, concerns evident in the refusal of sacrifices from gentiles, the exclusion of the high priests from temple worship, their later withdrawal into the temple, and the choice of a new high priest by lot.

These hints from Josephus' narrative suggest that the Zealot party which was formed in the winter of 67–68 C.E. included some of those priests and lay revolutionaries who were responsible a year earlier for instigating the war.[11] It may be assumed that the constituency altered somewhat as a result of the change of leadership from Eleazar, son of Ananias, to Eleazar, son of Simon. And this revolutionary group may have increased in number when the whole nation joined the revolt and established the provisional government after the defeat of Cestius. With these considerations in mind, we may conjecture that many of those who initiated the war were part of the Zealot group which later formed to regain control of the war.

In addition to these hints about the composition of the Zealot party, Josephus also has an extended narrative which describes the rise of the Zealots as originating with brigands from the countryside. He begins this narrative by describing the widespread dissension in Judea caused

10. A talmudic story considers this latter priest responsible for the cessation of sacrifices (*Babylonian Talmud*, Gittin 56a), a further support of the connection between the Zealots and the earlier coalition of lower priests and revolutionaries at the beginning of the war.

11. Baumbach argues that the Zealots were a predominantly priestly group. He cites their presence in the temple (*War* 4:151–52, 204, 216, 228, 577ff.; 5:5, 9–10) and their decision to choose a new high priest as the basic evidence: Baumbach, "Zeloten," p. 8.

by bands of brigands who plundered and raided to gain control of their various villages and districts (*War* 4:130–34). As Vespasian moved southward in the winter of 67–68 C.E. to subdue the areas around Jerusalem, these brigands moved into the city (*War* 4:135–37). Their rural terrorism was now transferred to the metropolis where they killed and imprisoned many of the aristocracy and the royalty, whom they charged with treason (*War* 4:138–46). They banded together in Jerusalem to suppress all who were suspected of opposing the impending war with Rome.

Josephus goes on to say that these brigands, fearing a revolt of the populace against their efforts to control the city, then made the temple their headquarters and used it as a refuge and fortress from the assault of the populace (*War* 4:151–57). They abandoned the traditional high priestly succession by choosing a new high priest by lots. This new high priest, from the village of Aphthia, was brought to Jerusalem and instructed in the high priestly procedures. At this point, the traditional high priests and leaders of the people condemned the populace for tolerating such actions and incited them against the Zealots. ". . . for so these miscreants called themselves, as though they were zealous in the cause of virtue and not for vice in its basest and most extravagant form" (*War* 4:161).[12] This lengthy description of the rise of the Zealots presumes that they were brigands from the countryside who used their terrorism to get authority in the city.

If this picture of the origin of the Zealots is combined with the conjectures we have made based on other passages, a composite picture of the Zealots emerges. Eleazar, son of Simon, had been the chief revolutionary leader during the siege by Cestius, and after the Jewish victory he controlled the money and spoils gained from it. He was probably supported by his own group of priests and lay people, mostly revolutionaries from Jerusalem (*War* 2:564). Many of these may have participated earlier in the cessation of sacrifices and the civil war in Jerusalem. Perhaps Eleazar had been joined by like-minded revolutionaries from the countryside who had remained in Jerusalem after

---

12. Josephus never explains the peculiarly Jewish significance of the word "zealot" to his Hellenistic readers (see above pp. 84–87). Rather, he interprets it to mean "emulators" of good, which was a common meaning of the Greek word. Compare the parallel occurrence of the word "copied" in *War* 7:268. The fact that Josephus notes that they claimed to be zealous for the good shows that among the members of the party the title was honorific.

participating in the battles against Cestius (*Life* 28, 100).[13] They desired control of the city and the war. However, this desire was thwarted when, after the defeat of Cestius, the high priests joined the revolution and became the leadership of the provisional government. Eleazar, son of Simon, was excluded (*War* 2:564).

Eventually, Eleazar and the group around him, as well as the revolutionary brigands who had pressed for war in the countryside and were now in Jerusalem, began to suspect that the provisional government was moderate in its prosecution of the war. When Ananus threatened to influence the populace to suppress the terrorism in the city, Eleazar persuaded these revolutionary groups to take their stand in the temple, where they could also make use of the weapons seized from Cestius. Then they initiated their own "democratic" government with the choice of a high priest by lot—an innovation acceptable both to the lower priests and the Judean peasants.[14]

It thus appears that at the time of their formation the Zealots were made up of a majority of persons from outside Jerusalem (*War* 4:241). Later, most Zealots, perhaps many of the brigands from the countryside, joined John of Gischala when he broke away to form his own group. A core of Zealots continued to occupy the inner temple until the end of the war period. The leadership of Eleazar, son of Simon, along with several notables (*War* 5:6), continued to be prominent among this diminished group of Zealots. It may be conjectured that Eleazar's closest followers, perhaps lower priests and lay revolutionaries from Jerusalem, made up the majority of this core of Zealots who endured as Zealots in the temple through the war years.[15]

It is important to add that the Judean peasants who entered Jerusalem to comprise part of the Zealot coalition in 67–68 C.E. were not in any

13. Some of these may in fact have been representative contingents from cities or regions of the country. We know of one unit of six hundred men from Galilee who remained in Jerusalem after the battle with Cestius (*Life* 200). Later, a contingent of two thousand men from Tiberias came to defend Jerusalem (*Life* 354).

14. This is similar to Hengel's view which is that the Zealots were basically a priestly group but their formation as an independent party was possible only because of the strengthening of their forces by these fugitives from Vespasian's conquest in Galilee, Idumaea, and Peraea: Hengel, *Zeloten*, pp. 375, 379.

15. Smith argues that the Zealots were primarily Judean peasants, not priests. He points to (1) the influx of Judean "brigands" from Vespasian's conquests, (2) the attack on aristocracy, seizure of temple, and choice of new high priest, which reflect peasant piety, and (3) the fact that Zealots were opposed by the Jerusalem populace (*War* 4:162, 193–207), suggesting that they were not natives of Jerusalem.

way associated with Menahem and the Sicarii, who also probably originated from Judea. Had they been followers of Menahem they would not have been likely to unite with that priestly faction which had earlier been responsible for Menahem's murder.[16] Also, when these Judean peasants of the Zealot party in Jerusalem later appealed for help, they turned not to the Sicarii on Masada, but to the Idumaeans. And the Sicarii on Masada did not join the Judeans in Jerusalem when they took over the city as part of the Zealot faction. Consequently, it is clear that the Sicarii and Zealots were entirely different factions of revolutionary Jews.

The takeover of the temple by the Zealots was a strategic move which enabled them to operate from the most impregnable fortress in the city. It also enabled them to occupy the headquarters of the national government. The appointment of a new high priest was indicative of their intention to topple the provisional government and to replace it with their own. Perhaps also this abrogation of traditional, upper-class, high priests expressed the desire of lower-class, tithe-paying, anti-Roman citizens for a less expensive administration of the temple. Thus, the Zealots were a nationalistic group of revolutionaries which formed in order to overthrow the traditional government suspected of treason and in order to make certain that the war would be zealously prosecuted.[17]

The democratic tendencies of the Zealots' government may also be noted; for example, they chose the new high priest by lot.[18] Perhaps they conceived of the high priest as God's representative to be the central national figure. Unfortunately that was in one sense impossible, since the person to whom the lot fell was an ignorant country peasant (*War* 4:155). Elsewhere the Zealots are described as having several leaders (*War* 5:6–7), and in one passage the "equality" among the Zealot leaders is contrasted with the "monarchical" designs of John of Gischala (4:389–93). These democratic tendencies may be one of the distinguishing characteristics of the Zealots, one which perhaps prevented them from having the strong central leadership of the followers of Simon and John.

16. Smith, "Zealots and Sicarii," p. 13.
17. See S. Zeitlin, "The Slavonic Josephus and the Dead Sea Scrolls: An Exposé of Recent Fairy Tales," *Jewish Quarterly Review* 58 (1968): 195; idem, "Masada and Sicarii: The Occupants of Masada," *Jewish Quarterly Review* 55 (1965): 317.
18. Cecil Roth, "The Constitution of the Jewish Republic of 66–70," *Journal of Semitic Studies* 9 (1964): 315.

The religious motivations for the actions of the Zealots can also be inferred.[19] The temple was the center of worship, and proper control of the temple would ensure God's favor for their cause.[20] In this sense, the occupation of the temple may be seen as an attempt to purify the cultus, similar to the refusal of gentile sacrifices. The Zealots had "zeal" for the purity of the sanctuary and the realization of a new order in the temple.[21] The choice of a new high priest, for example, was probably more than a simple abrogation of the traditional priests. It may have been an effort to reestablish an older and more legitimate line of high priestly descendants to conduct the cultic worship.[22] They may have thought that their reinstitution of proper worship in the temple on God's behalf foreshadowed the imminent fulfillment of God's promises on their behalf.

In any case, after the Zealots had established their own democratic, high priestly government, the populace rose up and began to besiege the temple where they were located (*War* 4:193–209). The Zealots, expecting the provisional government to betray the city to the Romans and fearing an attack upon themselves by the populace, sent for the Jews from the region of Idumaea to come to their aid. This action had been suggested to the Zealots by John of Gischala, who had pretended to support Ananus and the provisional government and had subsequently been sent as their envoy to the Zealots in the temple (*War* 4:208–35). An army of Idumaeans promptly appeared at the gate of the city only to be prevented from entering by the chief priests. However, under the cover of a nocturnal rainstorm, some Zealots managed to escape their temple hold-out and let them into the city. The Zealots were freed from their confinement in the temple, and by morning Jerusalem was in their hands (*War* 4:288–313). Josephus tells us that thousands were killed and the city looted by the fury of the Zealots and the Idumaeans, who believed that the populace and the chief

19. Zeitlin denies that the Zealots were motivated by a religious ideology: Zeitlin, "Masada," p. 317; idem, "Zealots and Sicarii," *Journal of Biblical Literature* 81 (1962): 397.
20. "Command of the Temple was the key to victory": Cecil Roth, "Zealots in the War of 66–73," *Journal of Semitic Studies* 4 (1959): 343.
21. So Baumbach who suggests that the new order was based on the promises of Ezekiel 40–48: Baumbach, "Zealots," p. 9.
22. Hengel suggests they were trying to restore the unbroken zadokite line of descendency from the time of the Seleucids (cf. 1 Chronicles 24:12): Hengel, *Zeloten*, p. 225; cf. also Baumbach, "Zeloten," p. 8. Baumbach refers to this action as an attempt on their part to achieve a measure of "realized eschatology": Baumbach, "Zeloten," p. 13.

priests had arranged to surrender Jerusalem. The Idumaeans then killed the high priest Ananus along with Jesus, his immediate subordinate in the provisional government. Many of the populace were slaughtered by the Zealots. The youth among the nobility were imprisoned (*War* 4:326–27), some being tortured and others killed. Eminent citizens were brought before a newly summoned Sanhedrin on charges of treason. When the citizens refused to cooperate by condemning the accused, the defendants were killed anyway (*War* 4:334–44).

Josephus accuses the Zealots of bringing about the "dissolution of their [Jewish] laws and their laws courts" (*War* 4:223). Certainly it is true that the Zealots established their own government in the city and used it to execute those suspected of treason. Josephus, however, may have exaggerated the excesses of the Zealots. Nevertheless, the Idumaeans are an independent witness to their terrorism. Josephus records that some Idumaeans could "no longer continue to lend support to men who were subverting the institutions of their forefathers" (*War* 4:348, cf. 385–86). They therefore liberated two thousand citizens from prison and left the city.

The Zealots, along with John of Gischala and the remaining Idumaeans, maintained control of the city. They continued their reign of terror against the wealthy and prominent, including one Gurion and Niger of Peraea, whom Josephus says might have deposed them from power (*War* 4:354–65). They also had various battles with Simon Bar Giora, who was threatening to overrun the countryside and then take over the city (*War* 4:514–55).[23] All this took place during the year 68 C.E.

Also during that year, John of Gischala broke away from the Zealots and formed his own faction. Josephus tells us that he disdained equality with the Zealot leaders and wanted to establish his own absolute power (*War* 4:389–90). John was supported by those Idumaeans who had remained in the city and by a Galilean contingent. It may be that he also took with him many of the brigands who had initially

---

23. Simon bar Giora was apparently prepared to challenge any other Jewish authority. The two thousand young nobles who were released from Zealot prisons had fled to join Simon's forces. They may have encouraged Simon to gain control of Jerusalem from the Zealots. In any case, their escape to him may help to explain the antipathy between the Zealots and Simon.

joined Eleazar, son of Simon, in the temple when the Zealot party was formed, for John's group was apparently the larger. However, the two factions now in the city—the Zealots and John's following—seldom fought with each other (*War* 4:396).

Then in the early spring of 69 C.E. the Idumaean contingent broke away from John's group. They enlisted the support of the chief priests and invited Simon bar Giora into the city to lead them to overthrow the Zealots and John, who now reunited in the temple for their own defense (*War* 4:577ff.). For some time, the group led by Simon fought against John and the Zealots for control of the city, neither side gaining much ground (*War* 4:584). Soon Eleazar, indignant at "the enormities daily perpetrated by John," seceded from the coalition along with several influential men and their following of Zealots (*War* 5:5–8). They withdrew into the inner temple, placed their weapons above the holy gate, and held their ground. There were now three factions fighting in the city—the forces of Simon, the forces of John, and the Zealots.

Eventually John's group in the outer area of the temple was in need of supplies (*War* 5:104). When the Zealots opened the inner temple for the feast of unleavened bread, those of John's followers who would not be recognized entered with concealed weapons (*War* 5:99ff.). They took possession of the sanctuary, which gave them control of the Zealots and access to the supplies. From this point on the Zealots remained a subordinate group under John. And although the Zealots retained their identity as a distinct unit fighting against the Romans (*War* 6:92), Josephus writes that there were only two factions now in the city—John's group and those under Simon bar Giora (*War* 5:105).

Of the fate of the Zealots we cannot be certain. Although their numbers were small, they participated in the defense of the city against the Roman siege in the summer and fall of 70 C.E. (*War* 6:92, 148). Among the Zealots, Josephus cites Simon and Judes, sons of Ari, as men who distinguished themselves in battle. Eleazar, son of Simon, is not again mentioned. However, since the Zealots included priests among their number, they may have been among those priests who held out in the sanctuary after the temple had been burned (*War* 6:278, 318; cf. Dio Cassius 66:6, 3)[24] and who bargained for their

24. Baumbach, "Zeloten," p. 9.

lives with the temple treasures (*War* 6:387ff.). Others apparently fled to the forest of Jardes which was later overrun by the Romans, for Josephus reports that Judes, son of Ari, was killed there (*War* 7:215). No Zealot leader is mentioned along with John and Simon as prize Roman captives. This may indicate that the Zealots did not play so significant a military role as other revolutionary groups in the Jewish resistance to the Roman siege of Jerusalem.

Summary

It is probable that the Zealots were a "democratic" group composed of lower-class priests and laymen from Jerusalem, along with peasant "brigands" from the countryside. The priests provided the main leadership for the group, although the democratic tendencies of the Zealots would imply that the leadership was shared. Many of those from the countryside may have split off from the Zealots to join with John of Gischala. The social nature of their struggle for power is evident in the overthrow of the upper-class provisional government and establishment of their own organs of government. Firmly nationalistic, they were determined to press the war for liberation against Rome and suppress with violence all those who were suspected of moderation. From a religious point of view, they saw the temple as the key to victory. It was to be purified of all illicit contact with gentiles and traditional high priests who had cooperated with the Romans; the restoration of true priesthood and the right sacrifice would assure God's aid in the holy war against Rome and deny supernatural benefits to the Romans. There is no indication of the presence of any messianic figures among their number.

The terrorist methods of the Zealots apparently lost them the support of the populace of Jerusalem as well as that of the Idumaeans. They provided poor leadership for the war years and were in no way able to unify the nation or city. Their main historical significance lies in their toppling of the provisional government. Although they could not have done so without the aid of John of Gischala or the Idumaeans, they were the main force in the city which enabled the overthrow to take place. In the final battle with the Romans over the city, their numbers had become small, and they did not play a significant military role.

THE SICARII

In the summer of 66 C.E., at about the same time that Jewish priests in Jerusalem suspended the daily sacrifices which were offered on behalf of the Roman emperor, "some of the most ardent promoters of hostilities" (*War* 2:408), who are later identified by Josephus as the Sicarii (4:400), took possession of the fortress Masada by stratagem and replaced the Roman garrison stationed there with their own garrison.

Shortly thereafter Eleazar, the son of Ananias, who had instigated the rejection of the Roman sacrifice, was, along with his following, in armed conflict with the high priests and aristocracy for control of Jerusalem (*War* 2:409–24). When Eleazar opened the temple to the populace for the feast of wood carrying, a day designated for families to bring wood to the temple for use in making offerings and sacrifices, some *sicarii* flowed into the temple along with the unarmed populace and were subsequently enlisted to join the attacks against the high priests and royalists who accupied the upper city (*War* 2:425–26). The narrative shows clearly that the *sicarii* and Eleazar's group were originally separate and perhaps mutually hostile groups. Since the *sicarii* had to conceal their weapons and enter by stealth with the populace, the implication is that they would not have been allowed to enter if they had been recognized as *sicarii*.

Their presence now enabled Eleazar's forces to outnumber the royalist troops which had been sent by Agrippa II. The attacks were pressed more boldly against the upper city and the royalists were forced to evacuate to the palace of Herod (*War* 2:429). It was probably the *sicarii* who then set fire to the house of Ananias the high priest and to the palaces of Agrippa and Berenice. The public archives building, which held the record of debts, was also fired, "in order to win a host of grateful debtors and to cause a rising of the poor against the rich, sure of impunity" (*War* 2:427). Their terrorism forced the chief priests and notables into hiding (*War* 2:428).

At about the same time, Menahem, the son (grandson?) of Judas of Galilee, whose followers are later designated as "Sicarii" by Josephus, went to Masada to arm his fellow townsmen (presumably from a village in Judea) and other brigands with weapons from Herod's arsenal there. He then "returned like a veritable king to Jerusalem, became the leader of the revolution, and directed the siege of the palace" (*War* 2:434).

111

It may be argued that the ease with which Menahem entered Jerusalem and assumed charge of the siege implies that he was already the recognized head of the revolutionary movement in the prewar period.[25] However, it is not necessary to assume that. The fact that Menahem raided an arsenal and then used his armed companions as a bodyguard indicates that he took over the leadership of the revolutionary forces by intimidation, not by popular acclaim.[26] This suggestion is even more plausible in light of the observation that the revolutionaries in Jerusalem, in the midst of their initial struggle for freedom from Roman domination, would have had few weapons of their own with which to challenge Menahem's armed band. Thus the most that can be inferred is that Menahem was one of the prewar revolutionaries who had enough support among "initimate friends" to seize arms by taking Masada from a Roman garrison (*War* 2:408).[27] The fact that it was taken by a stratagem suggests that the number of Menahem's band was not large.

In any case, Menahem's presence in Jerusalem did strengthen the siege. The royalists and other Jews requested and were permitted to surrender and leave the palace. The Romans now retreated to the towers (*War* 2:427–28). The attacks on authorities, begun by the earlier *sicarii*, were continued by Menahem. Josephus tells us that he himself took refuge in the inner temple from Menahem and the brigands (*Life* 21). Then the high priest Ananias and his brother Ezekias, who had hidden in an underground passage, were caught and killed by the brigands (*War* 2:441).

These attacks upon the political authorities and the upper class imply that this was a social uprising of a predominantly lower-class group. They burned the archives to create impunity for an uprising of the lower class (*War* 2:427). Menahem was considered by some of the priests under Eleazar to be "far below themselves" (*War* 2:443). The house of Ananias and the palaces of Agrippa and Berenice were burned by the *sicarii* (*War* 2:426), and Menahem and his followers were responsible for the deaths of Ananias the high priest and his brother Ezekias (*War* 2:429). Like other revolutionary groups, they plundered

---

25. Hengel, *Zeloten*, p. 369. Against this is the fact that he is later opposed by Eleazar's faction and the populace of Jerusalem. So Smith, "Zealots," p. 14.
26. Smith, "Zealots," p. 12.
27. Hengel rightly observes that the two references to the seizure of Masada are a doublet (*War* 2:408 and 2:433) and refer to the same event: Hengel, *Zeloten*, p. 365, n. 2.

the wealthy (*War* 7:261). The Sicarii were the only revolutionary sect which survived the war, and their activities in the postwar period outside Palestine continued to have social revolutionary characteristics. In Alexandria of Egypt, many in authority were killed (*War* 7:411). In Cyrene, on the coast of North Africa, impoverished people made up the following of a certain Jonathan, while the rich were attacked and accused (*War* 7:438, 441).

It may also be possible to infer a religious rationale for these attacks against the wealthy and the authorities who cooperated with the Romans. In a similar way in which the Zealots wanted to purify the temple, the Sicarii may have struggled for a new order in the land, involving the elimination of inequality and the reestablishment of the original God-given condition. This rationale may be rooted in biblical passages such as Leviticus 25 and Deuteronomy 15.[28] This is an interesting possibility, especially in light of the motif of God's lordship over the people and the land in these two passages, a motif which we know to have been shared by the Sicarii in light of their historic connection with Judas the Galilean and the fourth philosophy. The author of Leviticus affirms that the people of Israel "shall do my statutes, and keep my ordinances and perform them; so you will dwell in the land securely" (25:18) and adds, "The land shall not be sold in perpetuity, for the land is mine" (25:23; cf. 25:55). The Deuteronomic writer asserts that "there will be no poor among you (for the Lord will bless you in the land which the Lord your God gives you for an inheritance to possess), if only you will obey the voice of the Lord your God" (15:4–5); and he adds that "you shall rule over many nations, but they shall not rule over you" (15:6). These thoughts seem to be consistent with the fourth philosophy "no Lord but God," which was the rationale employed in 6 C.E. in opposition to a Roman census and which was later influential among the Sicarii.

Although there is no direct evidence for it, the Sicarii as well as the Zealots may have shared an imminent eschatological expectation, albeit with different content. While the Zealots may have attempted to usher in the age of fulfillment by cleansing the temple and restoring a legitimate high priesthood, the Sicarii worked for the realization of a

28. So Günther Baumbach, "Zeloten und Sicarier," *Theologische Literaturzeitung* 90 (1965): 733; cf. Baumbach, "Das Freiheitverständnis in der Zelotischen Bewegung," *Das Ferne und Nahe Wort*, no. 105 in *Beihefte zur Zeitschrift für die Alttestamentliche Wissenschaft* (Berlin: Alfred Töpelmann, 1967), pp. 11–18.

radical obedience to God's sole dominion over the holy land under the leadership of a political messiah.[29]

After Josephus describes the various terrorist activities of Menahem and his brigands, he then records the assassination of Menahem by the followers of Eleazar:

> But the reduction of the strongholds and the murder of the high-priest Ananias inflated and brutalized Menahem to such an extent that he believed himself without a rival in the conduct of affairs and became an insufferable tyrant. The partisans of Eleazar now rose against him; they remarked to each other that, after revolting from the Romans for love of liberty, they ought not to sacrifice this liberty to a Jewish hangman and to put up with a master who, even were he to abstain from violence, was anyhow far below themselves; and that if they must have a leader anyone would be better than Menahem. So they laid their plans to attack him in the temple, whither he had gone up in state to pay his devotions, arrayed in royal robes and attended by his suite of armed fanatics. When Eleazar and his companions rushed upon him, and the rest of the people to gratify their rage took up stones and began pelting the arrogant doctor, imagining that his downfall would crush the whole revolt, Menahem and his followers offered a momentary resistance; then, seeing themselves assailed by the whole multitude, they fled whithersoever they could; all who were caught were massacred, and a hunt was made for any in hiding. A few succeeded in escaping by stealth to Masada, among others Eleazar, son of Jairus and a relative of Menahem, and subsequently despot of Masada. Menahem himself, who had taken refuge in the place called Ophlas and there ignominiously concealed himself, was caught, dragged into the open, and after being subjected to all kinds of torture, put to death. His lieutenants, along with Absalom, his most eminent supporter in his tyranny, met with a similar fate. (*War* 2:442–48)

The reference to "royal robes" suggests that Menahem may have been expressing messianic pretensions. He had taken over the leadership of the rebel forces which now had virtual control of the city. Ananias, the high priestly head of state, was dead. Menahem was filling the vacuum to exercise authority over temple and state. And the earlier "royal" entrance into the city with his followers from Masada implies that he may have had messianic intentions from the outset.[30]

---

29. So Baumbach, "Zeloten," pp. 12–13. He clarifies most fully the social and religious point of view of the Sicarii.

30. The "royal" terminology here does not necessarily mean that Menahem made messianic claims. Josephus may have used the terms sarcastically to refer to the "tyrannical" methods of some revolutionary leaders. However, they represent one of the few clues from Josephus about the possibility of messianic claims among revolutionaries.

Josephus tells us that he was killed by Eleazar's group because of his assumption of absolute authority in affairs of state and because of the excesses of violence, which included the death of Eleazar's father Ananias. Eleazar and his following may have feared that they themselves would be the next victims of his terrorism. They also considered Menahem to be "far below themselves," which implies that his family, class, or social background made him unacceptable for leadership in the eyes of the partisans of Eleazar. Josephus tells us that the Jerusalem populace supported their actions, thinking that Menahem's death would end the revolt. Many of Menahem's followers were killed. Others escaped to Masada, where they are subsequently designated by Josephus as the "Sicarii."

This passage which describes Menahem's death has a significant reference to Menahem's entourage as "his suite of armed fanatics" (*War* 2:444). The Greek word *zelotas,* here translated "fanatics," can also mean zealots or "Zealots." If this phrase were to be translated "his armed Zealots," it would imply that this descendant of Judas the Galilean and his followers were members of a party of Zealots and were therefore in some way connected with the Zealot party of priests and Judean peasants which emerged during the war period. One might conclude that the revolutionary movement was originally unified as one party of Zealots in the prewar period. The assassination of Menahem would then have served to split the party in two, one group subsequently being referred to as Sicarii, the other as Zealots. This split might also be seen as the cause of later dissension within the revolutionary movement.[31]

However, several factors militate against the translation of this significant phrase as "armed Zealots" and imply that Josephus did not intend to refer here to any such sect. Nowhere else is the term *zelotai* ever applied to Menahem, his followers, or his relatives. When they are identified as a distinct faction, they are always referred to as "the Sicarii." The term *zelotai* in the *War* is, with this one exception, always related to Eleazar, son of Simon, and his compatriots who came to be located in the temple. This term is not used by Josephus of any revolutionaries in the prewar period. And he describes the formation of the Zealot party a year and a half after the event described here at

---

31. This is the position put forth by Hengel, *Zeloten,* p. 371.

the opening of the war.[32] Thus, it is highly unlikely that Josephus intended his use of *zelotas* in this passage to imply that Menahem's followers were members of a Zealot party.

The phrase might be translated "armed zealots." We have indicated that Menahem and his followers were probably motivated in part by religious zeal. It makes sense to think that in the prewar era and the early period of the war many of the activities of Menahem and his followers would have gained for them, along with other revolutionaries, the epithets of *sicarii* and "zealots" as they were used in the functional, nonsectarian sense.[33] The early Latin translator rendered *zelotas* as "devotees,"[34] despite the fact that elsewhere in the *War*, when the term refers to Eleazar and his followers, he translated the same word, "Zealots."[35] Thus, the Latin translator did not consider the use of *zelotas* in this passage to be a sectarian designation. The context also favors the translation "armed fanatics" or "devotees." If Menahem was making a messianic entrance to the temple, he would have likely been accompanied by those most ardently attached to him. In addition, the "devoted followers" of Menahem provides a parallel contrast to "the partisans of Eleazar." Thus, the passage is best translated "his suite of armed fanatics" or its equivalent.[36]

32. This observation, that the Zealot party in Jerusalem was not formed until 67–68 C.E., is the main counter to Baumbach's view that Menahem was accompanied by "armed Zealots" of the priestly faction.

33. It is easy for confusion to arise from the prewar nonsectarian use of zealots and *sicarii* (perhaps applied to the same persons) and the use of Zealots and Sicarii to refer in the war period to two distinct revolutionary factions. This confusion may be the origin of passages in later writings which presume that these terms were always intended to be proper nouns or that the titles, Zealots and Sicarii, referred to the same faction. See the first and second recensions of *The Fathers According to Rabbi Nathan*, trans. Judah Goldin (New Haven: Yale University Press, 1955). For the text, see *Aboth de Rabbi Nathan*, ed. Solomon Schechter (London: D. Nutt, 1887). See also Hippolytus, *Refutation of All Heresies* (9:22) in *The Anti-Nicene Fathers*, ed. A. Roberts and J. Donaldson (New York: Charles Scribner's Sons, 1926), vol. 5. For the Greek text, see *Refutatio Omnium Heresium* in *Die Greichischen Christlichen Schriftsteller Der Ersten Drei Jahrhunderte*, trans. P. Wendland (Leipzig: H. C. Hinrichs, 1916), vol. 3. Compare also *Mishnah Machshirin* 1:6, *Lamentations Rabbah* 4:4, and Acts 21:38.

34. *Suique studiosos armatos secum trahens*. See Smith, "Zealots," p. 7; and Zeitlin, "Zealots and Sicarii," pp. 397–98. In an entirely different context (*Antiquities* 20:47), Josephus has the same use of *zeloten* as "devotee," which again the Latin translator has rendered *studiosus*.

35. With one exception, *War* 2:564, referring to the followers of Eleazar, son of Simon, which the Latin translator renders *sectari*, or "followers" (cf. *Life* 12). See above, note 8.

36. Hengel argues that the presence of a possessive is necessary for this translation, "Zeloten and Sikarier," *Josephus Studien*, ed. Otto Betz, et al. (Göttingen: Vandenhoeck and Ruprecht, 1974), p. 185. That is however supplied by the use of the article as a possessive pronoun.

Thus, this passage cannot be used as evidence for an original party of Zealots which was split by the conflict between Menahem and Eleazar, son of Ananias. It would be useful to summarize the other arguments against the recognition of a unified party at this time: (1) There is no reference to the use of "Zealots" as a party name before this time in any literature. (2) There was no unity or central leadership to the prewar movement in the country before 66 c.e. Therefore, there is little reason to think there was a unified party at this point. (3) Menahem was the leader of only one band of revolutionaries, not the whole movement, and his leadership of the siege in Jerusalem was forced upon the other revolutionaries, being accepted neither by them nor by the Jerusalem populace. (4) There were radical differences between Eleazar, son of Ananias, and Menahem. Eleazar was from the city, Menahem from the country; Eleazar did not share Menahem's terrorist tactics, and he did not recognize his messianic claims. All these arguments show that this passage does not bear witness to an original unity to the movement. Rather, the assassination of Menahem exposes the irreconcilable gulf already existing between the revolutionary factions.[37] Thus, the followers of Menahem, who are called "Sicarii" by Josephus, are a distinctly different revolutionary group from the core of priests who came to make up a significant part of the Zealot party when it was founded in Jerusalem in the winter of 67–68 c.e.

The survivors of Menahem's group remained at their desert refuge on Masada for the remainder of the war. They held out there until they were conquered by the Romans in 74 c.e., four years after Jerusalem was destroyed. During the war, they were removed from the center of any Jewish conflict with Romans. They neither came to the aid of their fellow Jews at the final siege of Jerusalem by Titus nor were they summoned to the assistance of other revolutionaries when help was needed. In fact, their main activity was to harass other Jews around the area of Masada, venturing out when they were certain of the inactivity of the Romans and of the coalition government in Jerusalem (*War* 4:401). At first their raids were limited to procuring supplies. Later, Josephus tells us, they attacked the village of Engaddi, most of whose inhabitants were at Jerusalem for a feast of unleavened bread. With little resistance the Sicarii killed the inhabitants and took off great

---

37. Baumbach, "Zeloten und Sicarier," p. 734.

spoils to Masada (*War* 4:401–404). It may be that Engaddi was an object of attack because it played host to a Roman garrison,[38] perhaps the one which had formerly been at Masada. The destruction of the town and supplies would undercut its use as a Roman station and remove a threat to their refuge. It appears that the tactics used by the Sicarii were similar to those attributed to brigands before the war, perhaps with the intention of cleansing the land of any who cooperated with Romans. New recruits apparently joined them for similar raids on the other villages in the district (*War* 4:404–405).

Also Simon bar Giora and his following, another revolutionary group, took refuge with the Sicarii on Masada to escape the Jewish government in Jerusalem:

> At first they regarded him with suspicion, and permitted him and his following of women access only to the lower part of the fortress, occupying the upper quarters themselves; but afterwards, as a man of congenial disposition and apparently to be trusted, he was allowed to accompany them on their marauding expeditions and took part in their raids upon the surrounding district. (*War* 4:504–506)

It is obvious that the two groups had had no previous contact with each other. The Sicarii were at first suspicious of Simon. Their refusal to allow him access to their upper quarters may indicate the "exclusive" character of their group.[39] Eventually they included him in their raids. Although they lived together for a time as fugitives from the provisional government in Jerusalem, they did not become one group. When the high priest Ananus was killed, Simon left Masada for more ambitious undertakings. The Sicarii continued their raids upon the surrounding area, especially Idumaea (*War* 4:516).

Josephus does not again mention the Sicarii until he describes the Roman assaults of 71–74 C.E. on those few fortresses which had held out after the war was over—Herodium, Machaerus, and Masada (*War* 7:163–64; cf. 4:555). Flavius Silva was the commander who conducted the siege and conquest of Masada. Although access to the quarters on top of the rock was difficult, Silva built a huge ramp to provide passage for his troops. Josephus tells us that when it appeared that the Romans would gain the wall the following day, Eleazar, a relative

---

38. This is suggested by Appelbaum, who notes that a Cohors Thracum was stationed at Engaddi between 70 C.E. and the time of Hadrian: Shimon A. Appelbaum, "The Zealots: The Case for Revaluation," *Journal of Roman Studies* 61 (1971): 165.

39. Appelbaum, "Revaluation," p. 165.

of Judas of Galilee and leader of the Sicarii, made a speech to enjoin his community to mass suicide. Although the speech is undoubtedly composed by Josephus and much of it can be attributed to him, the author clearly ascribes to this group the philosophy of "no Lord but God," which originated with Judas of Galilee (*War* 7:323). On this basis the Sicarii were encouraged to die by their own hands rather than submit to the horrors of Roman slavery (*War* 7:336, 381). In death they would find the true freedom of God (*War* 7:344). "This [suicide]" he concludes, "our laws enjoin, this our wives and children implore us" (7:387). And so, burning their belongings and casting lots, they killed one another. Only several women and children who had hidden from the others survived to tell the story to the stunned Romans on the following day (*War* 7:402–406).

The archaelogical findings at Masada from this period of occupation by revolutionaries confirm the religious devotion of the Sicarii to which Josephus draws attention. A *mikve* or small pool specified for ritual bathing among strict Jews was uncovered there. Also, numerous scrolls or fragments of biblical and other Jewish writings were discovered. And a synagogue, apparently built earlier, was used by the Sicarii.[40] These finds are also evidence for the similarity between the Sicarii and conservative Pharisees (cf. *Antiquities* 18:23).

Some of the faction of the Sicarii apparently had fled Masada to Alexandria in Egypt where they "sought to induce many of their hosts to assert their independence, to look upon the Romans as no better than themselves and to esteem God alone as their lord" (*War* 7:411). After murdering some Jewish leaders who opposed them and pressing for a revolt, they were finally turned over to the Romans by the Jewish community who desired to remain at peace with the Romans. Josephus describes with admiration the refusal of the Sicarii to call Caesar "lord," even under the worst of Roman tortures (*War* 7:417–19).

Josephus tells us that the "madness of the Sicarii" was also manifest in the cities around Cyrene, where a certain Jonathan, a weaver, led some of the poorer Jews into the desert to see signs and visions (*War* 7:437–38). When the leading Jews alerted Catullus, the Roman gov-

---

40. See Y. Yadin, *Masada: Herod's Fortress and the Zealots' Last Stand* (New York: Random House, 1966). For the probable date of the fall of Masada at 74 C.E., see W. Eck, "Die Eroberung von Masada und eine neue Inschrift des L. Flavius Silva Nonius Bassius," *Zeitschrift für Neutestamentliche Wissenschaft* 60 (1969): 282–89.

ernor, he dispatched troops to overcome the crowd of unarmed Jews. Jonathan was later captured and, at the instigation of Catullus, made false accusations against leading Jews, which led to their crucifixion. This led to further charges against Jews in Alexandria and Rome, including Josephus. These charges were exposed, however, and came to nothing. Jonathan was executed and Catullus reprimanded (*War* 7:450–51).

An overall look at some passages about the Sicarii enables us to estimate their numbers. One might think that the group which took over Masada from a Roman garrison would have been sizable. However, Josephus notes that it was taken by a stratagem, implying that it may not have involved an imposing number. The group of *sicarii* who joined Eleazar in the temple tipped the balance to outnumber the two thousand royalist troops sent by Agrippa II during the civil conflict early in the war (cf. *War* 2:421, 425). Menahem's armed following from Masada were imposing enough to assume leadership of the siege (*War* 2:434). However, it may not have been the numbers, but the arms, which intimidated the forces in Jerusalem. In any case, the partisans of Eleazar were easily able to overcome the followers of Menahem once their leader had been eliminated. Presumably all of Menahem's followers who were able to escape fled to Masada upon his death (*War* 2:446–47).

We do not know if any Sicarii remained in Judea or participated in the later part of the war in Jerusalem. On the basis of Josephus, there is no evidence for such a supposition.[41] There were nine hundred and sixty who died on Masada, including women and children (*War* 7:399). Some Sicarii had apparently escaped to Egypt, where more than six hundred Sicarii, including women and children (7:416), were caught and turned over to the Romans (7:416). However, this group may have included recent converts from Alexandria who did not join the sect until after the war. And most of those who participated in the episode in Cyrene were probably local residents. Thus, the Sicarii probably did not, at any one time, number more than one or two thousand heads of families at most.[42] As such, they were the smallest of the revolutionary groups (*War* 5:248ff.).

41. Menachem Stern, however, thinks that after the Sicarii fled to Masada, many of them swelled the ranks of the other revolutionary groups ("Zealots," p. 138).
42. Cf. Smith, who says they "may have numbered several thousand, but hardly more": Smith "Zealots and Sicarii," p. 14.

Concerning the significance of the Sicarii, it would be important to note that Eleazar's speech includes the sentence: "For we were the first of all to revolt, so are we the last in arms against them" (*War* 7:324). This passage may be referring to the historical connection between Eleazar and the revolt of his ancestor, Judas the Galilean. However, that is not necessarily the case. Even if we think of the activity of the *sicarii* in the fifties and sixties before the war, they were still the first in order of time among the five revolutionary groups listed by Josephus (see also *War* 7:254, 262).

Eleazar also refers to his faction as "we who have been instructors of the rest" (*War* 7:330). This is not a basis for arguing that the Sicarii philosophy of "no Lord but God" informed the other revolutionaries. Rather, this is part of Josephus' polemic which occurs in the context of a confession of the crimes of the Jewish revolutionaries. It is equivalent to an earlier statement of Josephus that "the Sicarii were the first to set the example of this lawlessness and cruelty to their kinsmen . . ." (*War* 7:262). Thus these references do not place a priority of importance upon this group except insofar as it came first in order of time.

The narrative of Josephus confirms the separateness and distinctiveness of the Sicarii. And neither its adherents nor its teachings were a basic cause for the existence or rationale of the other revolutionary groups.[43] This is not to say, however, that the Sicarii did not in themselves play a significant role in the Jewish revolution.

Summary

The Sicarii were lower-class revolutionaries from the Judean countryside with a prewar history of resistance to the Roman presence in Palestine. Their leadership was made up of the descendants of Judas of Galilee, although it was not limited to them (*War* 2:448). The Sicarii were primarily devoted to the religious teaching of "no Lord but God" which pitted them against their wealthy overlords and the Jewish authorities who cooperated with the Romans. They killed, plundered, and burned to rid the land of such idolatry, and thus to assure continued lordship of God's protection over Israel. Their struggle was a holy war. Like the Zealots, they must have seen control of the city and the temple as important, for when their attempt to take over the temple

43. See Smith, "Zealots and Sicarii," p. 11.

failed, they retired to their desert refuge at Masada. Menahem, in whom they had put their messianic hope, had been assassinated. At Masada, they were a close-knit exclusive group who ultimately chose to die by suicide rather than submit to Roman slavery. Their efforts to promulgate their religious teaching continued in Alexandria after the war. They were perhaps Pharisaic in religious practice and devotion.

The historical significance of the Sicarii rests primarily in the contribution they made to the resistance against Roman authority in the city of Jerusalem and the surrounding countryside in the prewar period. Along with the activity of other brigand groups of that time, they caused the breakdown of law and order in the land by the Roman procurator and contributed to the dissension and anarchy in the city. Their importance also lies in the support which they gave to the priestly faction in the city at the opening of the war. Although Menahem proved to be unacceptable as a leader over the whole revolution, he did provide the military force which enabled the royalists to be defeated. Also, their assassination of Ananias the high priest removed one of the most powerful foes of war in the city at that time. Apart from these activities, they contributed nothing to the battles with the Romans, either against Cestius at the opening of the war or against Titus at the siege of Jerusalem.

JOHN OF GISCHALA

An adequate historical reconstruction of the life of John of Gischala is extremely difficult. There are two accounts, one in the *War* and one in the *Life*, of John's activity in Galilee during the early part of the war. These accounts contain two different and often contradictory portrayals of John. We must remember that in these two accounts Josephus is also depicting his own role as the Jewish commander of Galilee. The two portrayals of Josephus differ, and both are probably distortions. In fact, since Josephus is describing events involving himself and since he is defending his image to Jews and Romans, these accounts may be among his most unreliable narratives. Because John was inextricably involved in the same events as Josephus, the portrayal of John must be viewed in relation to the portrayal of Josephus.

In the *War*, Josephus presents himself as a great Jewish general who raised and trained an army in Galilee, fortified its cities, and prepared for battle with the Romans. This picture of himself may have been intended to impress upon the Romans how great they were for having defeated him and how fortunate it was for them that he came over to their side. He may also have been impressing his Jewish readers with the dedicated, competent service he had given Israel before his prophetic insight and surrender to Vespasian. As a contrast, John of Gischala is described as "an intriguer . . . the most unscrupulous and crafty of all who ever gained notoriety . . . a ready liar and clever in obtaining credit for his lies, he made a merit of deceit and practiced it among his most intimate friends; while affecting humanity, the promise of lucre made him the most sanguinary of men; always full of high ambitions, his hopes were fed on the basest of knaveries" (*War* 2:585–87). In the *War*, John is also described as a brigand and is made out to be a revolutionary determined to undermine Josephus' authority in Galilee: "He had his heart set on war in order to obtain supreme power" (*War* 4:85). From this extremist position, he accuses Josephus of being a traitor to Rome (*War* 2:599). Thus, in the official account of the *War*, Josephus focuses on his formal role as Galilean general, and John is portrayed as an extremist revolutionary.

Josephus wrote the *Life* some twenty years after the *War*. Although it was well known from the *War* that Josephus had opposed Rome as commander in Galilee, a certain Justus of Tiberias wrote a history (no longer extant) of the Jewish war, which included a malicious depiction of Josephus' anti-Roman activities during this period.[44]

In defense of himself, Josephus wrote the *Life*, portraying his Galilean activities as secretly pro-Roman, or at least moderate in nature. He claims that his covert mission as commander of Galilee was to disarm the extremists and take a "wait and see" attitude toward Rome (*Life* 29). However, Josephus was unable to disarm the extremists. So, in order to maintain control in his overt role as commander in Galilee, he was contrained to appear more and more pro-war and tyrannical, until he was accused by John of Gischala of overstepping the bounds of his mission in Galilee. Although in the *Life* John is still considered an opponent of Josephus, the characterization of him is milder than it is in the *War*. In the *Life*, there is no malicious portrayal of John, and nowhere is he termed a "brigand." In the *Life*, Josephus includes a reference to the fact that John initially opposed the war with Rome. Also, the affirmation that John was thereafter committed to war with

44. See T. Rajak, "Justus of Tiberias," *Classical Quarterly* 23 (1973): 245–68.

Rome is not so definite as it is in the *War*. John's accusations against Josephus in the *Life* are limited to maladministration and tyranny, and do not include treason. Thus, in the *Life*, John is portrayed less like a revolutionary extremist and more like a moderate who competed with Josephus for the command of Galilee.

It is obvious from this brief sketch that these two differing accounts create problems for a historical study of John. In addition to the accounts of John's early activity in Galilee, we have in the *War* Josephus' description of John's role as a revolutionary leader in Jerusalem during the last years of the war. This portrayal is also to be considered an especially biased one, in light of the hostility Josephus must have had toward John from their conflicts in Galilee. Despite these difficulties, it is possible to construct a conjectural portrait of John that will explain most of Josephus' reports, but there is no way of making sure that the facts reported are true, still less that our conjectural explanations of them discussed below are the correct ones.

Josephus writes that at the beginning of hostilities with Rome:

> John, son of Levi, observing that some of the citizens were highly elated by the revolt from Rome, tried to restrain them and urged them to maintain their allegiance. His earnest efforts, however, proved unavailing; for the inhabitants of the neighbouring states, Gadara, Gabara, Sogane and Tyre, mustered a large force, stormed and took Gischala, burnt and razed it to the ground, and returned to their homes. Incensed at this outrage, John armed all his followers, made a determined attack on the aforesaid peoples and defeated them. He then rebuilt Gischala on a grander scale than before and fortified it with walls as a security for the future. (*Life* 43–45)

This opening reference to John of Gischala in the *Life* indicates that his initial reaction was to oppose the war with Rome. The subsequent accounts of John, especially in the *Life*, are best understood if we assume that, as a result of these early events, John changed from a pro-Roman position to that of a moderate, like Josephus, and only later became a revolutionary. A moderate is understood here as one who supported military preparations for defensive purposes, but who was not bent on instigating war (a revolutionary) and who would have settled for a peaceful reconciliation with Rome.

Josephus was sent to Galilee as the general appointed by the provisional government in Jerusalem to prepare that district for the coming war with Rome (*War* 2:568). However, since the provisional government was moderate in its attitude to the war, they unofficially instructed Josephus to attempt to disarm the brigands and carry out a "wait and see" policy regarding the actions of Rome (*Life* 29). Also, he was instructed not to encourage a pro-war attitude among those cities which had maintained their allegiance to King Agrippa II (and therefore to Rome), and he was to discourage civil conflict in Galilee over the war issue (*Life* 28; cf. 265).

There is reason to believe John knew these facts from the outset. From his moderate position, he did not hesitate to ask Josephus for support to rebuild the walls of Gischala in preparation for the defense of his native city. And Josephus writes that he was eager to meet John and to discern his attitude, indicating that they had some previous indirect knowledge of one another. In any case, Josephus tells us that John was "eager for revolution and desirous of obtaining command" (*Life* 70). However, as we shall see, the revolution of John in Galilee was not against Rome, but against Josephus. And his ambition for command was already evident in his control of upper Galilee.

Josephus informs us that John was poor at first (*War* 2:590) and requested Josephus to allow him to sell the imperial corn stored in upper Galilee and to use the profits to rebuild the walls of Gischala (*Life* 71). Although Josephus opposed this, he was outvoted by his two colleagues from Jerusalem who, he alleges, had been bribed by John (*Life* 73). Then John asked permission to sell Galilean oil to the Jews of Caesarea Philippi who had been cut off from other Jews by the royalist forces in that region (*Life* 74–75; *War* 2:590–92). Ostensibly, he wished to keep them from having to use gentile oil which was forbidden by Jewish law. Josephus writes that he allowed John to do this out of fear of the multitude. He also asserts that John made huge profits from this enterprise (*Life* 76). Apparently John also profited from the wealthy citizens of Gischala in his project to rebuild the city walls (*War* 2:590). Josephus attributes these enterprises to greed. More likely, however, they served John's desire for power.

While at Gischala, Josephus summoned the leaders of the brigands and decided that it would be impossible to disarm them as he had originally intended. So he decided to pay them as mercenaries and had them vow that they would not enter the district except to collect their pay (*Life* 77–78). Since he could not disarm the brigands, he began to raise an army from the Galilean cities in order to gain control of the territory (*War* 2:569–70; *Life* 79–80). This latter action, along with Josephus' popularity among the pro-war Galileans, naturally appeared to be contrary to the moderation unofficially expected of him by the Jerusalem authorities. Perhaps envious of Josephus' position of power, John now attempted to induce the city of Tiberias to abandon their allegiance to Josephus and to join him (*Life* 84). When Josephus went there to dissuade the populace from this, he was attacked by some of John's men and narrowly escaped to Tarichaea (*Life* 96).[45] Josephus had to restrain this city, along with the Galileans of the district, from taking revenge on the Tiberians and exterminating John (*Life* 97–103). John fled to Gischala and subsequently wrote to Josephus denying any responsibility for what had occurred (*Life* 101).

At this point, Josephus made further efforts to secure his authority in Galilee. He threatened the pro-Roman city of Sepphoris with plunder if its inhabitants were not loyal to him (*Life* 111). He also confronted a force sent by King Agrippa and prevented them from destroying the fortress Gamala (*Life* 114–19). These actions must have implied to John of Gischala that Josephus was trying to win the whole of Galilee for personal allegiance to himself and that he had turned extremist in his attack on Agrippa's troops. John then went to the three largest cities in Galilee to persuade them to shift their allegiance to him (*Life* 122–25). Gabara secretly went over to him, and Tiberias befriended him although it remained under Josephus. Sepphoris desired to be under neither John nor Josephus.

Josephus' position in Galilee was then threatened from another quarter. One of the Galilean units plundered the caravan baggage of the wife of Agrippa's overseer (*Life* 126–27). When Josephus failed to return to the Galileans a share of the spoils which they relinquished to him, they suspected him of sympathy with the king and began to spread the word that Josephus was a traitor (*Life* 132). He escaped death at the hands of the Galileans in Tarichaea only by promising to use the spoils to fortify that city along with Tiberias and several other cities (*Life* 132–54). Suspicion of his commitment to Judaism was also raised when he allowed several nobles who had deserted the king to live among the Galileans without being circumcised. Thus, when Tiberias

---

45. In *Life* 95, Josephus tells us that the overall number of John's men at this time was about a thousand, but in *War* 2:588, he places the number at four hundred, adding that they were mostly fugitives from the region of Tyre.

decided to shift its allegiance to King Agrippa, Josephus, already under great suspicion, had little choice but to oppose Tiberias (*Life* 155–56). By means of a ruse, he got the leaders of the city apart and had them taken to Tarichaea for imprisonment.

This latter action appeared even more tyrannical and revolutionary to John, who now sent an appeal to Jerusalem to have Josephus removed from his post:

> Meanwhile, the hatred, borne me by John, son of Levi, who was aggrieved at my success, was growing more intense, and he determined at all costs to have me removed. Accordingly, after fortifying his native town of Gischala, he dispatched his brother Simon and Jonathan, son of Sisenna, with about a hundred armed men, to Jerusalem, to Simon, son of Gamaliel, to entreat him to induce the national assembly of Jerusalem to deprive me of the command of Galilee and to vote for his appointment to the post. This Simon was a native of Jerusalem, of a very illustrious family, and of the sect of the Pharisees, who have the reputation of being unrivalled experts in their country's laws. A man highly gifted with intelligence and judgment, he could by sheer genius retrieve an unfortunate situation in affairs of state. He was John's old and intimate friend, and, at the time, was at variance with me. On receiving this application he exerted himself to persuade the high-priests Ananus and Jesus, son of Gamalas, and some others of their party to clip my sprouting wings and not suffer me to mount to the pinnacle of fame. He observed that my removal from Galilee would be to their advantage, and urged them to act without delay, for fear that I should get wind of their plans and march with a large army upon Jerusalem. Such was Simon's advice. In reply, Ananus, the high priest, represented the difficulties of the action suggested, in view of the testimonials from many of the chief priests and leaders of the people to my capacity as a general; adding that to accuse a man against whom no just charge could be brought was a dishonourable proceeding. (*Life* 189–93)

This passage is the key to John's position in Galilee. John was a man of high reputation who was known among some of the Jerusalem leaders.[46] Perhaps John had felt from the outset that he was better qualified than Josephus, and, as a native of Galilee, ought to have been appointed general for that district by the provisional government. John's antiwar actions prior to Josephus' arrival in Galilee indicate he would have been sympathetic to the moderate position of the provisional government. Seeing Josephus' attempts to gain absolute control of Galilee and his efforts to win popularity with the Galileans by his pro-war

---

46. The long-time close relationship which John had with Simon ben Gamaliel suggests that John may have been a Pharisee. See Hengel, *Zeloten*, p. 38.

activity, John was alarmed that Josephus might even try to approach Jerusalem and dislodge the moderate provisional government. John's own ambitions are evident in his request to get himself appointed general.

This interpretation of the passage from *Life* presumes that John was a moderate at the time, an assumption which is open to question, since that is nowhere explicitly stated. Others have argued that John became a revolutionary when Gischala was attacked and razed by fellow Jews at the opening of the war before Josephus arrived in Galilee.[47] On that assumption, John's accusations against Josephus would have been motivated by his conviction that Josephus had maladministered and had attempted to gain absolute power in Galilee for himself. This latter charge of tyranny would have been supported by the fact that Josephus dismissed two colleagues who had been sent to Galilee with him (*Life* 77). But, if John had been a revolutionary bent on war at this point, it is surprising that the provisional government was willing to appoint him as general to Galilee to replace Josephus. To do so they would have had to change their own moderate position with respect to war against Rome—which is unlikely.[48]

It is much more convincing to suppose that the initial attack on Gischala forced John to change from an anti-war position to that of being a moderate, much as the popular tide of war led the conservatives in Jerusalem to assume a moderate position.[49] John's intimate friendship with Simon ben Gamaliel suggests that he may have known their strategy from the outset. John's moderation is also implied by the fact that he was consistently opposed by the Galilean populace who favored war (e.g., *Life* 102-103). More important, Josephus says (in the above cited passage) that the delegation from John brought no real charges that could justify Josephus' dismissal but simply said that it would be to Ananus' "advantage" to have Josephus removed from his

---

47. See Paul Kingdon, "Who Were the Zealots and Their Leaders in A.D. 66?" *New Testament Studies* 17 (1970): 72; Hengel, *Zeloten,* p. 381. Shaye Cohen argues that John of Gischala was not ever a pro-Roman or a moderate. He asserts that this reference to an initial pro-Roman attitude by John (*Life* 43–45) is due to Josephus' apologetic claim that the Jews were forced into the war in part to defend themselves against Hellenists ("Josephus in Galilee and Rome: His *Vita* and Development as a Historian" [Ph.D. dissertation, Columbia University, 1975], pp. 389–99).

48. Against R. J. Shutt, *Studies in Josephus* (London: SPCK, 1961), p. 39.

49. Many people were forced to join the war effort to defend themselves from attack by the non-Jewish population in Israel (cf. *War* 2:457–86; *Life* 27).

post. The fact that the leaders acted to dismiss Josephus without the sanction or knowledge of the populace—who were in favor of the war —implies that they were acting out of the same dual role which Josephus carried out in Galilee: that is, overtly prosecuting the war but secretly pursuing a policy of moderation. Thus, they were alarmed at Josephus' revolutionary behavior and feared the extent of his power over Galilee.

Josephus could hardly have admitted that John was a moderate. To do so would have made it clear that he, Josephus, had been under attack as a revolutionary extremist. This would have run counter to his purpose for writing the *Life*, namely, to controvert the attacks by Justus of Tiberias that he (Josephus) had been responsible for the revolutionary posture of Tiberias; therefore his "apology" was a response to attacks of extremism leveled against him. He thus attempted to explain Ananus' subsequent efforts to relieve him of his post as being due to bribery and envy (*Life* 196), both of which are extremely unlikely.[50] Josephus was thereby repressing the fact that he was accused of being a revolutionary in his actions in Galilee. As such, it is most cogent to assume that John and the Jerusalem leaders—the source of the attacks—were operating as moderates. It was probably only later that John moved from a moderate to a revolutionary position.

A delegation was sent by these Jerusalem leaders, without the sanction or knowledge of the public assembly, to relieve Josephus of his Galilean post and to replace him with John (*Life* 196). When Josephus learned of this plan, he thwarted their attempts to dislodge him and to gain control of the major Galilean cities. He was supported by the Galilean populace, whose leaders carried to Jerusalem a report of his actions (*Life* 266–67)[51] and, with the backing of the Jerusalem populace, succeeded in getting confirmation for Josephus' appointment as general of Galilee (*Life* 309–10). John then suggested to the delegation from Jerusalem, which was still in Galilee, that charges of maladministration against Josephus be brought before the populace in

50. S. Zeitlin, "A Survey of Jewish Historiography: From the Biblical Books to the *Sefer Ha-Kabbalah* with Special Emphasis on Josephus," *Jewish Quarterly Review* 60 (1969): 45.

51. Richard Laqueur argued that the *Life*, written late in the first century, was based on this report which Josephus sent to Jerusalem to defend his conduct against John's accusations: Richard Laqueur, *Der judischer Historiker Flavius Josephus*, with epilogue by Otto Michel (Darmstadt: Wissenschaftliche Buchgesellschaft, 1970; originally published 1920). See also Zeitlin, "Historiography," pp. 37–68.

Jerusalem in order to persuade them to reverse their decision (*Life* 315). This plan, too, was blocked by Josephus, who managed to get the delegation under his control and had them escorted back to Jerusalem (*Life* 317–35).

The confirmation of Josephus' position enabled him to act immediately to disarm John (*Life* 368–72). He sent letters to those towns where John had followers, threatening to destroy their houses and confiscate their property if they did not transfer their allegiance to him. Thereupon three thousand of John's followers deserted him, leaving John with a band of about fifteen hundred men, mostly fugitives from the region of Tyre. From this point on, John remained in Gischala for fear of Josephus (*War* 2:632). No doubt he was also disillusioned by the lack of support he had received from Jerusalem, perhaps even feeling betrayed by the reversal of the provisional government's decision to support him. All through Vespasian's Galilean campaign, we hear nothing of John. Even after Josephus surrendered at Jotapata early in the war and Galilee was without a general, John did not emerge to take charge.[52]

Gischala was the last city to be taken by the Romans in their Galilean campaign. When Titus approached, John and his followers were in charge of the city. Titus called for a surrender, whereupon John asked that the agreement be made the following day, since it was the sabbath and Jews were not permitted either to bear arms or make a treaty (*War* 4:99–100). However, that evening under cover of darkness, John led numbers of the inhabitants of Gischala out of the city toward Jerusalem (*War* 4:106–20). Many perished at Roman hands before they were able to reach the capital the next morning. John and his close companions, who had gone on ahead, made it to the city, where they were eagerly greeted by the populace.

When it became apparent that John had abandoned Gischala and fled the Romans, some of his Jerusalem supporters deserted him (*War* 4:125):

> But John, little abashed at the desertion of his friends, went round the several groups, instigating them to war by the hopes he raised, making out the Romans to be weak, extolling their own power, and ridiculing the ignorance of the inexperienced; even had they wings, he remarked, the Romans would never surmount the walls of Jerusalem,

52. Zeitlin, "Historiography," p. 62.

after having found such difficulty with the villages of Galilee and worn out their engines against their walls. (*War* 4:126–27)

John's decision to abandon Gischala may show that he felt he had a greater mission in Jerusalem,[53] namely, to fight the war with Rome on more secure grounds. His instigation of war in Jerusalem was based, Josephus tells us, on the very practical consideration that he felt the Romans could be defeated in the capital in light of the difficulties which the Romans had met in overcoming the Galilean cities. Perhaps John came to that conviction within the walls of Gischala and was therefore prompted to move from a position of moderacy to commitment to war.[54] Or, it may simply be that an ambitious man like John fled to Jerusalem rather than fight or surrender not because of any ideological considerations, but because he saw a commitment to war in Jerusalem as a promising opportunity. Certainly, once in Jerusalem, he almost needed to favor war in order to justify his flight from Gischala.

However, John did not immediately join with the more revolutionary factions. Rather, he became Ananus' close associate and sought to increase his support in the provisional government (*War* 4:213). The acceptance of John into the inner circle of the provisional government was perhaps due to his earlier contacts with and support of that government, and to the fact that he may still have been considered by them to be a moderate. Josephus also says that John had support within the provisional government, partly because he was not a man of low birth (*War* 4:213).[55] Meanwhile, the provisional government was coming under suspicion because of Josephus' surrender and the failure of the government to go out aggressively after the Romans during their Galilean campaign. Rumors were widespread that the government was making plans to betray the city to the Romans. In the winter of 67–68 C.E., the opposition party of revolutionary Zealots finally broke from the government, took control of the temple, and elected a new high priest. John continued to support, at least overtly, the provisional

---

53. Ibid., pp. 62–63.
54. Zeitlin argues that John shifted from a moderate to a revolutionary position later, at the time of his defection from the provisional government to the Zealots: Zeitlin, "Historiography," pp. 63–64. See below pp. 132–33.
55. Baumbach combines this reference to John's aristocratic origins at birth with the assertion that John was not a man of means at the beginning of the war (*War* 2:590). He concludes that John may have belonged to the class of landed nobility who had been impoverished by Hellenistic forms of economy in Palestine: Baumbach, "Zeloten und Sicarier," p. 731.

government, but began now secretly to betray to the Zealots the government's plans to dislodge them and regain control of the temple (*War* 4:209). Although the government began to suspect him of such duplicity, he reassured them by an oath of loyalty (*War* 4:214–15). He nevertheless continued his contact with the Zealots.

The fact that John was participating in the provisional government at the time the Zealot party was formed is a clear refutation of the notion that John himself was a Zealot.[56] He is consistently distinguished from the Zealots (e.g., *War* 4:208–25; 5:5–7; 98–103; 358; 7:263–74), except during the period when the city was controlled by the Zealots, "to whom John had attached himself" (*War* 5:528).[57] Nor, of course, is John to be considered among the Sicarii.[58]

John was now appointed by the provisional government to negotiate with the Zealots (*War* 4:215). He proceeded to alarm the Zealots by falsely accusing Ananus and the government of having sent an embassy to betray the city to the Romans and of preparing an attack on the Zealots' holdout the following day (*War* 4:216–27). At John's suggestion, they sent secret emissaries to the Idumaeans to come and rescue them (*War* 4:228–29).

Josephus tells us that John carried out these ploys from "a dire passion for despotic power" (*War* 4:208). That may, in part, have been the case. Examples of John's opportunistic desire for power are too numerous to be dismissed (e.g., *Life* 45, 122–25, 190; *War* 4:213, 389). He already had a grievance with the provisional government from the Galilean episode.[59] Realizing he could not get supreme command over Ananus within the provisional government, John may have determined to try to take advantage of the opportunity for leadership should the war party be able to topple the government.

On the other hand, John may have wanted to overcome the moderate position of the provisional government. Josephus tells us they were accused falsely by John of betraying the city to the Romans, and sub-

---

56. Lake calls John the founder of the Zealot party: Frederick Foakes-Jackson and Kirsopp Lake, eds., *The Beginning of Christianity*, 5 vols. (London: Macmillan, 1920), vol. 1, p. 423.

57. See also Kingdon, "Who Were the Zealots and Their Leaders," p. 70, n. 1; and Roth, "The Zealots in the War," p. 346.

58. Baumbach argues ("Zeloten und Sicarier," p. 735) that John was a Sicarius because (1) he was distinguished from Zealots (but that does not make him a Sicarius), (2) he was from Galilee (but Sicarii were active in Judea), and (3) his followers used daggers (but so did Josephus—*Life* 293).

59. Zeitlin, "Historiography," pp. 63–64.

sequent events showed that an embassy had not been sent to Vespasian by them. Although John probably lied about an embassy to Vespasian, he may have done so to alarm the Zealots about the ultimate dangers of the moderate position. He was close to Ananus and probably knew his mind on these matters. He may have sensed that if negotiations with the Zealots broke down, the provisional government would resort to betrayal in order to maintain control. Certainly it was an opportune time to invite the Romans into the city: the Zealots were contained within the temple area; there was occasion to sway the populace against the revolutionaries; and the moderate leaders had access to the gates. To avert such a possibility, John alarmed the Zealots into acting immediately to invite the Idumaeans to rescue them.

The plan to rescue the Zealots succeeded and they took over the city. There is no mention of John's participation in the slaughter which followed, and he apparently was not the prominent leader that he had perhaps expected to be. Soon John was dissatisfied with sharing the .leadership with the Zealot chiefs, so he broke away from them.

> But now John, aspiring to despotic power, began to disdain the position of mere equality in honours with his peers, and, gradually gathering round him a group of the more depraved, broke away from the coalition. Invariably disregarding the decisions of the rest, and issuing imperious orders of his own, he was evidently laying claim to absolute sovereignty. Some yielded to him through fear, others from devotion (for he was an expert in gaining supporters by fraud and rhetoric); a large number thought that it would conduce to their own safety that the blame for their daring crimes should henceforth rest upon one individual rather than upon many; while his energy both of body and mind procured him not a few retainers. On the other hand, he was abandoned by a large section of antagonists, partly influenced by envy —they scorned subjection to a former equal—but mainly deterred by dread of monarchial rule; for they could not expect easily to depose him when once in power, and thought that they would have an excuse for themselves if they opposed him at the outset. (*War* 4:390)

Josephus uses the terms "despotic power" and "absolute sovereignty" to describe the intention of John in contrast to the "equality" of the democratic polity of the Zealots. Apparently John wanted supreme command, and he seems to have held the upper hand in the city at this time (*War* 4:503, 564). The two groups did not engage in battle with each other in spite of their rivalry (*War* 4:395ff.). Josephus tells us that John's supporters were "a group of the more depraved" (*War* 4:389) who are identified later as the "Galilaean contingent." Perhaps the two thousand men representing the city of Tiberias were among them (*Life* 354). They are accused by Josephus of the worst abuses of oppression in the city: looting the houses of the wealthy, transvestism, murder, and immorality (*War* 4:560–64). Josephus claims that John had obtained the allegiance of this group, which had promoted him to power, by giving them freedom to carry out these excesses (*War* 4:559).

The Idumaeans, who along with John had broken away from the Zealots, now mutinied from him to unite with the chief priests and the populace (*War* 4:566–67). They succeeded in confining the Zealots and John to the temple and proceeded to invite Simon bar Giora into the city in hopes that he would be able to dislodge John and the Zealots. John, however, held his ground against Simon and even tried to regain control of the city. He attempted this by burning the food stores to which Simon had access in order to force Simon to turn to him (John) for supplies which were in the temple (*War* 5:21–23). Meanwhile, the Zealots broke from John and occupied the inner temple. John, in order to regain access to the supplies there, caught the Zealots unaware when they had opened the temple for the populace at feast time, and he took complete control of the temple and its environs.

Josephus points out that John was guilty of some offenses against Jewish religious tradition. He misappropriated sacred timber which had been purchased to underpin the sanctuary and he used it to build towers for his battles against his rivals (*War* 5:36–37). Some of his followers who were unpurified were allowed to enter the temple (*War* 5:100), where blood was shed in his skirmish against the Zealots (*War* 5:101–102). John also melted down many of the temple offerings and vessels required for worship and used them as weapons (*War* 5:563). The wine and oil used for sacrifices were taken from the inner temple and given to John's warriors who "anointed themselves and drank therefrom" (*War* 5:565; cf. 7:264).

However, Josephus does tell us that John's rationale for these actions was based on the notion that "they should not scruple to employ divine things on the Divinity's behalf, and that those who fought for the temple should be supported by it" (*War* 5:564). John apparently felt that he had divine support for his activity, for later he responded at the wall to one of Josephus' appeals to surrender by saying that he himself "could never fear capture, since the city was God's" (*War* 6:99).

John and Simon thus shared the rule of the city, and Josephus tells us that they both tyrannized over the people and plundered the wealthy (*War* 5:439–41). During the siege of the city John and Simon both fought against the Romans, and it was Simon, not John, who had made the first concession in their rivalry by allowing John's men to go to the wall to fight (*War* 5:278). Nevertheless, Simon's force was large and he was the main Jewish commander. John's forces were, however, active in the defense of the fortress Antonia (*War* 6:15–92). After the temple was burned and the Romans took over the lower city, the Jews removed to the upper city. There Titus offered the revolutionaries a pledge of their lives in return for their immediate surrender:

> To this they replied that they could not accept a pledge from him, having sworn never to do so; but they asked permission to pass through his line of circumvallation with their wives and children, undertaking to retire to the desert and to leave the city to him. (*War* 6:351)

The desire to retreat to the desert was not, as we have seen, an abandonment of religious commitment. Jews would have interpreted the burning of the temple as God's judgment on his people, not a rejection of them. If God had failed to protect the temple and had left the city, a devoted Jew could only want to go into the wilderness where God had first made a covenant with Israel.[60] Titus refused that request and proceeded with his conquest of the upper city. John hid in some underground passages hoping for an opportunity to escape. However, when he and his companions began to perish from hunger, they requested the pledge of protection which they had earlier refused (*War* 6:432). John was conveyed to Rome along with Simon and was sentenced to life imprisonment (*War* 7:118; 6:434). Simon, who was treated as the Jewish general, was executed.

Summary

On the basis of evidence from Josephus' accounts, which are less than reliable, we have attempted to reconstruct a portrait of John which depicts him as a moderate during his activity in Galilee and as a revolutionary while in Jerusalem. In general, these seem to be the most plausible conjectures, and they are qualified by the fact that many of

60. William R. Farmer, *Maccabees, Zealots, and Josephus* (New York: Columbia University Press, 1956), pp. 116–24.

John's actions seem to have been motivated as much from personal ambition as from any ideological considerations relative to the war.

John is the only person among the revolutionaries, apart from Eleazar the son of Ananias, who was of the same ilk as the traditional Jewish authorities. Although he was from Galilee, he had a close friendship with a leading Pharisee, Simon ben Gamaliel, and he had support among the members of the provisional government. He joined with them upon his entry into Jerusalem and was a confidant of Ananus. As such, John shows no evidence of being a social revolutionist. He was strongly nationalistic, but in a practical way. He probably favored the war because he believed the Romans could not conquer Jerusalem. He believed himself to be a capable chief, able to provide the nation effective leadership in the war. He used his cleverness at every occasion to realize his destiny. He was an opportunist in his strong desire for power. His religious commitment was probably typical of many Jews in the war period in that he believed that he had God's aid in the defense of the city and temple. John was not a messianic figure, and he may have viewed the war more as a nationalistic one than as a holy war. He does not appear to have been fanatical, as one might characterize the Zealots or the Sicarii. Although he took an oath never to submit to the Romans, in the end he gave himself up to them.

Although the Galileans, Idumaeans, and others who made up John's following looked to him for strong leadership, he did not provide it. He was unable to unify the city, alienating the moderates, the Idumaeans, and in the end even the Zealots with whom he had cooperated. Although he may not have engaged in the terrorist tactics of the Zealots, he suppressed the wealthy and moderates when he came to power. He did not exercise strong discipline over his troops; in fact, the excesses of the Galilean contingent under him may have contributed to the defection of the Idumaeans. Some of his opportunistic methods, especially the burning of the siege supplies in order to overcome Simon, contributed to the downfall of the city.

John was most important for his machinations with the Zealots which resulted in the overthrow of the provisional government. If the provisional government did have plans to storm the temple and call in the Romans, it was John's actions which prevented them. And he did play a significant military role in the resistance of the city against the siege by Titus.

THE IDUMAEANS

Idumaea was a territory to the south of Judea which had formerly been the kingdom of Edom. Near the end of the second century B.C.E. John Hyrcanus, one of the Maccabean rulers, conquered this kingdom, forced circumcision upon its inhabitants, and incorporated it into the state of Israel. The territory was treated as part of the kingdom of Judea under the Hasmonaeans and the Herodians, and in 6 C.E. was included in the Roman province of Judea. By the time of the war period, Idumaea had come to share the Jewish allegiance to nation, religion, and culture. At the formation of the provisional government in 66 C.E., Eleazar, son of Ananias, was designated as the general of the Idumaean territory. It was expected that the Idumaeans would participate in the defense of the nation and the city.

Josephus emphasizes the loyalty of the Idumaeans to the Jewish state. At the time he was writing the *War*, Josephus may have held hopes for the restoration of Israel as a Herodian kingdom under Agrippa II. The former kingdom under Herod the Great had included Idumaea. Josephus may have feared that the Romans would think of Idumaea primarily as a territory which had been conquered by the Maccabeans and exclude it as separate and non-Jewish. Stressing the loyalty of the Idumaeans to the Jewish cause in the war may have been Josephus' way of assuring their inclusion in a restoration of the Herodian state.[61]

In any case, Josephus tells us that when the contingent from Idumaea was summoned by the Zealots in the winter of 67–68 C.E. to rescue them from their temple refuge, they were told that Ananus and the leaders of the provisional government were about to negotiate with Vespasian for the surrender of the city (*War* 4:228). The Idumaeans immediately raised a large force under the command of four generals and went to Jerusalem to free the city and the Zealots from the threat of treason (*War* 4:233–35). Finding the gates barred against them, the Idumaeans exchanged accusations with the Jews on the wall, especially with Jesus, the high priest who was second in command to Ananus. Simon, son of Cathlas, an officer, was spokesman for the Idumaeans.

61. This suggestion comes from Morton Smith in private correspondence, 1975.

He charged the high priests with treason (*War* 4:281) and with imprisoning the "champions of liberty" (the Zealots) in the temple (*War* 4:272). The Idumaeans had come to Jerusalem, Simon said, for the "defence of liberty" and "the protection of the mother city" (4:274). If Josephus has accurately depicted the motives of the Idumaeans in these speeches, their intention was to "preserve God's house and fight to defend our country from both her foes, the invaders from without and the traitors from within" (*War* 4:281).

The city remained closed to the Idumaeans, and they huddled that night outside the gate under their shields in a driving rainstorm. The Zealots within the temple used the cover of bad weather to elude the guards watching the temple exits and admitted the Idumaeans through a gate nearest them. The Idumaeans then led the onslaught of the populace and their leaders. After looting and killing many of the common people, they went in search of the high priests whom they believed to be traitors. Josephus claims that it was they who killed Ananus and Jesus, an event from which Josephus was happy to exonerate his fellow Judeans, since he considered it to be a key event in the course of the war:

> I should not be wrong in saying that the capture of the city began with the death of Ananus; and that the overthrow of the walls and the downfall of the Jewish state dated from the day on which the Jews beheld their high priest, the captain of their salvation, butchered in the heart of Jerusalem (*War* 4:318).

Josephus considered the death of Ananus to be significant because of his conviction that Ananus might have persuaded the Jews to come to terms with the Romans (*War* 4:320). Josephus also apparently felt that, had Ananus been unable to bring the nation to terms, he would have made a superior military leader (*War* 4:321). The Idumaeans cast out the slain bodies of Ananus and Jesus without burial (*War* 4:316).

As the Zealot reign of terror continued, some Idumaeans began to regret the Zealot abandonment of traditional institutions (*War* 4:349) and to suspect that Ananus was not guilty of treason as they had supposed. Liberating two thousand of those citizens who had been imprisoned by the Zealots, they departed for Idumaea (*War* 4:353). The remaining Idumaeans joined with John when he broke from the Zealots. Later they rebelled against John, pursued him into the temple and subsequently plundered the treasures he had stored in the palace of Grapte (*War* 4:566–67).

The Idumaeans then met with the traditional chief priests who yet remained in the city. They decided to attempt to regain control of Jerusalem by inviting Simon bar Giora and his forces to enter. Simon, who had conquered the area around Jerusalem including the territory of Idumaea (*War* 4:511–37; 552–56), was besieging Jerusalem, waiting outside the walls for an opportunity to enter the city and take over leadership of the nation and the war. The chief priests and Idumaeans in the city now welcomed Simon as the one who would deliver them from John's forces and the Zealots (*War* 4:571–76).

The fact that a contingent of Idumaeans released a large number of citizens from Zealot prisons and left the city in reaction to the excesses of the Zealots provides evidence that there was a popular reaction against the Zealots and their methods. Likewise, the revolt against John on the part of those Idumaeans who remained in the city supports the notion that he was unacceptable as a leader to many people. The Idumaeans had entered the city to overthrow the high priests who headed the provisional government, but they eventually joined with the high priests in order to overthrow John and the Zealots. The reference to the Idumaeans' mutiny against John follows immediately after a catalogue of the immoral actions of John's Galilean contingent— plunder, carousing, transvestism, assassination (*War* 4:558–65). Perhaps the offensiveness of this behavior and the permissiveness of John (*War* 4:559) led them to unite with a more disciplined leader, Simon. And, given Simon's conquests in the countryside, they may have turned to him as the one who might provide the best leadership for the nation in its struggle with Rome.

During the remainder of the war, the Idumaeans fought as a distinct contingent under Simon bar Giora (*War* 5:358; 6:92, 148). John, their own commander, was killed by a Roman arrow while walking near the wall (*War* 5:290). Alexas, Gyphthaeus, James, son of Sosas, and Simon, son of Acatelas, are singled out by Josephus for valor in battle against the Romans. In the final days of the siege, after the temple had been razed and the revolutionaries were holding out in the upper city, the Idumaean chiefs planned secretly to surrender to Titus. However, Simon bar Giora discovered the plot, put to death the emissaries who had parleyed with Titus, and incarcerated the Idumaean leaders. The rank and file soldiers from Idumaea continued to fight, under guard, with Simon's troops. No Idumaean leader is cited as a prize Roman prisoner after the war.

Summary

The Idumaeans were made up of the citizen force from the territory of Idumaea, just south of Judea. They were not part of a social movement, except insofar as they shared with other country folk the distrust of the traditional city authorities. Perhaps that is why they were so ready to believe the claims of the Zealots that the high priestly authorities were seeking terms with the Romans. They came to Jerusalem to liberate the Zealots from these authorities and to assure the prosecution of the war, which they viewed primarily as a war of national liberation. They led the purge against the moderates which followed the takeover of the city by the Zealots. Their presence was crucial to the downfall of the provisional government, and their assassination of Ananus removed the only moderate leader who might have put a quick end to the war. The subsequent defection of some Idumaeans from the Zealots attests to the Zealot excesses. When other Idumaeans later broke off from John's group, they destroyed whatever unity there was in the city at that point, but they also succeeded in introducing into Jerusalem a stronger military leader, Simon, and his superior military forces. Under Simon's leadership the Idumaeans played a significant role in the defense of the city.

SIMON BAR GIORA

Josephus informs us that Simon bar Giora was "a youth less cunning than John [of Gischala] . . . but his superior in physical strength and audacity" (*War* 4:503–504). The name "bar Giora" may mean "son of a proselyte," implying that his father was of non-Jewish origin.[62] His native place was a town of Gerasa in Transjordan, a town of mixed population (*War* 4:503).

We first hear of Simon as the head of a band of Jewish revolutionaries who attacked the rear of Cestius' troops on their approach to Jerusalem in 66 C.E. (*War* 2:521). Josephus says that he seized some of the Roman baggage and brought it with him into the city of

62. So Cecil Roth, who notes that nowhere is Giora met as a proper name: Cecil Roth "Simon bar Giora, Ancient Jewish Hero," *Commentary* 29 (1960): 52.

Jerusalem. Thus we know that Simon was head of one of the many bands of brigands who were operating in the countryside before the war period, and that he joined with the rest of the Jews in the battles against Cestius.

When he is next mentioned, Simon is in the region of Acrabetta in northeast Judea, raising a band of revolutionaries who plundered and maimed the wealthy (*War* 2:652), presumably because of their pro-Roman sympathies. Ananus, in accordance with his moderate policy of attempting to disarm the brigands (*Life* 28–29), sent out an army against him, whereupon he fled to the Sicarii at Masada (*War* 4:503–504).

This seems to have been the first and only contact between Simon and the Sicarii. There is therefore no reason to think either that Simon was a part of their group or that he espoused their philosophy of "no Lord but God."[63] Although Simon and the Sicarii were profoundly different, they were united by their common antipathy to the Jerusalem government and their opposition to Rome. Their unfamiliarity with one another before this time supports the argument that the prewar revolutionaries were disparate bands of brigands with no central leadership.

At first Simon and his followers, including some women, were regarded with suspicion by the Sicarii, and were permitted only to occupy the lower quarters away from the actual fortress at the top of Masada (*War* 4:505). However, he was soon found to be "a man of congenial disposition and apparently to be trusted," so they allowed him to accompany them in their raids on the surrounding district. Simon was unable to persuade the Sicarii to join him for more ambitious enterprises (*War* 4:507), since they did not want to go far from their refuge:

> His efforts to tempt them to greater enterprises were, however, unsuccessful; for they had grown accustomed to the fortress and were afraid to venture far, so to speak, from their lair. He, on the contrary, was aspiring to despotic power and cherishing high ambitions; accordingly on hearing of the death of Ananus, he withdrew to the hills, where, by proclaiming liberty for slaves and rewards for the free, he gathered around him the villains from every quarter. (*War* 4:507–508)

Apparently Simon saw the death of Ananus and the civil war in Jerusalem as his opportunity to embark on a full-scale military operation. Therefore, he expanded his social program of opposing the rich and championing the poor to include the freeing of slaves, many of whom joined him.

63. Against Baumbach, "Zeloten," p. 23; and Zeitlin, "Masada," p. 311.

It is clear that Simon did have a social program of some kind. In addition to attacking the wealthy (*War* 2:652; 5:439–41), he liberated slaves and offered rewards to the free (*War* 4:508). And Josephus tells us that in his early activity his following was made up of serfs and brigands (*War* 4:510). Perhaps his origin as son of a proselyte means that Simon was from the lower class himself[64] and that his opposition to Ananus and the provisional government was because of class conflict.

The religious rationale for Simon's social program may have come from Isaiah's call "to bring good tidings to the poor . . . to proclaim liberty to the captives . . . to proclaim the year of the Lord's favor, and the day of vengeance of our God." (Isaiah 61:1, 2). As such, the divine vengeance on the Roman enemy was to be accompanied by the freeing of slaves. If this was Simon's understanding he would have viewed himself in the messianic role of the liberator.[65]

However, the freeing of slaves may have been less a part of his social program than a function of his military discipline. Like King Zedekiah (Jeremiah 34:8–11), who proclaimed liberty to all Hebrew slaves as a result of the national crisis with the Babylonians, so Simon announced their liberty as a result of his pact with God to fight the Roman enemy. As such, liberation would have been a "royal" ordinance from one who had a mandate to fight a war in an eschatological time of crisis.[66] This view is supported by the fact that after citizen recruits, in contrast to serfs and brigands, began to make up a majority of his force, we no longer hear about this social message. Later, in Jerusalem, it is not his social program that is evident but his strict military discipline. Thus, his social program may have been part of his response to the national crisis, a response which changed somewhat when he received a broader base of support from the citizenry.

After Simon left the Sicarii to expand his operations, he and his forces overran the hill country. Soon, he became bold enough to extend his activities into the lowlands. His strength and success now won him numerous citizen recruits, so that his army was no longer comprised only of serfs and brigands (*War* 4:510). Among those who

---

64. Roth, "Zealots in the War," p. 349.
65. So Roth, "Simon," pp. 54–55.
66. So Otto Michel, "Studien zu Josephus," *New Testament Studies* 14 (1968): 403.

joined him were the two thousand young nobles of Jerusalem who had been released from Zealot prisons by the Idumaeans when they left the city (*War* 4:353). Their presence in his company must have reinforced his ambitions and encouraged him to wrest Jerusalem from the Zealots—whom these nobles had opposed. It also probably did a lot to discourage him from offering freedom to slaves and attacking the rich. In any case, Simon now conquered Acrabetta and the regions south of Idumaea. He built a fortress at Nain to secure his position, filled the storehouses with supplies, and prepared to march on Jerusalem (*War* 4:513).

One can infer from Simon's assertiveness that he may have had a strong personal ambition to gain control of Israel and to lead a war against Rome. Josephus informs us that his followers were "subservient to his command as to a king" (*War* 4:510).

This comment by Josephus might be perceived as an indicator that Simon was a messianic pretender.[67] However, there is no clear evidence that Simon aspired to royalty.[68] Even the reference just cited states that Simon's followers were subservient to him "as to a king," not that he actually had a recognized kingship. Also, there are no overt messianic demonstrations by Simon such as Menahem's wearing of royal robes to the temple. In addition, Simon's origins would have prohibited him from claiming a royal heritage.[69]

However, if Simon had a messianic consciousness, it may not have been of the Davidic type. Perhaps the key messianic element came from the "strong man" tradition in Israelite history, a tradition which emphasized the mighty warrior.[70] Josephus' reference to the corporeal strength and the courage of Simon (*War* 4:503–504) may place him in this tradition of outstanding military leaders.[71] As such, he would have seen his religious mission as a matter of faithfulness in battle and in the execution of God's law. However, there is need for caution

67. So Hengel, *Zeloten*, p. 304.
68. Appelbaum, "Revaluation," p. 168.
69. Michel, "Studien," p. 403
70. This is suggested by Michel, "Studien," p. 403. For the possible messianic significance of this strong man (*gibbor*) tradition, see Geza Vermes, *Scripture and Tradition in Judaism* (Leiden: E. J. Brill, 1961), pp. 56–60; and William H. Brownlee, "The Servant of the Lord in the Qumran Scrolls, II," *Bulletin of the American Schools of Oriental Research* 135 (1954): 36–38.
71. Cf. the similar types of figures which arose after the death of Herod (*War* 2:57, 60).

regarding this interpretation since a connection with the "strong man" tradition is nowhere explicitly stated.

Whatever Simon's self-understanding was, he appears to have had a mandate to carry on a war against the Romans and against all Jews who opposed him. His assumption of leadership in this holy war involved his carrying out a role in which strong military discipline was central.[72]

The Zealots became alarmed at Simon's growing strength and went out from Jerusalem in arms to defeat him. Although Simon prevailed in the battle and drove the Zealots back into the city, he decided not to attack the city at that time. Perhaps he feared that the Zealots would again request help from the Idumaeans. So he decided to first subdue Idumaea, which he proceeded to do (*War* 4:515–37). This renewed the apprehensions of the Zealots, whereupon they ambushed Simon's forces in a mountain pass, captured his wife and her entourage, and returned to Jerusalem (*War* 4:538–54). Simon was enraged. He came to the walls of the city and vented his fury by torturing or killing any innocent person who ventured outside Jerusalem, threatening to tear down the walls and do the same to those within the city if they did not return his wife. The Zealots did return his wife, and Josephus writes that he then "paused for a while from his ceaseless slaughter" (*War* 4:544).

Perhaps the pause in Simon's activity was due to the renewed presence of Roman troops in Palestine, who now subdued the very territories in which Simon had been successful—Acrabetta and Idumaea (*War* 4:550–55). Simon then began to harass the countryside again and drove many people into Jerusalem. He himself then camped with his forces outside the city walls where, Josephus tells us, he provoked a terror without the walls which equaled the oppression within Jerusalem (*War* 4:557–58). Perhaps Simon hoped that when the Romans came to besiege the city, the Zealots would become desperate enough to seek his support. More likely, he had contacts within the city which led him to think that he might somehow gain entrance to the city. Perhaps the young nobles from Jerusalem who had joined Simon were in touch with the vestiges of the high priestly provisional government which had been overthrown by the Zealots. Also, some of the refugees to Jerusalem from recent Roman conquests may have considered Simon to be a leader who was preferable to the Zealots and John. In any case, the

72. Michel, "Studien," p. 406.

Idumaean forces in the city, who were under John of Gischala, revolted from John and succeeded in containing him and his forces along with the Zealots within the temple area (*War* 4:566). Meanwhile, the Idumaean leaders consorted with the high priestly representatives of the populace and voted to invite Simon and his stronger forces into the city in order to enable them to overcome the rebel forces in the temple (*War* 4:571).

So the high priests and the Idumaeans threw their lot in with Simon, who now, Josephus writes, "became master of Jerusalem" (*War* 4:577). This took place in the spring of 69 C.E. At his entrance into the city, he was hailed by the people as "saviour and protector"[73] from the oppressors of the city (*War* 4:574–75). Thereupon he began a vigorous attack against John and the Zealots in the temple area. Being on lower ground, Simon's forces were at a disadvantage, but their superior numbers enabled them to hold their position (*War* 4:577–84). For a year the hostilities between these groups continued. The battles between them resulted in the destruction of most of the city's supplies for the siege (*War* 5:23–26). Josephus tells us that both of them tyrannized the populace, plundering and killing the wealthy and those suspected of treason (*War* 5:29–30; 439–41). Their dissension continued even after the Romans came on the scene (*War* 5:255). The Roman threat did, however, lead Simon to allow John's men access to the besieged walls (*War* 5:278).

In the siege of the city by the Romans in 70 C.E., Simon was the main commander of the Jewish forces. Josephus speaks admiringly of his leadership, saying that he was one who commanded great loyalty and for whom subordinates were willing to risk their lives (*War* 5:309).

From the beginning, Simon seems to have carried out a strict discipline appropriate to the extreme situation of war. Although Josephus accuses him of cruelty, it may have been precisely this discipline which made Simon's leadership appealing in comparison with the rebel leaders in the temple.[74] As we have indicated, the Idumaeans may have abandoned John of Gischala in favor of Simon because of John's permissiveness with his troops. They may have joined with the high priests to invite Simon into the city because they saw in him a true war leader. As

---

73. This phrase, "saviour and protector" (*War* 4:575), cannot be used as evidence that Simon was understood messianically. Josephus uses such phrases frequently of a variety of leaders, including himself (*Life* 259).
74. Michel, "Studien," p. 404.

such, it would have been this strict "discipline in war" which distinguished Simon from the other revolutionary leaders and characterized any messianic self-understanding he might have had.[75]

Simon's strict discipline resulted in the penalty of death for many. When Matthias, the high priest who had invited him into the city was suspected of desertion, Simon executed him without allowing him to defend himself. His three sons were executed with him, and they were all denied burial (*War* 5:527–31). Seventeen other eminent men were executed on suspicion of desertion; still others were imprisoned (*War* 5:532). A proclamation was issued by Simon, presumably to prevent desertion, that citizens would not be permitted to congregate on penalty of death (*War* 5:533). Simon also discovered a plot by ten of his underlings to surrender the ramparts to the Romans. These men were also slain and their bodies were cast over the ramparts (*War* 5:534–40).

There are clues, however, which indicate that Simon's discipline was not a matter of a ruthless tyranny. For example, there were a number of upper-class persons, including chief priests, who were still actively prosecuting the war through most of 70 C.E. (*War* 6:112–14),[76] a fact which suggests that Josephus may have exaggerated the number of executions ordered by Simon. Also, when a plot to desert on the part of the Idumaean leaders was exposed to Simon, he only imprisoned the Idumaean chiefs, although he did kill the five men who had been emissaries to Titus (*War* 6:380–81). And he retained his prisoners even while hiding from the Romans in underground passages of Jerusalem (*War* 6:432). A further indication of restraint in Simon's discipline is that Josephus' own parents, though put under arrest, were unmolested and accompanied by their attendants in prison (*War* 5:533, 544–45).[77] Also, Simon probably did not ruthlessly deny burial, since there was a public fund, operative even to the end of the war, which was intended to provide burial for the poorer classes (5:567; cf. 5:532). Thus, we are given the impression that Simon may not have been the capricious tyrant that Josephus often claims he was (*War* 4:576; 5:528–29; 7:33).

After the temple was burned and the lower city taken by the Romans, Simon joined with John in asking Titus for pardon and a safe exit from

---

75. Michel clearly depicts this discipline as the key to our understanding of Simon and his possible messianic role: Michel, "Studien," p. 405.
76. Two chief priests, Joseph and Jesus, are mentioned by name, in addition to eight sons of high priests, all of whom ultimately escaped to the Romans.
77. See also Roth, "Simon," p. 57.

the city to go with their families to the desert (*War* 6:326, 366). When this request was refused, Simon began the defense of the upper city. Eventually, as the Romans took over the whole city, Simon took some stonecutters, along with sufficient provisions, into one of the secret passages underneath the city to attempt an escape (*War* 7:26–27). This, however, proved impossible.

Then Simon emerged from under the city into the temple area dressed in white robes. He asked the Roman guards to summon their general and voluntarily surrendered (*War* 7:28–29). Josephus suggests that Simon emerged in the temple area in white robes in order to frighten the Roman guards and effect an escape which he could not accomplish through the underground passages.[78] However, it may be that Simon was voluntarily surrendering in order to take responsibility for his defeat and to share the burden of the consequences with the Jews who were so loyal to him. As such, the white robes would symbolize the role of a martyr who gives up his life for his people.[79] This interpretation of Simon's action is possible, although its power is diminished by the fact that Simon presumably would have escaped through the underground passages if that had been possible.

After his capture, Simon was transported to Rome where he was paraded in the triumphal march as the enemy's chief commander. Then he was executed in the Roman Forum (*War* 7:153–54). This treatment of Simon shows that he was considered by the Romans to be the predominant war leader among the Jews in the siege of Jerusalem.[80]

Summary

Simon was a military leader originally active in the region of Acrabetta in northeast Judea. From the time of the siege by Cestius, he was fighting the Romans. At first, his movement was made up of slaves and brigands. Eventually his successes gained him citizen support. He ap-

---

78. This explanation is accepted by Roth, "Simon," p. 58.

79. This interpretation is suggested by Michel, who compares Simon to Jesus of Nazareth as one who suffered the humiliation of public death by the Romans in order to lighten the load of the Jews: Michel, "Studien," pp. 406–408.

80. Appelbaum adds that his capital punishment (in contrast to John's life imprisonment) might have also been due in part to his egalitarian actions in freeing the slaves: Appelbaum, "Revaluation," p. 166. The Romans feared slave revolts, several of which they had experienced in the empire during the previous two centuries: S. A. Cook, F. E. Adcock, and M. P. Charlesworth, eds., *Cambridge Ancient History*, vol. 9, *The Roman Republic 133–44 B.C.* (New York: Macmillan, 1932), pp. 11–16, 153–56, 200–206.

pears to have had a mission, perhaps understood messianically, to gain control in Israel and to fight the war against Rome. Although he was opposed by the provisional government and then the Zealots, he eventually gained the confidence of the Idumaeans and the remaining high priests so as to be given authority in the city. The acceptance of him by these latter groups was due mainly to his capability as a military leader and to the firm discipline he exercised, a discipline demanded by the crisis of the war.

Simon's main significance lies in his role as general of Jewish forces. Although he was unable to dislodge John and thereby gain absolute control of the city, he nevertheless provided the main resistance to the Roman siege. In this regard, he gave excellent leadership to the very end of the war.

CONCLUSIONS

From these historical sketches, it is obvious that each revolutionary group was distinct. The differences among them apparently account for the constant factionalism and infighting during the war, and they explain the lack of unity in the Jewish resistance against the Romans. If one argues that these factions resulted from a split in an originally unified movement, there is a tendency to reduce the differences between the groups to only one factor. However, when we abandon that thesis and embrace the point of view propounded here, namely, that each group had its own distinct origin and history, then it becomes clear that many factors contributed to the internecine struggle among the revolutionaries. Among these factors were: the conflict between the urban and rural areas,[81] the differences due to regional particularism,[82] antagonism between social classes,[83] the distinctions in religious practices,[84] the variety of expectations in regard to eschatological hopes,[85] the differences in belief about messianic figures,[86] the distinctive methods employed to achieve freedom,[87] the conflict of alternative social and political pro-

---

81. Hengel, *Zeloten*, p. 371.
82. Appelbaum, "Revaluation," p. 162.
83. Roth, "Zealots in the War," pp. 341–42; and Appelbaum, "Revaluation," p. 168.
84. Baumbach, "Zeloten," p. 11.
85. Hengel, *Zeloten*, p. 371; and Appelbaum, "Revaluation," p. 168.
86. Appelbaum, "Revaluation," p. 168; and Hengel, *Zeloten*, p. 383.
87. See above, p. 87.

grams,[88] the difference between a nationalistic movement and an ideological commitment to revolution,[89] and the conflict of personalities in the struggle for power.[90] These same factors also at times united different groups. What they all shared, however, was a commitment to fight for national freedom from the Romans.[91]   In this, they fought together for national freedom with the conviction that God was on their side.

It is not easy to assess the relative historical significance of the various revolutionary groups. The Sicarii were most important in the prewar period.   Their brief coalition with the priestly group under Eleazar, son of Ananias, at the opening of the war enabled the revolutionary forces to bring the nation to war.   Eleazar and the Jerusalemites were significant in initiating the war by the action which they took in rejecting the sacrifices to foreigners and by their victory over Cestius.   The next crucial event was the Zealots' takeover of the city.   Their overthrow of the provisional government assured the prosecution of the war.   This could not have been done, however, without the help of John of Gischala and the Idumaeans.   Simon does not figure so much in the infighting, but his strong presence in Jerusalem in the last year of the war period may have prevented many from deserting to the enemy.   Simon was most prominent in the battles with the Romans, along with John and the Idumaeans. It is clear that no one faction emerges as being more crucial to the revolution than any others were. And it is also evident that no one group could have forced the war issue by itself, or gained control of the revolt without the assistance of other groups   In a sense, the various groups never did become united even at the end.   Josephus may have been right to argue that it was sedition which lost the war for the Jews and not the might of the enemy, although the might of the enemy would presumably have prevailed in the end, even if the Jews had been united.

88. Appelbaum, "Revaluation," p. 168; Hengel, *Zeloten*, p. 383.
89. Zeitlin, "Fairy Tales," p. 195.
90. Heinrich Graetz, *History of the Jews* (Philadelphia: Jewish Publishing Society of America, 1893), p. 301; and Hengel, *Zeloten*, p. 373.
91. Baumbach, "Zeloten," p. 8.

V

MOTIVES FOR THE WAR

We have already dealt with the purposes and motives of the different revolutionary groups in our delineation of the histories. In this chapter, we will deal first with an analysis of the role which moderates and quietists played in the war. Then we will discuss the motivations for the revolt which can be inferred from the disparaging terms which Josephus applies to the revolutionaries and the polemical accusations he makes against them.

MODERATES IN THE WAR

Moderate Sadducees, including chief priests and lay members of the aristocracy, made efforts to prevent the cessation of sacrifices which opened the war (*War* 2:411–18) and subsequently engaged in civil war against these revolutionaries to prevent them from taking over the city. Later, some leading citizens under Ananus, son of Jonathan, tried to turn the city over to the Romans when it was beseiged by Cestius Gallus (*War* 2:533–34). These efforts failed. When the revolutionaries returned to Jerusalem from the victory over Cestius, they did so on a wave of popular support for independence which won over all but those die-hard Herodians and pro-Romans who fled the country (*War* 2:556–58). Yet the traditional Sadducean government, headed by Ananus, son of Ananus, was elected to power by the populace (*War* 2:562–68).

It may seem surprising that the chief priests, who as we saw earlier had acted so independently of Rome in the prewar years, would attempt to prevent or halt the revolution when it came. Yet it may have been one thing to resist the maladministration of the procuratorial system and quite another to face the Roman legions. But if the behavior of the chief priests implied such a realistic acceptance of Roman rule, it may be wondered why they consented to head the provisional government of independence and proceeded to prepare the nation militarily against the eventual return of Roman troops. Perhaps it was because the Sadducees traditionally provided the leadership in Jewish government that they were reluctant to abandon their national responsibilities. If the populace wanted war, then they may have felt it was their obligation to provide leadership.

In any case, by this time the nation may have gone too far to ask for terms from the Romans. They could not simply surrender to the Romans and expect the nation to be exonerated for its actions. The province of Judea was too important to the Roman Empire as a protection on the eastern front for this rebellion to be treated lightly. Besides, the Hellenistic pogroms against Jews in many cities, such as Caesarea, Scythopolis, and Damascus (Life 24–27; War 2:457–98; 559–61), must have led many otherwise pro-Roman Jews to support the war cause for reasons of self-defense. These events probably increased the expectation that Roman reprisals were inevitable.

Also, it may have been that some Sadducean leaders were convinced at the beginning of the war that the Jews could successfully defend their homeland. They might have thought they could depend upon the support of the Jews throughout the empire. Letters were sent to the large and influential Jewish communities in the Parthian Empire to the east, encouraging them to persuade the Parthians to wage war against the Romans (War 6:341; cf. 2:388–89). And there was dissatisfaction with the Emperor Nero on the part of nations within the empire. Perhaps, the Jewish leaders may have reasoned, other revolts against Roman domination might follow their own. In any case, having initially driven the Romans out of Israel in 66 C.E., the Jews now had time to make more adequate preparations for war.

If Ananus and other traditional Sadducean leaders had been making such preparations for war, why do we continue to refer to them as "moderates," as persons who would have accepted surrender? Perhaps Ananus made preparations so enthusiastically because it increased the Jews' chances of coming to acceptable terms with Rome rather than having

151

to capitulate. Jerusalem could be made into a fortress which was almost impregnable (*War* 2:378; 4:89–90). Before the stores were burned by John and Simon, the city had siege supplies which would have lasted a number of years. There was also the outside possibility that Roman troops and supplies might be depleted in subduing the rest of the country even before approaching Jerusalem. And revolts in other parts of the empire might limit the military resources which Rome could mobilize in the reconquest of Palestine. If Israel could present a formidable threat or if the siege of Jerusalem could prove to be a long-term military operation for the Romans, the Jews might just be able to bargain for favorable terms, enabling them to avoid an all-out war with Rome which would probably end in a Jewish defeat. The fact that other cities, such as Tiberias (*War* 3:455; cf. 1:21), were able during the war years to sue for terms of peace with the Romans, increased the possibility that the same might be done for Jerusalem. And if no such terms could be reached, they would still be prepared for war (*War* 4:318–25).

Perhaps it was this ambiguity in their position which explains some of the political maneuvers of the Sadducean high priests. For example, they included some of the revolutionaries in the provisional government, perhaps in order to persuade them to soften their attitudes (*War* 2:651). The active presence of revolutionaries in the governmental preparations for war would also have satisfied that segment of the populace which most favored war. There is reason to think this coalition between moderate high priests and revolutionaries was mutually beneficial. The lower priests who had led the revolution at the opening stages probably needed the authority and prestige of the high priests in the wartime government in order to win over that portion of the population which might not have favored the war.[1] Together, these groups excluded the most radical revolutionaries, headed by Eleazar ben Simon, from the government. They feared that he had the means and influence to control the government if allowed to be a part of it (*War* 2:564–65). Yet it may have been this exclusion which suggested to many revolutionaries that the provisional government headed by the Sadducees was not prepared to press the war to its ultimate conclusion.[2]

---

1. I owe this suggestion to S. Safrai in private conversation, 1975.
2. We have identified as "moderates" those who remained in Jerusalem preparing to defend against the Romans but who would have been willing to accept the

It was just this suspicion that the provisional government was moderate, that it would be willing to revert to former methods of diplomacy and bargaining, which led to its downfall. High priestly actions, which before the war were seen as mediations on behalf of Jews, clearly would have been viewed during the war as actions of betrayal. As a result, the traditional leaders were overthrown by the revolutionary forces under Eleazar, son of Simon. Ananus, Jesus, and other moderate leaders were killed, while many others of aristocratic origin were imprisoned. Some priestly leaders within the revolutionary group of the Zealots, who would accept no compromise with Rome, may have been of the same Sadducean origin as those whom they were now persecuting.

It is surprising that we find no mass escape to the Romans on the part of the two thousand nobles who were subsequently released from Zealot prisons by the Idumaeans. Rather, the nobles left the city to join the forces of Simon bar Giora. Others from among the high priestly families remained in Jerusalem and eventually arranged for Simon to enter the city on their behalf. By now they had apparently abandoned their hopes of reinstituting the traditional government and sought restoration of their power through the monarchical leadership of Simon, who they hoped would overcome John and the Zealots. In the end, many high priests and aristocrats also became disillusioned with Simon and near the later stages of the siege tried to escape the city. Some were caught and executed by Simon as traitors.

Any Sadducees who were still alive when the city was being conquered, including those who may have been among the Zealot party, had by this time been absorbed into the groups under John and Simon. At the last, nothing was left of the authority or influence of the traditional Sadducean government.

---

right kind of terms, were they offered. It is important to note the variety of positions included among "moderates," from the more militant Ananus who headed the provisional government (*War* 4:320) to those who initially attempted to stop the revolt but joined it when it seemed inevitable.

Shaye Cohen denies that those who headed the provisional government were ever moderate, asserting that they participated in the war from the beginning and only appeared moderate in retrospect when more extreme figures came to the fore. He argues that Josephus does not call them "moderates," but reserves that term for the "peace" party ("Josephus in Galilee and Rome: His *Vita* and Development as a Historian" [Ph.D. dissertation, Columbia, University, 1975], pp. 323–415).

In assessing the role of Pharisees in the war, it is interesting to note that despite the paucity of explicit references to any sects in Josephus' works, there is one important mention of the political activity of the Pharisees at the opening of the war. After Josephus records the decision made by Eleazar, son of Ananias, and his priestly followers in 66 c.e. to reject the sacrifices to Caesar, he writes: "the principal citizens assembled with the chief priests and the most notable Pharisees to deliberate on the position of affairs now that they were faced with what seemed irreparable disaster" (*War* 2:411).

The Pharisees may have been included in these deliberations primarily because of their expertise in legal matters. But judicial experience is not emphasized as the reason for their presence here. In fact, that role was carried out by the "priestly experts" who were subsequently produced in a public meeting to persuade Eleazar and his followers to reverse their decision (*War* 2:417). Rather, the Pharisees were brought in at the point of the earliest deliberations presumably as an important part of the decision-making process of the Jerusalem establishment. The leading Pharisees apparently participated as influential representatives of their sect in order to bring as much political weight as possible to bear against the dissident priests. Their presence was especially important if there were conservative Pharisees in the ranks of those priests.

This reference to the Pharisees occurs in the *War*, where there is no apparent attempt to exaggerate the role of that sect. If this passage is accurate, then a similar passage in the *Life* might also be considered trustworthy. In the *Life*, Josephus writes that when he returned from Rome and during the civil war in Jerusalem, he took asylum in the temple for a brief time for fear of the revolutionaries. Then, he writes, "I ventured out of the temple and once more consorted with the chief priests and the leading Pharisees" (*Life* 21). If the Pharisees had been included in the initial efforts of the national leaders to prevent the revolt (*War* 2:411), it would seem reasonable to take this passage as an accurate depiction of a later event in which they were included in attempts by moderates to halt the revolt once it had begun. In both cases, the participants are cited in such a way as to suggest they were included because they were leaders and representatives of the Pharisaic party.

154

This analysis may provide the context for an understanding of Simon ben Gamaliel's activity in the war years. This Simon, Josephus writes, was "a native of Jerusalem, of a very illustrious family, and of the sect of the Phariseses . . ." (*Life* 191). Josephus characterizes him as a man gifted with "intelligence and judgment." He also describes the role he played in the attempt by Jerusalem leaders to remove Josephus from his post as general of Galilee (*Life* 192ff.). As a Pharisee according to the house of Hillel, Simon most likely worked for the cause of peace, in this case as an important moderate figure in the political process.

Undoubtedly, Simon took an important part in the moderate government because of his family background and his diplomatic ability to "retrieve an unfortunate situation in affairs of state" (*Life* 192). But also, he must have been influential because he was a Pharisee. He may have been one of the leaders of the Pharisees who were consulted in the early war years. It is not clear whether he held an office in the Sanhedrin, but he did work within the inner circle of power in close cooperation with Ananus the high priest (*Life* 192, 216; *War* 4:160).[3] He is identified as one of two outstanding leaders of the provisional government who urged the populace to take measures against the Zealots entrenched in the temple (*War* 4:159). Surely his words of counsel bore the weight of other Pharisees who agreed with him and whom he represented.

In addition to Simon being involved in the provisional government, the three-man delegation sent to Galilee to relieve Josephus of his post were members of the Pharisaic party (*Life* 197). Josephus implies that their presence in Galilee as Pharisees was designed to sway the populace (*Life* 198). Their inclusion may also have been a measure of the authority which the Pharisees had attained in the coalition government.[4] However, we need to be cautious here in light of Josephus' tendency in the later *Life* to exaggerate the historical role of the Pharisees.

Yohanan ben Zakkai was representative of other Pharisees of the house of Hillel who opposed the war. He was apparently not involved

---

3. Cecil Roth, "The Pharisees in the War of 66–73," *Journal of Semitic Studies* 7 (1962): 67–68.
4. Ibid., p. 69.

in the political process and his voice of protest was not heeded. Yohanan remained in Jerusalem until it was clear that no terms would be made with the Romans. He then escaped the city surreptitiously in 68 C.E. and asked the besieging general Vespasian if he could be granted leave to settle in Jamnia and establish a Pharisaic school there.[5] Yohanan was typical of many later Pharisees who condemned the war as a consequence of "baseless hatred." It was the Pharisaism of Yohanan ben Zakkai which survived the war and became instrumental in shaping subsequent Judaism.

Regarding the role of the Essenes in the war, Josephus tells us that many were tortured in the war with the Romans because they refused to blaspheme their lawgiver or to eat foods forbidden to them (*War* 2:152–53; cf. 2:141, 145). However, there is no indication that they suffered because of active opposition to the Romans. They are depicted as passive victims, not belligerents.[6] On the other hand, one wonders why the Romans would have tortured them unless the Essenes had actively opposed them.[7]

In Josephus' historical narrative of the period under consideration, there is reference to only one Essene. "John the Essene" was appointed in 66 C.E. by the provisional government as general "to the province of Thamnia, with Lydda, Joppa, and Emmaus also under his charge" (*War* 2:567; cf. *War* 3:11–19). There is no other evidence of active Essene participation in the war, so we do not know if John was an exception to or typical of other Essenes. However, it would not be surprising if other Essenes had followed John's example and caught the national contagion of war, joining this as a holy war against the Romans.

There is some evidence for a possible connection between the Essene community at Qumran and the revolutionaries in Jerusalem at the beginning of the war. Jewish coins from the first three years of the revolt (66–68 C.E.) were found on the Qumran site. It has been suggested that the *Copper Scroll*[8] found at Qumran may contain an actual record

---

5. For a full treatment of Yohanan, including the stories of his escape, see Jacob Neusner, *A Life of Yohanan ben Zakkai*, 2d ed. (Leiden: Brill, 1970).

6. So Marcel Simon, *Jewish Sects in the Time of Jesus*, trans. James H. Farley (Philadelphia: Fortress Press, 1967), pp. 63–64.

7. So Menachem Stern, "Zealots," *Encyclopedia Judaica*, supplementary volume (1972), p. 150, n. 17.

8. J. Allegro, *The Treasure of the Copper Scroll* (Garden City, N.Y.: Doubleday, 1960).

of treasures hidden in the temple area. We know that Eleazar ben Simon controlled the public treasury from the time of the defeat of Cestius (*War* 2:564), and that he, along with other Zealots, occupied the temple in the winter of 68 C.E. They may have hidden the temple treasury from the Romans or possibly from moderate Jews. As a record of places where the treasury had been hidden, they might have then sent this *Copper Scroll* to Qumran for safekeeping until a later time.[9] If that was the case, then there was some connection between the revolutionaries in Jerusalem and the Qumran sect.

In this regard, we may also note that the Qumran group and the revolutionaries in Jerusalem under Eleazar ben Simon were priestly-oriented, and both were concerned with the legitimate restoration of the Zadokite priesthood.[10] The Qumran sectarians may have been in touch with the lower priests in Jerusalem, who in 68 C.E. participated in the overthrow of the traditional priests and in the selection of a new high priest by lot. Some of those from Qumran may have gone to Jerusalem and participated in the Zealot takeover of the temple. The presence of the *War Scroll* among the Qumran scrolls, along with the idea pervasive among the scrolls that there would be a "day of vengeance," may suggest that the Qumran sectarians joined in battle with other Jewish revolutionaries because they saw the revolt against Rome as the final eschatological war.[11]

However, all of these considerations are very tenuous. There is no evidence that members of the Qumran community were in Jerusalem. There is no reason to think the Qumran community would have accepted the legitimacy of the high priest chosen by Zealots any more than they accepted the legitimacy of the traditional high priests. And there is no connection made in the scrolls between the final day of vengeance and the Jewish War against Rome. The *Copper Scroll* was probably a fictitious record of treasures that was part of Jewish lore

---

9. H. H. Rowley, "Qumran: The Essenes and the Zealots," *Von Ugarit nach Qumran: Beitrage zur alttestamentischen und altorientalischen Forschung*, ed. Johannes Hempel and Leonard Post (Berlin: Alfred Töpelmann, 1958), p. 192.
10. Günther Baumbach, "Die Zeloten: ihre geschichtliche und religionspolitische Bedeutung," *Bibel und Liturgie* 41 (1968): 18–19.
11. For the date of the *War Scroll* and its significance for the community, see especially A. Dupont-Sommer, *The Essene Writings from Qumran*, trans. G. Vermes (New York: World Publishing Company, 1961), pp. 165–68; and J. T. Milik, *Ten Years of Discovery in the Wilderness of Judaea*, trans. John Strugnell (London: SCM Press, 1959), pp. 122–23.

from the remote past,[12] and the coins of the revolt at Qumran could have been brought by fugitives from the civil conflicts in Jerusalem. The *War Scroll*, while expressing the hatred borne toward the Roman oppressors, may have been mostly visionary and apocalyptic rather than practical.[13]

Some evidence suggests a connection between the Essene community at Qumran and the Sicarii at Masada. One of the Essene sectarian writings, the *Songs of the Sabbath Sacrifices* was discovered at Masada. However, the geographical obstacles between the two sites make any close contact unlikely. Perhaps no more can be inferred than that some Essenes fled to Masada from the Romans when their own refuge at Qumran had been destroyed in 68 c.e.

The fact that the Romans destroyed the Qumran center does not necessarily mean that the Essenes there made a stand against them, since the Romans destroyed many villages and locales where people had gone simply for refuge. The community may have remained inactive up to the last; they may not have viewed this war as the apocalyptic battle for which they had been waiting. Perhaps the most that can be inferred from our information about the Qumran sect and the Essenes in general is that they may have participated in a limited way in the war against the Romans.

Later traditions tell us that the Christian community remained in Jerusalem for some of the war period and then, like Yohanan ben Zakkai, fled the city, and they established a community at Pella in the Transjordan.[14] Probably this group represented the majority of the Jerusalem church, including its leadership. Although we have no evidence for it, there is the possibility that some rank-and-file Christians remained in the city to fight to the end for national independence.

It is possible in a general way to characterize the political involvement of the major sects in Israel. The Sadducees, as leaders of the

---

12. See F. M. Cross, *The Ancient Library of Qumran* (Garden City, N.Y.: Anchor, 1961), pp. 22–23.
13. Ibid., pp. 61–62.
14. Eusebius, *Ecclesiastical History*, with trans. by Kirsopp Lake (New York: J. P. Putnam's Sons, 1949–1953), 3.5.3. For recent treatments of the Pella traditions, see S. Sowers, "The Circumstances and Recollection of the Pella Flight," *Theologische Zeitschrift* 26 (1970): 305–20, and John Gunther, "The Fate of the Jerusalem Church," *Theologische Zeitschrift* 29 (1973): 81–94.

nation, were in the midst of the political life of Israel; hence, they were involved in many forms of resistance, including the war. The Pharisees were primarily oriented toward religious practices, but their political involvement at various levels contributed to the course of events. The Essenes were withdrawn from political life, and the extent of their participation in the war is uncertain.

Beyond these general observations, however, there was great diversity within each sect. During the prewar period, there were many attitudes toward the war, and there were differing levels of participation in the various forms of resistance. Nor did the subsequent stances during the war run along sectarian lines; there were probably revolutionaries, moderates, and quietists from each sect. Factors such as class or economic status were probably more important than sectarian beliefs and loyalties in the determination of attitudes toward the war. And it would be fair to say that many adherents of the sects changed their political position toward Rome in response to the developing course of events. Our observations about the sects, like our study of the revolutionary groups, encourages us to appreciate the diversity of people who were involved in the resistance against the Roman overlords.

INFERENCES FROM JOSEPHUS' VOCABULARY

Much can be learned about the character and motives of the revolutionaries by a study of the pejorative terms which Josephus employs against them. *The Jewish War* was addressed to Jews, living in the eastern Roman Empire and in Parthia, who might have been tempted to revolt against Rome in the aftermath of the Roman conquest of their homeland. Josephus is critical of the revolutionaries in order to dissuade his readers from identifying with these revolutionaries in Palestine.

In his historical narrative, Josephus uses derogatory terms to portray the revolutionaries and their actions, thereby conveying to his readers that the war was throughout misconceived and misdirected. These words include: "brigands," "insurgents," "tyrants," "conspirators," "wicked ones," and "imposters."

Brigands

In those portions of Josephus' works which relate to the period from

6 to 74 C.E., various forms of this noun occur eighty-four times.[15]   In its classical meaning, "brigands" refers to robbers operating in bands to attack caravans or travelers, plunder homes, or on a larger scale, raid villages.[16]   In Roman parlance, this term was also used for patriots who resisted the Romans in the lands which they occupied and who used the methods of robbers.   By applying this term to various revolutionary groups, Josephus was impugning their motives, implying falsely that they were no different from common highway robbers and that their intentions were solely a desire for material gain.   He writes: "When raids are made by great hordes of brigands . . . it is supposed to be the common welfare which is upheld, but the truth is that in such cases the motive is private gain" (*Antiquities* 18:8).

It is clear from a close reading of Josephus' narrative that many of the brigands were not ordinary robbers.   In one passage, the "brigands" are political revolutionaries who suppressed those Jews "who submitted to Roman domination" (*War* 2:264).   In another instance, the "brigands" who attacked a Roman caravan in the *War* (2:228) are called "seditious revolutionaries" in the parallel passage in *Antiquities* (20:113).   The Sicarii, who entertained the religious motivations of the fourth philosophy, are frequently termed "brigands" (*War* 2:434; 4:505).   Other occurrences, as we have seen, relate to economically and socially deprived people who had turned to brigandage for survival or dissension (e.g., *War* 2:652; 5:439; 7:261).   Sometimes, "brigands" does refer to ordinary robbers, some of whom must have taken advantage of participation in the revolutionary movement to do their own plundering and raiding (*War* 2:278; *Antiquities* 20:215).[17]   However, by applying "brigand" to all groups which used robber methods without regard to their principles or lack of them,[18] Josephus was imputing to them the mercenary motives and the disregard for law of common rob-

---

15. For the Greek words and comparative occurrences related to each of the terms discussed here, see appendix. For a fuller explication of these terms, see D. Rhoads, "Some Jewish Revolutionaries in Palestine from A.D. 6 to 73 According to Josephus" (Ph.D. dissertation, Duke University, 1973), pp. 177–224.
16. See K. H. Rengstorf, *"Lēstēs," Theological Dictionary of the New Testament,* 9 vols., ed. Gerhard Kittel, trans. Geoffrey Bromiley (Grand Rapids: Eerdmans, 1964), 4:257ff.
17. Bernard H. Jackson, *Theft in Early Jewish Law* (Oxford: Clarendon Press, 1972), p. 36.
18. See also Morton Smith "Zealots and Sicarii, Their Origins and Relation," *Harvard Theological Review* 64 (1971): 9–10, n. 52.

bers. In this way, he suppresses the honorific, religious, political, and social attitudes which characterized many of them.

The countryside is the locus for almost all activity of brigands in Josephus' prewar narrative.[19] When brigands are located in Jerusalem, Josephus indicates that they entered there from the countryside.[20] This makes sense if we observe that robber methods—raids, plunder, and so forth—were only possible in rural areas and small villages, not in a city like Jerusalem. When "brigands" entered Jerusalem, they were forced to adopt new methods, such as assassination with a dagger, which were more effective in a metropolitan situation (*War* 2:254). Thus, Josephus uses "brigands" to refer only to those groups which originated in the countryside.

This distinction continues into the war period. The revolutionaries originating in Jerusalem—those who opposed Florus (*War* 2:295, 325, 330), the priestly-lay coalition under Eleazar, son of Ananias (*War* 2:411, 422, 424), and those who defended the city against Cestius Gallus—are not called "brigands," but "insurgents" (*War* 2:517–40). The term "brigand" is employed only during that part of the narrative when *sicarii* and the forces of Menahem were present in Jerusalem (*War* 2:431, 434, 441).

The fact that Josephus uses different terms for revolutionaries from the countryside and those from the city indicates that he was making a distinction between rural and city revolutionaries. His distinction implies there were two kinds of revolutionaries, "brigands" and "insurgents," who may have differed in their methods, ideologies, or social dissatisfactions. This implied city/country disparity may help to explain some of the numerous conflicts between certain of the revolutionary groups. It also reinforces the view that the revolutionary movement in Israel was never a united monolithic group.

As Josephus describes how group after group of brigands entered the city during the subsequent years of the war, he laments the fact that their presence in Jerusalem, with their appetites sapping the resources of the city, contributed to the downfall of Jerusalem (*War* 4:135–37). In the final siege, the brigands so permeated the revolutionary ranks that Josephus came to refer to all revolutionaries as "brigands." At

19. *War* 2:125, 142, 228, 229, 235, 239, 253, 264, 271, 273; *Antiquities* 20:5, 121, 124, 160, 161 (2), 172, 185, 215, 255–56.
20. *War* 2:254; *Antiquities* 20:163 (2), 165, 167, 186, 210. *War* 2:275 is an analogical usage.

this point, the term serves to set the revolutionaries apart from the general populace, who are depicted as the innocent victims of the brigands' exploits (*War* 4:241–42).

Insurgents

Despite the variety of English translation which Thackeray, for example, employs (rebels, revolutionaries, insurgents, malcontents, rival parties, factions) to depict revolutionaries from the city, there is usually one Greek word which stands behind them. This word occurs sixty-eight times[21] and refers with few exceptions,[22] to revolutionaries in and from Jerusalem.

In addition, the term is almost exclusively limited to the period of the war. Initial occurrences refer to those Jerusalemites who opposed Florus (e.g., *War* 2:295), to the followers of Eleazar, son of Ananias (e.g., 2:411), and subsequently to the Jerusalem natives who defended the city against Cestius Gallus (*War* 2:517–40). The fact that the term "insurgents" is limited to the war period may imply that there was no organized revolutionary group within the city before the war began.

Josephus' use of this term refers not to insurrection against Rome,[23] but against the traditional government of Israel. As such, he maligns the revolutionaries by claiming it was their internal sedition and factionalism which plagued the nation throughout the war period and which was a contributing factor in its demise (*War* 5:257; cf. 1:10; 4:376). During his description of the final siege of the city, Josephus employs the word "insurgents," as he does "brigands," of all revolutionaries. In so doing, he sets them off from the "peace-loving populace" who are depicted as being caught in the crossfire of their factional conflicts (*War* 4:362; 5:14; 6:369).

Tyrants

This term, used thirty-three times of the revolutionary leaders, car-

---

21. For statistics, see below pp. 182–83. If the parallel occurrences of "brigand" in the *War* and *Antiquities* are taken into account, "insurgents" occurs more frequently for revolutionaries than "brigands."

22. War 2:484, 290; 3:449, 542. Three of these four exceptions clearly refer to revolutionaries from other cities, not the countryside.

23. Josephus uses other terms for the revolt of the whole nation from Rome. For "revolt," see *War* 2:118, 264, 283, 347; 5:183; 6:290; 7:257; *Life* 17, 25; and cf. *War* 2:371, 385; 7:75, 77, 411. For "revolution," see *War* 2:318, 332, 513; 5:152; 6:329, 343; 7:4, 421, 447 and cf. *War* 3:109; 6:239.

ries the reproach of those who seize and misuse power.[24]   Josephus depicts the overthrow of the traditional government, as well as the power struggles among the revolutionaries, in a pejorative way by ascribing to them a lust for absolute power (e.g., *War* 5:5–6).

Josephus' use of this term also serves his biased efforts to portray the populace as helpless victims of a ruthless tyranny (*War* 5:439–44), implying that ordinary Israelites were forced by the revolutionary leaders into an unpopular war.   In this regard, Josephus lists tyranny, along with famine, war, and sedition, as major causes of the downfall of the state (*War* 4:397).

Conspirators

The term "conspirator" is used a number of times for leaders of the revolutionary movement.   In the *War*, it refers to plots against the provisional government rather than against the Romans (e.g., *War* 4:151, 154, 208).   Thus, Josephus maligns the revolutionaries by portraying them as conspirators against Jewish institutions such as the "state" (*War* 4:208) and the "mother city" (*War* 4:267 cf. 5:21).

Wicked Ones

This term is used numerous times of the revolutionaries and their leaders. It asserts that the revolt was carried on by the criminal, lawless element of the Jewish society.

Imposter

Josephus uses the term "imposter," along with "false prophet" and "deceiver," to refer to the prewar prophetic figures whom we have discussed.   Prophetic figures also emerged in the war period.   When the temple burned, a "false prophet" led Jews up to the temple's portico to receive signs of their deliverance (*War* 6:285).   Two other passages make a general reference to false prophets and deceivers who arose near the end of the war period (*War* 6:286, 288).

Josephus throughout clearly distinguishes between "revolutionaries" and "imposters." The imposters of the prewar period are said not to have shared the terrorist methods of the revolutionaries (*War* 2:258). Even when it is said that "imposters" and "revolutionaries" were active

24. This term was important to Josephus.   It occurs five times for revolutionaries in the prologue to the *War* (1:10, 11, 24, 27, 28) in comparison to one occurrence each of "insurgents" (1:10) and "brigands" (1:11).

during the same period and that their activity created a similar effect, they are nevertheless identified as distinct types (*War* 2:264). None of the revolutionary leaders of the war period was called an "imposter."[25] Josephus states, however, that some leaders did suborn prophets in the late stages of the war in order to check desertions and provide encouragement to the loyal (*War* 6:285–86). Even in this situation the distinction between the two is preserved. Thus, it would be mistaken to lump the imposters indiscriminately with the revolutionaries.

Yet by applying derogatory terms to the prophetic figures, Josephus clearly wishes to malign their motives as well as the motives of the revolutionaries who cooperated with them. He depicts them as victimizing the populace, who, he writes, "were deluded at the time by charlatans and pretended messengers of the deity" (*War* 6:288).

Summary

An examination of Josephus' use of these words we have discussed indicates they may have originated from his aristocratic heritage. His point of view as a historian was not so much that of his Roman patrons as that of the wealthy, upper-class family of Jerusalem from which he came. He used the derogatory terms not mainly as a spokesman for the Roman general, but as a member of the Jewish provisional government threatened by subversive elements from within the nation. The "exploits," "tyrannies," "conspiracies," and "deceptions," as Josephus describes them, are directed against the Jewish state and people, and only indirectly against the Romans. These terms may thus have been a part of Josephus' vocabulary and perspective before he became a historian, and may simply reflect the point of view of the ruling aristocracy of which he had been a part.[26]

Other aristocratic Jews seem to have shared Josephus' point of view. We note that, in the prewar period, Jewish officials in Judea were expected to pursue and punish "brigands" (*War* 2:229, 273). We are told that during the war period the traditional provisional government wanted to disarm the "brigands" (*Life* 28–29). Ananus, as head of that

---

25. John of Gischala is called an "imposter" (*War* 4:85). However, it refers only to his cunning with no prophetic overtones whatsoever (cf. *Life* 40 and *War* 2:565; 5:317).

26. Against Hengel, who thinks Josephus borrowed the term "brigand" from one of his sources, Nicholas of Damascus: M. Hengel, *Die Zeloten* (Leiden: E. J. Brill, 1961), p. 46.

government, sent forces against Simon bar Giora and his brigands (*War* 2:653). Also, several times in the speeches of the high priests to the populace, the revolutionaries are referred to as "brigands" (*War* 4:199, 242, 244, 261). Although there is no evidence for it, the term "insurgent" may have been used by the ruling class in a similar way. If so, the use of these two terms reflects the attitudes of the class struggle which figured so prominently in the war.

Other terms may have been part of the verbal weapons used by both the aristocracy and the revolutionaries to attack each other in the war period. Ananus accused the revolutionaries of tyranny (*War* 4:179), but the revolutionaries also accused the traditional government of tyranny (*War* 4:278; cf. 2:294). Ananus called the Zealots conspirators against "liberty" (*War* 4:185) and the "mother city" (*War* 4:267). But the revolutionaries accused the aristocracy of conspiracy, in regard to their suspected efforts to betray Jerusalem to the Romans (*War* 4:365; 5:439). We also know that there were conflicting attempts to interpret signs and prophecies in support of a position favoring or rejecting war (*War* 2:650; 6:312–313). It may be that "imposter" was also a derogatory term used by both sides to denigrate the other. Thus, these terms may have originated from the intra-Jewish struggles, rather than from a Roman perspective.

A word of caution in general is necessary regarding Josephus' derogations. The terms which Josephus uses may not of course have been altogether inaccurate. There may have been enough truth to these disparaging epithets to explain Josephus' use of them. Criminals and robber bands may have attached themselves to the revolutionary movement. The revolutionary leaders used some unscrupulous means to undermine the provisional government and may well have been tyrannical. This observation is a caution against dismissing the characterizations of the revolutionaries as if their significance could be exhausted by a consideration of Josephus' purposes and prejudices. It would be just as mistaken to portray all the revolutionaries as righteous Jews, inspired by trust in God, who lived unselfishly for the Jewish nation, as it was for Josephus to portray them all as scoundrels and criminals. And it would be mistaken to suppose that because any one revolutionary or group of revolutionaries had religious—or even fanatical—motives, they had no others. Human motivation is almost never simple, and it is presumable that the economic rewards of robbery and the psychological satisfactions of violence were no less important to ancient than they are to modern revolutionaries.

INFERENCES FROM JOSEPHUS' POLEMICAL ACCUSATIONS

In addition to employing derogatory terms to malign the revolutionaries, Josephus also makes some recurring accusations against them which, as we shall see, take the form of a "reverse polemic"; that is, he turns the arguments of the revolutionaries against themselves.[27]   In these passages, Josephus accuses the Jewish revolutionaries of the very offenses for which they blamed the Romans, and conversely he attributes to the Romans the very motives which the revolutionaries claimed for themselves.

The reverse polemic is the main technique which Josephus uses to deal with honorific reasons for which the war was fought, reasons which Josephus might have feared his readers would support.   When we encounter this polemic in Josephus' writings, it is often a signal to us that Josephus is dealing wtih what must have been an important issue of the war.   Our analyses of these issues may help to clarify some of the purposes and grievances of the Jewish revolutionaries which underlie the polemic.

Josephus' reverse polemic is most explicit in a passage which recounts his speech before the walls of Jerusalem.   In this speech he is addressing himself to the revolutionaries, whose spokesman, John of Gischala, had just claimed that he "could never fear capture, since the city was God's" (*War* 6:98):

> At this Josephus cried aloud: "Pure indeed have you kept it for God! The Holy Place too remains undefiled! Your looked-for Ally has suffered no impiety from you, and still receives His customary sacrifices!   Most impious wretch, should anyone deprive you of your daily food, you would consider him an enemy; and do you hope to have God, whom you have bereft of His everlasting worship, for your Ally in this war?   And do you impute your sins to the Romans, who, to this day, are concerned for our laws and are trying to force you to restore to God those sacrifices which you have interrupted? Who would not bewail and lament for the city at this *amazing inversion*, when aliens and enemies rectify your impiety, while you, a Jew, nurtured in her laws, treat them more harshly even than your foes?   (*War* 6:99–102)

27. Hengel suggests that Josephus may have used such a "polemical reversal" in regard to the sanctuary, but he does not treat it as a general method of argumentation: M. Hengel, *Zeloten*, p. 223.

In this passage Josephus accuses John and the revolutionaries of defiling the holy city and temple, abandoning Jewish laws and customs, and being unfit to have God as an ally. Yet these are the very accusations the revolutionaries had made against the Romans. That these were Jewish accusations can be inferred from Josephus' assertion that the revolutionaries imputed these sins to the Romans. In addition, when he emphasizes that it is really the Romans who have concerns for the city, the law and the customs, it may be inferred that these were concerns which the Jewish revolutionaries claimed to have for themselves Josephus' reference to the "amazing inversion," when gentiles and enemies rectify the impiety of Jews, suggests that he is aware of the dynamics of the argument which he is using.

Defense of the Law

Such a reverse polemic is apparent with regard to several specific issues, such as the issue of upholding the Jewish law. We have the explicit statement that one of the purposes of the revolutionaries was to keep their "religious rules from contaminations" (*War* 2:391) and "to preserve inviolate all the institutions of your forefathers" (*War* 2:393). Josephus reverses this stated purpose of the revolutionaries. He blames the Zealots for the fact that "every human ordinance was trampled underfoot, every dictate of religion ridiculed by these men" (*War* 4:385); and he accuses them of "subverting the institutions of their forefathers" (*War* 4:348; cf. 2:517–18, 391, 393; 4:382; 5:402; 6:94).

On the other hand, Josephus extols the Romans for having permitted the Jewish laws to continue (*War* 6:333–34; cf. 5:405) and for having observed those laws themselves (*War* 4:181–82) even to the point of forgoing many of their own customs in deference to them (*War* 5:402). Josephus concludes that the Jews treated their laws "more harshly even than their foes" (*War* 6:102). "Indeed," he writes, "if one must nicely fit the phrase to the fact, it is the Romans who may well be found to have been the upholders of our laws, while their enemies were within the walls" (*War* 4:184; cf. 6:101). This extensive reverse polemic designed to depict the Romans as righteous and the Jews as unrighteous (*War* 5:406) indicates that the Jews' own claim to be defending the law from Roman interference was probably an important purpose of the war.

God as Ally

The Jews based their hope for God's assistance (*War* 2:391) and their claim to have God as their ally in battle (*War* 6:99, 101) on the assertion that they were adherents and defenders of the law. Other passages indicate this was a pervasive claim among the revolutionaries (*War* 5:402, 413, 459; 6:73; 6:98). Josephus reverses this assertion by accusing the Jews of being unworthy to have God as an ally (*War* 6:100). He lists the Jewish offenses and concludes, "after all this do you expect Him, thus outraged, to be your Ally?" "My belief," Josephus writes, "is that the Deity has fled from the holy places and taken His stand on the side of those with whom you are now at war" (*War* 5:412). This reverse polemic is further illustrated by numerous references to the ways in which God cooperated with the Romans in their battles against the Jews (*War* 3:484; 4:366–70; 6:38–41, 110, 401, 411; 7:293, 319), and to the ways in which God frustrated the military efforts of the Jews (*War* 4:573; 5:39, 343, 555; 7:331, 359–60). Once more, we see the pattern of the revolutionaries' claims. Josephus' counterclaim serves to underscore the importance of this issue and to clarify the Jews' position on it.

Exclusions of Aliens (Gentiles)

We have already noted Josephus' reference to the amazing inversion when "foreigners and enemies rectify your [Jewish] impiety" (*War* 6:102). Josephus ascribes to the revolutionary ideology a commitment to eliminate gentile influence in Israel: the lower priests rejected sacrifices and gifts from gentiles (War 2:409); the Sicarii suppressed those Jews who cooperated with Rome as if they were "aliens" and "enemies" (*War* 7:255; cf. 7:266); and John of Gischala melted down foreign gifts for the temple to forge weapons for battle (*War* 5:562). As a reverse polemic to the Jewish suppression of gentiles, Josephus emphasizes the kindness of gentiles toward Jews. Some Jews, he writes, "fled from their countrymen to take refuge with aliens and obtained at Roman hands the security which they despaired of finding among their own people" (*War* 4:397; cf. 1:27).

The corollary to the Jewish elimination of alien influence is their commitment to the solidarity of their people. Yet Josephus attacks the Jews for mistreating their own people (*War* 1:27; 5:525; 7:266) and for killing Jews "whom even the Romans, if victorious, would have spared" (*War* 4:181; cf. 7:266). By contrast Josephus portrays the Romans as treating the Jewish deserters with compassion (4:184, 397; 6:115, cf. 6:333) and as desirous of saving the inhabitants of Jerusalem (*War* 4:410–12; 5:360, 456, 522; 6:324). This inference from Josephus' reverse polemic serves to underscore the significance of the revolutionaries' own motives.

Defense of God's City and Temple

When Josephus quotes John of Gischala as saying that he "could never fear capture, since the city was God's" (War 6:98), he attributes to the revolutionaries the purpose of defending Jerusalem as God's dwelling place. Josephus reverses the revolutionary commitment to defend "God's" city and temple by accusing John of having polluted both (*War* 6:99). He even claims that the Jews themselves were ultimately responsible for the destruction of Jerusalem and the temple by their insistence on carrying out a hopeless war to its devastating conclusion (*War* 1:10, 27; 5:362–64; 6:130, 214–15). By contrast, the Romans, including the soldiers, had great awe for the temple (4:184, 324; 5:402, 444; 6:123). The Roman commander Titus acted "against his will" when he took military measures against the temple edifice and its defenders (*War* 1:28; 6:128, 216, 266, 346; 7:112–13).[28] The Roman appreciation of the temple was so great, Josephus writes, that "the indignation which the Jews might naturally have displayed had the Romans inflicted such wanton outrages upon them was now manifested by the Romans against the Jews, for profaning their own sacred places" (*War* 6:122).

Cleansing of Temple

Although we have inferred that the refusal of gifts from foreigners and the establishment of a new high priest were both designed to purify the temple cultus, that purpose is nowhere explicitly stated as the intent of the Jewish revolutionaries. But it is strongly implied by the reverse polemic of Josephus. The revolutionaries are accused of polluting the sanctuary by entering with polluted feet and hands (*War* 4:150, 159, 163, 183, 242), killing in the temple (*War* 4:201; 5:17, 380–81, 402; 6:95, 126; *Antiquities* 20:165ff.), allowing corpses in the temple (*War*

---

28. See also Helgo Lindner, *Die Geschichtsauffassung des Flavius Josephus im Bellum Judaicum* (Leiden: E. J. Brill, 1972), pp. 120ff.

5:19; 6:110, 121–22, 126; cf. 4:382), and deferring sacred cultic customs (*War* 5:402; 6:95).

Josephus then argues that it was the fires of the Roman conquest which purged both temple and city from these pollutions: "God, it is then, God himself who with the Romans is bringing the fire to purge His temple and exterminating a city so laden with pollutions" (*War* 6:110). In other passages Josephus states that God used the Roman army to "cleanse" the temple (*Antiquities* 20:166; *War* 4:323; 5:17–19; cf. 4:159).

This polemic is so typical of his other reverse polemics that it is reasonable to assume that the intent of the Jews can be inferred from it; namely, that they blamed the Romans and Roman sympathizers for polluting the temple and sought to cleanse it of all contact with them. Indeed, this reverse polemic is so pervasive and specific that it may have been a predominant religious motive of the revolutionaries.

Eschatological Hopes

Although Jews looked to God as an ally who would aid them, the specific content of their eschatological expectation is not clear. Was it a Jewish victory, national supremacy, return of diaspora Jews to the holy land, an apocalyptic intervention, a final judgment, a new age, the advent of the Messiah? Josephus is silent about these. On the basis of our attempts to infer eschatological beliefs from the study of each of the revolutionary groups, it does seem clear that there were differences among them. By implication, the people entertained various eschatological hopes. Yet, in general, the Jews fought with the common hope that God would bring a decisive victory. Toward the end of the siege of Jerusalem, the Jews were claiming that the temple would yet be saved by God and that "while they had God as their Ally" any threat from the Romans which was "unsupported by action" would be derided. "For the issue," they concluded, "rested with God" (*War* 5:459).

The implication seems to be that the Jews believed they could count on God's decisive aid because they were supporting their commitment to him by aggressive military actions. Josephus reverses this by asserting that it was precisely their military action which caused them to lose God's aid. In a speech to the rebels before the walls of Jerusalem, Josephus argues that historically the Jewish resort to arms had invariably resulted in defeat (*War* 5:390, 399). Therefore, he writes, it is "the duty of the occupants of holy ground to leave everything to the arbitrament of God and to scorn the aid of human hands" (*War* 5:400). In his view, God is able to defeat the enemies of Israel without their military aid, when it is his will to do so.

The Jews themselves may have looked for a source of hope to God's destruction by plague of most of the Assyrian army when they had besieged the city centuries before (*War* 5:388).[29] The rebels might have claimed that it had been the Jewish military defense of the city which had won them God's aid. Josephus reverses this illustration by noting that the plague which killed 185,000 of the Assyrian army took place at night when Jewish hands were either at rest or raised in prayer. Thus, he concludes, if God had desired to defeat the Romans he would have inflicted "instant vengeance" on them long ago (*War* 5:407). The Jewish recourse to arms was therefore futile. In fact, Josephus claims, the Jewish insistence upon fighting and their refusal to respond to repeated Roman offers of surrender were bringing destruction upon the city and temple. By contrast, Josephus depicts the Romans as doing everything in their power to avoid war and avert the destruction which was to follow. Hence, Josephus reverses the Jewish claim for God's eschatological aid by arguing that the Jews had failed to leave the matter wholly in God's hands.

The eschatological-apocalyptic hopes of the Jews were articulated in part by the numerous prophetic figures of the period, whom Josephus calls imposters and deceivers. Josephus' own prophetic insights and the awareness among the Romans of their own imminent victory serve as a contrast to the words of these "charlatans and pretended messengers of the deity." The same reverse polemic is evident in Josephus' references to the fullfillment of prophecies and oracles. He refers to the oracle which more than all else incited the Jews to war, namely, that "one from their country would become ruler of the world" (*War* 6:312).[30] Typical of his using reverse polemic, Josephus emphasizes

---

29. See also W. R. Farmer, *Maccabees, Zealots, and Josephus* (New York: Columbia University Press, 1956), pp. 97–111.

30. The oracle is also referred to by Tacitus (*Histories* 5:13) and Suetonius (*Lives of the Emperors*, Vespasian 4). As to the origin of this oracle, which is "likewise found in their sacred scriptures" (*War* 6:312), scholars conjecture it might be either from Daniel 7:13–14 (so, for example, R. Meyer, *Der Prophet aus Galiläa* [Darmstadt: Wissenschaftliche Burchgesellschaft, 1970], pp. 52–57) or Numbers 24:17–18 (so Hengel, *Zeloten*, p. 243).

that many Jewish wise men went astray in their interpretation of it, and he affirms that the oracle really "signified the sovereignty of Vespasian, who was proclaimed Emperor on Jewish soil." Elsewhere Josephus refers to other oracles which the Jews interpreted to their advantage (4:387–88; 6:109–10; 310–12), but which they themselves helped to bring to fulfillment to their own disadvantage. Meanwhile, Josephus asserts, the Romans were the primary agents by whom and in whom these prophecies were fulfilled.

In addition to prophetic oracles, the Jews looked to signs and portents as indicators of their fate. Josephus lists the portents which preceded the fall of the city and the destruction of the temple. Some of these signs, Josephus writes, "the Jews interpreted to please themselves, others they treated with contempt" (6:315; cf. 2:650). Josephus reverses the meaning of these portents by interpreting them not as indicative of a Jewish victory but as God's way of forewarning his people of the impending disaster so that they would avert it (War 6:310).

The extent of the eschatological theme in Josephus' reverse polemic indicates that eschatological-apocalyptic hopes were important incentives for participation in the war. Other Jewish sources from the first century reinforce this impression that eschatology was an integral part of Jewish life in this era. Josephus himself says that "what more than all else incited them to war" was an oracle prophesying that a world ruler would emerge from Judea (War 6:315).[31] There is, however, need for caution here. This statement occurs in the context of a discussion of signs and oracles. As such, it may mean, not that the messianic hope was the major inspiration for the whole war, but that of all the signs and oracles which inspired the Jews to fight, this oracle was the most important one. Even then, it should be observed that nowhere else in the narrative is the messianic hope articulated as a cause of the war.[32] There is no unambiguous messianic claim among the

31. See the comprehensive article by Abraham Schalit which indicates the testimony from so many sources of this period to the widespread knowledge and significance of the messianic oracle which Josephus mentions here, "Die Erhebung Vespasians nach Flavius Josephus, Talmud und Midrasch. Zur Geschichte einer messianische Prophetie," in *Aufsteig und Niedergang der Romischen Welt. Geschichte und Kultur Roms im Spiegel der neueren Forschung* (Berlin: Walter de Gruyter, 1975), pp. 208–327.

32. One should note particularly that "nowhere in Agrippa's plea to the people to desist from rebellion does he (Josephus) deal with the messianic hope as one of the illusions held by the people. He merely stresses that God will not come to their aid." E. Rivkin, "The Meaning of Messiah in Jewish Thought," *Union Seminary Quarterly Review* 26 (1971): 395, n. 8.

revolutionaries and little evidence that the populace viewed any of the leaders as messianic figures. Although the fervor created by the prophetic figures who arose in this period fed the popular revolutionary commitment, Josephus clearly distinguishes the revolutionary leaders from the prophetic figures. Thus, while the importance of eschatological hopes should be clearly emphasized, we must be cautious, at least on the basis of the writings of Josephus alone, not to exaggerate them.

The reverse polemic was the major technique employed by Josephus to deal with some of the honorific motives of the revolutionaries. Josephus does not deny the validity of the purposes and hopes of the revolutionaries; he only claims that they were subverted by the revolutionaries themselves. He asserts, furthermore, that the Romans carried out these purposes better than did the revolutionaries themselves. This assertion serves to obviate the Jewish grievances against the Romans and to portray Rome as an empire which could be said to have the best interests of the Jews at heart. By portraying the matter in this -way, Josephus was discouraging his Jewish readers from identifying with the revolutionaries in their homeland and was encouraging their allegiance to the Romans.

VI

CONCLUSIONS

When Jerusalem was conquered in 70 C.E., the Romans set aside the strongest and most handsome of the youth for the triumphal march in Rome. The weak and feeble were killed, while the majority of captives were sent to be slave labor in Egypt or reserved for use in the Roman games. Those under seventeen were sold (*War* 6:414–19). The city of Jerusalem and the temple were razed to the ground, except for three towers and a portion of the wall (*War* 7:1–4). The conquering general Titus returned to Rome with his prisoners for the triumphal march (*War* 7:119–62). During the next four years, there were large numbers of Roman troops in Palestine conquering the several remaining fortresses which continued to hold out. The nation had been impoverished by the war, its numbers and productivity greatly reduced. And although Judea continued as a province under Roman governors, the Jewish institutions of self-government were no longer present.

What have we found to be the causes of this tragic war, and how much support did it have among the populace? This chapter is an attempt to draw together many aspects of this study of Josephus and to make some concluding remarks about the nature of the Jewish revolt against the Romans.

Our study has shown that there is little evidence for the presence or activity of a Jewish revolutionary sect in the prewar history of 6–44 C.E. We have seen that the faction of the Sicarii, led by the descendants of Judas of Galilee, may have been active in the two decades before the war; however, they did not organize or control other revolutionaries. Although their terrorist activities were often effective, their influence with the populace was not great; their attempt to take over the leadership of the revolt at the opening of the war failed; and they did not

174

participate in major battles with the Romans during the war. These conclusions contradict the commonly accepted view, which Josephus himself at one point suggests (*Antiquities* 18:8–10), that a major Jewish revolutionary sect founded in 6 C.E. gradually gained enough power and influence to win the nation over to war against Rome. That view, as we have seen, is due to Josephus' biased attempt to blame the war upon a small group within Judaism. It is not supported by the rest of Josephus' narrative in which he says only that the Sicarii were the first revolutionary group, the one which set the example—not that they were the group from which other revolutionary factions emerged.

Once we have discarded the conspiracy theory—that the origin of the war could be attributed to one group or sect—we are left with a very different picture of the nature of the revolt and its causes. Until the late forties, the nation was in a spirit of accommodation to Roman rule. In general, the leadership of the nation was effective. When conflict did arise, the Jews sought peaceful methods to overcome it. Dissatisfaction with Rome during this period was primarily made up of general resentment of Roman rule and of spontaneous responses of the populace as a whole to specific offenses committed by the Roman procurators. The more extreme forms of resistance in the fifties and sixties were expressive of the widespread discontent over the prevailing social, economic, and political conditions in Palestine. The failure of the Jewish and the Roman leadership in this period contributed greatly to the gradual breakdown of order, first in the countryside of Judea and then in Jerusalem. During the whole prewar period, resistance took many forms: nonviolent protests, popular clamor, riots, petitions, appeals, delegations, acts of defiance, strikes, plundering, assassinations, kidnapping, extortion, threats, bribery. In one way or another, a cross-section of the Jewish populace in Israel, including all classes as well as the major sects, participated in this resistance. In the war period, five separate revolutionary groups were active, each one with distinct origins and outlooks. Together, they represented a geographical cross-section of Palestinian Judaism.[1]

While various revolutionary groups at different times forced the issue of the war, the populace did not in general oppose their efforts. The

1. This observation obviates a traditional view that Jewish resistance against Rome centered primarily in Galilee. For other sources making this point, see Francis Malinowski, "Galilaean Judaism in the Writings of Flavius Josephus" (Ph.D. dissertation, Duke University, 1973); and Marc Borg, "Conflict as a Context for the Ministry of Jesus" (Dissertation, Oxford, 1972), p. 38.

popular discontent of the prewar period erupted at the opening of the war. Swarms of Jews from all over the countryside attacked Cestius in his retreat from the first major Jewish victory against the Romans (*War* 2:545; cf. 523). It was in the midst of this popular upsurge of support for the war that the coalition government was elected and generals were appointed to prepare for war in the various districts (*War* 2:562–68). Certainly many Jews saw the defeat of Cestius as a sign of their ultimate victory (cf. *War* 2:650). Others supported the war at this point in fear that the nation had gone too far to hope for amnesty (*War* 2:532; cf. 556). And numbers of villages joined the war effort because they were forced to defend themselves against the attacks of Roman and Greek residents of Palestine (*War* 2:457–86; *Life* 27). The popular army also rallied support to reconquer cities which had fallen out of Jewish control (*War* 3:9). There was a readiness in Galilee, except at Sepphoris and Tiberias, to fortify for the return of the Romans (*War* 3:40–41). And although many fled the rural areas in the face of the Roman legions, the Galilean troops took their stand in the cities which had been fortified the best in the brief time they had had to prepare for Vespasian's appearance. There was representative resistance in each territory of the nation, as exemplified by the readiness of the popular militia from Idumaea to oppose any attempt of the national leaders to surrender. Many Jews collected at the "impregnable fortress," Jerusalem, to defend the city there (*War* 4:61, 111, 123). And three other fortresses held out even after Jerusalem was conquered.

Thus, the war was for the most part supported by the populace. The nation was not entirely united, however, for Josephus indicates there was some division over the war almost everywhere (*War* 2:424; 4:128–32). The resistance outside Jerusalem was significant, but not sustained. Many fled for refuge at the appearance of the Roman armies, and a few cities surrendered. Yet the numerous active revolutionaries that appear to have emerged from such a cross-section of the nation seem to have represented a groundswell and were supported by many more who shared their attitudes and convictions. Thus, this war was not carried out only by "an active minority."[2] And when the populace in Jerusalem did oppose the Zealots in 68 c.e., it was not because

2. This phrase was employed by Elias Bickermann to describe the Maccabean Revolt in *From Ezra to the Last of the Maccabees* (New York: Schocken Books,

they opposed the war movement, but because they were disillusioned by the leadership and conduct of the war under the Zealots.

Since the war in general is to be seen as a popular war, it is necessary to reevaluate the causes of the revolt. We have seen that it was not primarily motivated by a revolutionary ideology by which the nation was determined to revolt against Rome. Certainly the persistence of a minority of religious militants, such as the Sicarii, was an important cause of the conflict. However, our study has shown that the widespread resistance to Rome was a reaction to the harsh realities of the actual presence of Rome in Palestine. Until the late forties, the Jewish discontent was expressed primarily in reaction to religious offenses, such as the introduction of Roman standards bearing images into Jerusalem, the attempt to place a statue of Gaius in the temple, and the burning of a copy of the Torah by Roman soldiers. During this period, there is little evidence of conspiratorial revolutionary activity. However, in the last two decades before the war, the Roman offenses were primarily of a political nature. The ineptness of Cumanus in handling the Galilean-Samaritan conflict resulted in a fundamental breakdown of Roman (and Jewish) authority in the countryside. The incompetence and insensitivity with which subsequent procurators handled the affairs of Judea only stimulated a deeper discontent. The corruption of the procurators eventually resulted in anarchy in Jerusalem, which encouraged corruption and conflict among the traditional Jewish authorities. And the instability of the political situation often led to the oppression of the lower classes by aristocratic Jews. In the midst of the loss of civil order, revolutionary activity emerged and became widespread.

Accompanying the lack of political order were the dire social and economic conditions which led many of the lower classes to seek to escape from their plight. We have indicated that much of the brigandage of the period may have been a consequence of intolerable taxes and confiscation of property by Romans and wealthy Jews. The popular following of the prophetic figures of this period demonstrates the longing of the people to find "salvation" from their troubles. Most of the revolutionary groups we have discussed had their origins in the ills of

---

1962), p. 102. Contrast Tacitus' description of popular support against the Roman siege of Jerusalem: "There were arms for all who could use them, and the number ready to fight was larger than could have been anticipated from the total population" (*Histories* 5:13).

the lower classes among the Jews. The Sicarii at the opening of the war burned the archives in which the record of debts was kept in order to rid the records of their own debts and to encourage an uprising of the poor against the rich. The Zealot party was composed of dissident peasants from Judea and lower priests in Jerusalem who had been oppressed by the chief priests in the decade before the war. The early followers of Simon bar Giora were slaves and brigands who plundered the rich. Even the Idumaeans who came to Jerusalem showed their distrust of the high priestly aristocracy by their readiness to support the Zealots. And the vengeance with which both the Zealots and the Idumaeans treated the Jewish aristocracy can best be understood as the expression of accumulated frustration resulting from grievances against the wealthy and traditional authorities.

The elucidation of these political, social, and economic conditions explains in large measure why the war was popular. The populace as a whole experienced the oppression of these conditions. They saw the presence of Rome as the root cause of their situation, and they longed for national autonomy to deal with their own affairs without the oppressive presence of a foreign power. Those who were bent on war against Rome only mirrored in an extreme way the discontent of all the people. Perhaps the revolutionaries, who were predominantly from the lower classes, were most determined to revolt because it was for them that the social conditions were the most intolerable. This fact would also help to explain the civil war in Jerusalem between revolutionaries and moderates, because the major difference between the moderates and the revolutionaries was a class distinction. Thus, the war was not only a national revolt against Rome, it was also a class war among the Jews. The majority of revolutionaries saw the war as an opportunity not only to exclude the foreign power, but also to overthrow the traditional aristocratic Jewish government. And that is exactly what they did. Freedom for them ultimately implied freedom from the traditional Jewish authorities who had been so closely aligned with the Romans. Only thus could they guarantee their freedom from oppression and the success of their cause. In this context, the conflicts among the revolutionaries are to be seen as the struggle between dissident groups to provide national leadership in the vacuum created by the absence of the Romans and by the weakness and downfall of the provisional government.

The intentions of the revolutionaries to overcome their social oppression were often accompanied by other personal motives. We have indicated that for some the war was an opportunity to gain wealth and to change their status in society. Slaves, for example, were freed. The political motive of overthrowing the Roman and Jewish authorities was accompanied by the personal desire for power; we have noted, for example, the opportunism of John of Gischala. Josephus also indicates that the youth, many of whom were daring and wanted to prove their military valor, played a significant role in the course of events. Many revolutionaries were convinced of the practical possibility of a victory over the Romans, certain that the walls of Jerusalem would withstand any siege. But there was also the fear, once the war had begun, that the consequences of a surrender would be horrible and that the only choice was to carry through the fight for freedom.

Throughout this work we have emphasized the pervasiveness of the religious dimensions of the revolutionaries' intentions and actions. We have indicated that in the most fundamental sense the beliefs and practices of Jews were integral to their identity as a nation. As God's chosen people, they believed they were meant for freedom, not foreign domination. The law and the temple were understood as religious as well as political institutions. Even the deteriorating relationship between Jews and Romans which threatened these institutions was interpreted by many as the suffering which was to precede God's deliverance.[3] It would be a mistake to isolate the religious dimension as the one determinative factor of the revolt.[4] Clearly, social and political ills were root causes of the war. Yet the religious understanding of their national life undoubtedly helped many Jews to articulate and deepen the institutional loyalties which the populace shared in common.

Josephus himself affirms the prophetic promises and eschatological

3. See M. Hengel, *Zeloten* (Leiden: E. J. Brill, 1961), pp. 253–55.
4. The religious motive dominates the historical studies of Farmer and Hengel, although Hengel has more recently taken into account social causes of the war in "Zeloten und Sikarier," from *Josephus-Studien*, ed. Otto Betz, et al. (Göttingen: Vandenhoeck and Ruprecht, 1974) pp. 181–82. For works which take account of the social, economic, and political dimensions, see Moses Aberbach, *The Roman Jewish War* (London: R. Golub and Company, 1966); Günther Baumbach, "Das Freiheitzverständis der zelotischen Bewegung," *Das Ferne und Nahe Wort*, no. 105 in *Beihefte zu Zeitschrift für die Alttestamentische Wissenschaft* (Berlin: Alfred Töpelmann, 1967); Shimon A. Appelbaum, "The Zealots: The Case for Revaluation," *Journal of Roman Studies* 61 (1971); and Heinz Kreissig, "Die Socialen Zusammenhange des Jüdischen Krieges" (Ph.D. dissertation, Humbolt University, 1965).

hopes which inspired and sustained the Jewish struggle for freedom and supremacy over the foreign foes. He also indicates that the Jews believed that they had God as their ally in the struggle. It is also clear from his narrative that the exclusion of Rome was understood by many revolutionaries in a religious way. The brigandage and assassination against the Jewish authorities on the part of the Sicarii especially were seen as a repression of idolatrous contact with heathen masters, perhaps to "cleanse the land" of those who refused exclusive allegiance to God.

We have seen that the war itself was initiated by the decision of the lower priests to purge the temple of all contact with the gifts and sacrifices of gentiles. The overthrow of the moderate Jewish establishment in 68 c.e. by the Zealots resulted in the reinstitution of the Zadokite priesthood. Simon bar Giora, among others, may have viewed the conflict as a holy war against God's hated enemies. There may have been messianic claims among the revolutionaries, although this is not certain. We have also seen how the desire of the revolutionaries to seek a new beginning in the wilderness after the burning of the temple implied that religious convictions and the centrality of the temple governed the revolutionaries' understanding of their cause.

In general, most Jews turned to their religious faith as a means to salvation from their troubles. They were convinced that without God as their ally they could not succeed. His aid would be assured, they believed, by a renewed devotion to their religio-national institutions, especially the temple and the law. This devotion took the form of the exclusion of all gentile influence or contact from those Jewish institutions and the willingness to battle against the foreign power which threatened them. It also often involved the violent repression of Jews who cooperated with the gentiles. But it is important to recognize that this religious exclusivism, which guaranteed the holiness of Israel and the absolute allegiance to God, coexisted with and served the purposes of the social and political struggle. All of these social, nationalistic, and religious motivations and desires came to be articulated together in the concept of "freedom." But no one factor, such as the religious, should be elevated to decisive preeminence as the cause of the war.

These concluding remarks are the barest statement of the motives that governed the revolutionaries: the evidence for them can be gleaned from the preceding pages. These motives were seldom isolated or singular. They were intertwined in a complex current of forces which cannot be easily differentiated. As these motives were at work, sometimes one motive predominated in a group or individual; but often they were all inseparably at work to bring about that course of events which constitutes the history of the Jewish War.

APPENDIXES

Archilēstēs—brigand, chief
  War 2:253, 275; 4:135; 5:30; *Antiquities* 20:5; *Life* 105.

Lēstēs—brigand
  War 2:125, 228, 229, 253, 254, 271, 425, 431, 434, 441, 541, 587,
  593(2), 653; 4:138, 199, 242, 244, 409, 504, 510, 555; 5:421, 448,
  515, 524, 546; 6:123, 129, 195, 324, 363; *Antiquities* 20:121, 124,
  161(2), 163(2), 165, 167, 172, 185, 186, 210, 215, 255, 256; *Life* 28,
  46, 47, 77, 106, 145, 175, 206.

Stasiastēs—insurgent
  War 1:10; 2:267, 289, 290, 295, 325(2), 330, 406, 411, 423, 424, 432,
  441, 452, 455, 484, 525, 529(2), 534, 538, 557, 651; 3:449, 542;
  4:410; 5:34, 72, 110, 277, 290, 334, 345, 348, 354, 420, 424, 431, 448,
  452, 517, 520, 522, 542, 547, 550, 572; 6:1, 72, 113, 116, 119, 157,
  177, 206, 207, 209, 227, 251, 259, 273, 316, 358, 363, 368, 392; 7:35;
  Antiquities 20:227.

Tyrannos—tyrant
  War 1:10, 11, 24, 27, 28; 2:208, 275, 442, 626; 4:166, 178, 258, 564,
  566, 573, 595, 596; 5:5, 11, 439; 6:98, 129, 143, 202, 227, 286, 323,
  325, 343, 370, 379, 394, 399, 409, 412, 432; 7:265.

Epiboulos—conspirator
  War 2:585, 615, 620, 622; 4:151, 185, 267, 365; 5:21, 27, 103, 183;
  Life 25

Ponēros—wicked one
  War 2:156, 258, 273, 275, 304, 352, 538, 539; 3:372, 373, 4:179, 187,
  238, 243, 328, 389, 407, 492, 508; 5:441, 535; 6:341, 343, 395, 7:34,
  185, 438, 453; *Life* 29, 86, 102, 133, 134, 151, 290, 355.

---

1. References are limited to the narrative of the period from 6 to 74 C.E. (*War*
1:1–30; 2:117–7:455; *Antiquities* 18–20; and the *Life*).

Goēs—deceiver
　War 2:261, 264; 4:85; 5:317; *Antiquities* 20:97, 160, 167, 188.

Sikarios—sicarius, Sicarius
　War 2:254, 425; 4:400, 516; 7:253, 254, 262, 275, 297, 311, 410, 412, 415, 437, 444; *Antiquities* 20:186, 204, 208, 210.

Zēlotēs—zealot, Zealot, devotee
　War 2:444, 564, 651, 4:160, 162, 193, 196, 197, 199, 201, 209, 215, 216, 224, 284, 291, 298, 302, 305, 307, 310, 326, 340, 342, 346, 355, 377, 387, 388, 490, 514, 538, 544, 556, 558, 567, 568, 570, 574, 575, 577, 579; 5:3 5, 7, 101, 103, 250, 314, 358, 528; 6:59, 92, 148, 268; *Antiquities* 20:47; *Life* 11.

Roman Emperors	Procurators and Rulers in Palestine			High Priests
	Herod the Great (37 - 4 B.C.E.)			
	Judea, Idumaea, and Samaria	*Iturea, Trachonitis, Batanea, and Auranitis*	*Galilee and Peraea*	
Augustus (31 B.C.E. - 14 C.E.)	Archelaus, son of Herod (4 B.C.E. - 6 C.E.)	Philip, son of Herod (4 B.C.E. - 33/34 C.E.)	Antipas, son of Herod (4 B.C.E. - 39 C.E.)	Jesus, son of See (3/4 B.C.E. - 5 C.E.)
	Coponius (6 - 9 C.E.)			Joazar, son of Boethus (5-6 C.E.)
	Marcus Ambibulus (9 - 12 C.E.)			Ananus, son of Seth (6 - 15 C.E.)
	Annius Rufus (12 - 15 C.E.)			Ishmael, son of Phabi (15 - 16 C.E.)
				Eleazar, son of Ananus (16 - 17 C.E.)
				Simon, son of Camith (17 - 18 C.E.)
Tiberius (14 - 37 C.E.)	Valerius Gratus (15 - 26 C.E.)			Joseph Caiaphas (18 - 37 C.E.)
	Pontius Pilate (26 - 36 C.E.)			
	Marcellus (36 - 37 C.E.)	Attached to Syrian Province (34 - 41 C.E.)		
Gaius Caligula (37 - 41 C.E.)	Marullus (37 - 41 C.E.)			Jonathan, son of Ananus (37 C.E.)
				Theophilus, son of Ananus (37 - 41 C.E.)
			Agrippa I (40 C.E.)	
Claudius (41 - 54 C.E.)	Agrippa I (41 - 44 C.E.)			Simon Cantheras (41 C.E.)
				Matthias, son of Ananus (41 - 44 C.E.)
	Fadus (44 - 46 C.E.)			Elionaeus, son of Simon Cantheras (44 - 46 C.E.)

Emperors	Governors / Events	High Priests
Nero (54 - 68 C.E.)	Tiberius Alexander (46 - 48 C.E.)	Joseph, son of Camith (46 - 48 C.E.)
	Ventidius Cumanus (48 - 52 C.E.)	Ananias, son of Nedebaeus (48 - 59 C.E.)
	Felix (52 - 60 C.E.)	
		Ishmael, son of Phabi (59 - 61 C.E.)
	Porcius Festus (60 - 62 C.E.)	Joseph Kabi, son of Simon (61 - 62 C.E.)
	Albinus (62 - 64 C.E.)	Ananus, son of Ananus (62 C.E.)
		Jesus, son of Damnaeus (62 - 63 C.E.)
		Jesus, son of Gamaliel (63 - 64 C.E.)
	Gessius Florus (64 - 66 C.E.)	Matthias, son of Theophilus (64 - 66 C.E.)
	Provisional Government of Israel (66–68 C.E.)	Ananus, son of Ananus [leader of the provisional government] (66 - 68 C.E.)
Galba (68 - 69 C.E.)	Zealot Coalition (68 - 69 C.E.)	Phineas, son of Samuel (by lot) (68 - 70 C.E.)
Otho (69 C.E.)	Simon bar Giora (69 - 70 C.E.)	
Vitellius (69 C.E.)		
Vespasian (69 - 79 C.E.)	Fall of Jerusalem (70 C.E.)	
	Fall of Masada (74 C.E.)	
Titus (79 - 81 C.E.)		

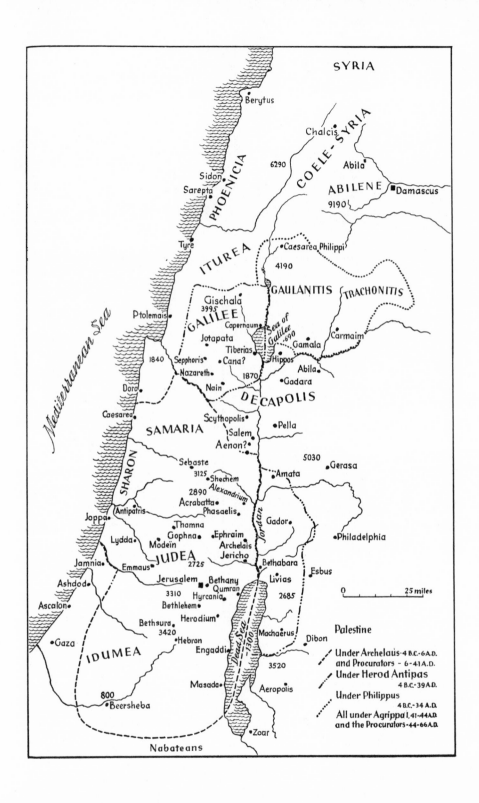

SYRIA

Berytus

Chalcis

Abila

6290

COELE-SYRIA

Sidon

Sarepta

ABILENE

Damascus

9190

PHOENICIA

Tyre

Caesarea Philippi

ITUREA

4190

GAULANITIS

TRACHONITIS

Gischala
3995

GALILEE

Capernaum

Sea of Galilee
.690

Carmaim

Ptolemais

Jotapata

Gamala

Tiberias

1840

Sephoris

Cana?

Hippos

Abila

Nazareth

1870

Gadara

Mediterranean Sea

Doro

Nain

DECAPOLIS

Caesarea

Scythopolis

Pella

SAMARIA

Salem

Aenon?

Sebaste

5030

Gerasa

3125

Shechem

Amata

Alexandrium

SHARON

2890

Acrabatta

Phasaelis

Joppa

Antipatris

Thamna

Gador

Philadelphia

Lydda

Gophna

Ephraim

Modeïn

Archelais

Jamnia

Emmaus

JUDEA

Jericho

Bethabara

Ashdod

Jerusalem

Bethany

Livias

Esbus

Qumran

2685

3310

Hyrcania

Ascalon

Bethlehem

Herodium

Machaerus

Dibon

Gaza

Bethsura
3420

Hebron

Engaddi

3520

IDUMEA

Masada

Aeropolis

800

Beersheba

Zoar

Nabateans

2725

Dead Sea
-1300

0   25 miles

Palestine

Under Archelaus-4 B.C.-6 A.D.
and Procurators - 6-41 A.D.
Under Herod Antipas
4 B.C.-39 A.D.
Under Philippus
4 B.C.-34 A.D.
All under Agrippa I, 41-44 A.D.
and the Procurators-44-66 A.D.

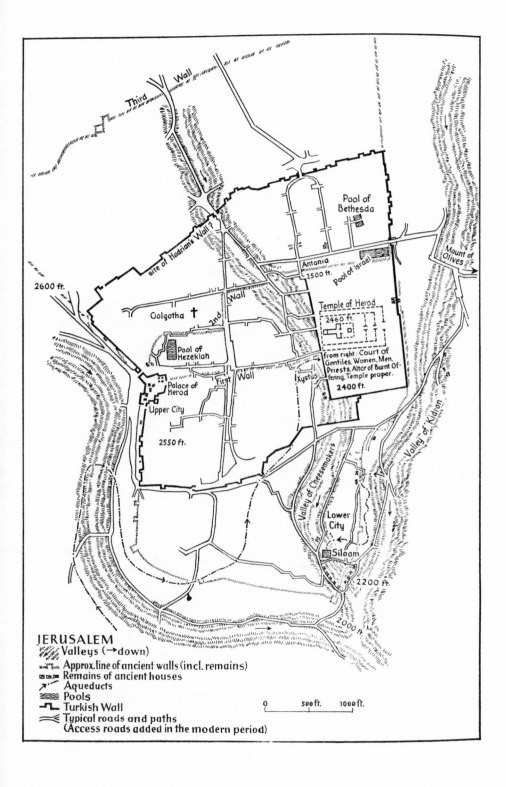

JERUSALEM

Valleys (→down)

Approx. line of ancient walls (incl. remains)

Remains of ancient houses

Aqueducts

Pools

Turkish Wall

Typical roads and paths
(Access roads added in the modern period)

0   500 ft.   1000 ft.

Third Wall

site of Hadrian's Wall?

2600 ft.

Golgotha

Pool of
Hezekiah

Palace of
Herod

Upper City

2550 ft.

2nd Wall

First Wall

Antonia
2500 ft.

Pool of
Bethesda

Pool of Israel

Temple of Herod
2460 ft.

from right: Court of
Gentiles, Women, Men,
Priests, Altar of Burnt Offering, Temple proper.
2400 ft.

Xystus

Valley of Cheesemakers

Lower
City

Siloam

2200 ft.

2000 ft.

Mount of
Olives

Valley of Kidron

INDEXES

INDEX TO THE WRITINGS OF JOSEPHUS*

THE JEWISH WAR

* This index contains the book-sentence references to Josephus' writings used throughout this work. It also includes the chapter-paragraph references employed in some editions of Josephus.

188

THE JEWISH ANTIQUITIES

LIFE

AGAINST APION

INDEX OF AUTHORS

INDEX OF SUBJECTS